T0202773

Communications
in Computer and Information Science   1887

Rationale

The CCIS series is devoted to the publication of proceedings of computer science conferences. Its aim is to efficiently disseminate original research results in informatics in printed and electronic form. While the focus is on publication of peer-reviewed full papers presenting mature work, inclusion of reviewed short papers reporting on work in progress is welcome, too. Besides globally relevant meetings with internationally representative program committees guaranteeing a strict peer-reviewing and paper selection process, conferences run by societies or of high regional or national relevance are also considered for publication.

Topics

The topical scope of CCIS spans the entire spectrum of informatics ranging from foundational topics in the theory of computing to information and communications science and technology and a broad variety of interdisciplinary application fields.

Information for Volume Editors and Authors

Publication in CCIS is free of charge. No royalties are paid, however, we offer registered conference participants temporary free access to the online version of the conference proceedings on SpringerLink (http://link.springer.com) by means of an http referrer from the conference website and/or a number of complimentary printed copies, as specified in the official acceptance email of the event.

CCIS proceedings can be published in time for distribution at conferences or as post-proceedings, and delivered in the form of printed books and/or electronically as USBs and/or e-content licenses for accessing proceedings at SpringerLink. Furthermore, CCIS proceedings are included in the CCIS electronic book series hosted in the SpringerLink digital library at http://link.springer.com/bookseries/7899. Conferences publishing in CCIS are allowed to use Online Conference Service (OCS) for managing the whole proceedings lifecycle (from submission and reviewing to preparing for publication) free of charge.

Publication process

The language of publication is exclusively English. Authors publishing in CCIS have to sign the Springer CCIS copyright transfer form, however, they are free to use their material published in CCIS for substantially changed, more elaborate subsequent publications elsewhere. For the preparation of the camera-ready papers/files, authors have to strictly adhere to the Springer CCIS Authors' Instructions and are strongly encouraged to use the CCIS LaTeX style files or templates.

Abstracting/Indexing

CCIS is abstracted/indexed in DBLP, Google Scholar, EI-Compendex, Mathematical Reviews, SCImago, Scopus. CCIS volumes are also submitted for the inclusion in ISI Proceedings.

How to start

To start the evaluation of your proposal for inclusion in the CCIS series, please send an e-mail to ccis@springer.com.

Carlos J. Barrios H. · Silvio Rizzi ·
Esteban Meneses · Esteban Mocskos ·
Jose M. Monsalve Diaz · Javier Montoya
Editors

High Performance Computing

10th Latin American Conference, CARLA 2023
Cartagena, Colombia, September 18–22, 2023
Revised Selected Papers

 Springer

Editors
Carlos J. Barrios H. ⓘ
Industrial University of Santander
Bucaramanga, Colombia

Esteban Meneses ⓘ
Centro Nacional de Alta Tecnología
San José, Costa Rica

Jose M. Monsalve Diaz ⓘ
Argonne National Laboratory
Lemont, IL, USA

Silvio Rizzi ⓘ
Argonne National Laboratory
Lemont, IL, USA

Esteban Mocskos ⓘ
University of Buenos Aires & Center for
Computational Simulation Aplicaciones
Tecnológicas
Buenos Aires, Argentina

Javier Montoya ⓘ
University of Cartagena
Cartagena, Colombia

ISSN 1865-0929   ISSN 1865-0937 (electronic)
Communications in Computer and Information Science
ISBN 978-3-031-52185-0   ISBN 978-3-031-52186-7 (eBook)
https://doi.org/10.1007/978-3-031-52186-7

This Springer imprint is published by the registered company Springer Nature Switzerland AG
The registered company address is: Gewerbestrasse 11, 6330 Cham, Switzerland

Paper in this product is recyclable.

Preface

CARLA, the Latin American High-Performance Computing Conference, is an international academic meeting aimed at providing a forum to foster the growth and strength of the High-Performance Computing (HPC) community in Latin America and the Caribbean. The conference has been running since 2014 and has become a leading event for HPC in the region. A key objective of the CARLA Conference is to disseminate the latest breakthroughs in HPC and HPC&AI (the intersection of HPC and Artificial Intelligence) to the global community, reflecting the significance of these domains in driving innovation and progress.

CARLA broadened its horizons this year by adding a third track to its program. This year, attendees could submit their work to the High-Performance Computing (HPC), Artificial Intelligence Using HPC at Scale, and High-Performance Computing Applications tracks. The objective was to provide a valuable platform for HPC users, system architects, and software developers to engage in meaningful discussions, ultimately increasing impact.

The 10th edition of the Latin American High-Performance Computing Conference (CARLA 2023) was a remarkable demonstration of the increasing maturity of the HPC Community in Latin America and the Caribbean, as well as its global importance. Furthermore, it was a prime illustration of the influential and vital academic network behind this conference. For ten consecutive editions, this network has come together to drive insightful discussions in the field, highlighting the strength and importance of collaboration. CARLA was held from September 18–22, 2023, and hosted by the Universidad de Cartagena, located in Cartagena de Indias, Colombia.

The conference program was not limited to the academic publications presented in this document. The conference featured eight workshops around advanced computing techniques and architectures, bioengineering, HPC practices, and HPC communities and inclusivity. Furthermore, it offered seven tutorials on advanced topics in HPC and AI, including its applications, programming models, and software development tools. The website[1] contains complete information about the conference and its schedule.

CARLA 2023 had 293 registered attendees from 29 countries from the majority of the continents, more than doubling the number of attendees from the year before. Eleven countries from Latin America and the Caribbean represented the vast majority of attendees, with the participation of 257 attendees. Fifty-five fellowships were provided across multiple countries in Latin America and the Caribbean to foster women-in-STEM participation and promote diversity in the conference.

The CARLA 2023 committee included 50 professionals divided into 15 committees. There were 35 meetings throughout the organization of the event. The event was sponsored and supported by SCALAC, RedCLARA, the Universidad de Cartagena, Universidad Industrial de Santander via SC3UIS, Universidad de Guadalajara via CADS, the Centro Nacional de Alta Tecnología (CeNAT) of Costa Rica, the RISC2 project,

---

[1] https://carla2023.ccarla.org.

and UNESCO via ICTP-Trieste. In addition, CARLA 2023 received sponsorship from eight companies and two professional societies. Compute resources were provided by Chameleon Cloud for some of the Tutorials. The committee also recognizes the role and support of the Science and Technology Ministry in Colombia (MinCiencias) and RENATA.

CARLA 2023 featured a total of three keynote speakers. In an effort to improve women's visibility in the field of high-performance computing (HPC), the committee made a conscious decision to select recognized female speakers for these keynotes: Ewa Deelman, Liliana Barbosa Santillan, and Trilce Estrada. The conference included three invited three invited talks by Fabrizio Gagliardi, Balaji Baktha, and Guido Araujo in addition to five industry talks given by different sponsors. The conference also encouraged attendees' participation and discussion through three panels featuring 12 international panelists. The panels were "EuroHPCLatam Panel: Policy and Global Actions", "Education HPC", and an Industry Panel.

This book contains 14 papers selected from 25 submissions and one invited paper from one of the keynote speakers. All manuscripts were peer-reviewed by at least three members of the Program Committee. The work by Johansell Villalobos and Esteban Meneses titled "Evaluation of Alternatives to Accelerate Scientific Numerical Calculations on Graphics Processing Units using Python" was selected for the Best Paper Award. Additionally, the poster by Kevin A. Brown and Robert Ross titled "Understanding HPC Network Behavior Using Low-level Metrics" was selected for the Best Poster award.

October 2023

Philippe Olivier Auguste Navaux
Carlos J. Barrios H.
Silvio Rizzi
Esteban Meneses
Esteban Mocskos
Jose M. Monsalve Diaz
Javier Montoya

Organization

Program Committee Chairs

Javier Montoya	Universidad de Cartagena, Colombia
Silvio Rizzi	Argonne National Laboratory, USA
Esteban Meneses Rojas	Centro Nacional de Alta Tecnología, Costa Rica
Carlos Jaime Barrios	Universidad Industrial de Santander, Colombia
Esteban Mocskos	Universidad de Buenos Aires, Argentina
Jose M. Monsalve Diaz	Argonne National Laboratory, Department of Energy, USA
Amaury Cabarcas	Universidad de Cartagena, Colombia
Plinio Puello Mafrrugo	Universidad de Cartagena, Colombia
Harold Castro Becerra	Universidad de los Andes, Colombia
Dario Yezid Peña Ballesteros	Universidad Industrial de Santander, Colombia
Lizette Robles Dueñas	Universidad de Guadalajara, México
Angie Fernández Olimón	Universidad de Guadalajara, México
Luis Alejandro Torres	Universidad Industrial de Santander, Colombia
Tania Altamirano	Cooperación Latinoamericana de Redes Avanzadas, Chile
Kevin Brown	Argonne National Laboratory, USA
Rafael Mayo-Garcia	Centro de Investigaciones Energéticas, Medioambientales y Tecnológicas, Spain
Claudio Chacón Arévalo	Corporación Ecuatoriana para el Desarrollo de la Investigación y la Academia, Ecuador
Esteban Hernandez	Cybercolombia, Colombia
Ginés Guerrero	Laboratorio Nacional de Computación de Alto Rendimiento, Chile
Gilberto Diaz	Universidad Industrial de Santander, Colombia
Álvaro L. G. A. Coutinho	Universida de Federal do Rio de Janeiro, Brazil
Nicolás Erdödy	Open Parallel, New Zealand
Elvis Rojas	Universidad Nacional, Sede Regional Brunca, Costa Rica
Jorge Luis Chacon Velazco	Universidad Industrial de Santander, Colombia
Oscar Carrillo	CitiLab, Francia
Lucas Schnorr	Universidade Federal do Rio Grande do Sul, Brazil
Philippe Navaux	Universidade Federal do Rio Grande do Sul, Brazil
Alfredo Cristobal Salas	Universidad Veracruzana, México

Gina Paola Maestre Gongora	Universidad Cooperativa de Colombia, Colombia
Edson Luiz Padoin	Universidade Regional do Noroeste do estado do Rio Grande do Sul-UNIJUÍ, Brazil
Robinson Rivas Suarez	Universidad Central de Venezuela, Venezuela
Carla Osthoff	Laboratório Nacional de Computação Científica, Brazil
Isidoro Gitler	ABACUS - CINVESTVA, México
Pablo Minini	Universidad de Buenos Aires, Argentina
Kary Ann del Carmen Ocaña Gautherot	Laboratório Nacional de Computação Científica LNCC, Brazil
Maria Pantoja	California Polytech, USA
Ulises Cortés	Barcelona Supercomputing Center, Spain
Verónica Vergara	Oak Ridge National Laboratory, USA
Aurelio Vivas	Universidad de los Andes, Colombia
Salma Jaelife	SCALAC: Servicios de computación Avanzada para América Latina y el Caribe, México
Luis Eliécer Cadenas	RedClara: Cooperación Latinoamericana de Redes Avanzadas, Chile
Mónica López	Universidad Nacional de Colombia, Colombia

Program Committee Members

Barrios H., Carlos J.	Universidad Industrial de Santander, Colombia
Carrillo, Oscar	University of Lyon, CPE, INSA Lyon, Inria, France
Castro, Harold	Universidad de los Andes, Colombia
Cazar Ramírez, Dennis	Universidad San Francisco de Quito USFQ, Ecuador
Cortés, Ulises	Barcelona Supercomputing Center, Spain
Cristóbal-Salas, Alfredo	Universidad Veracruzana, México
Garcia Henao, John Anderson	Nucleus AI, Switzerland
Gitler, Isidoro	ABACUS - CINVESTVA, México
Iturriaga, Santiago	Universidad de la República, Uruguay
Klapp, Jaime	Instituto Nacional de Investigaciones Nucleares, México
Martinez Abaunza, Victor Eduardo	University of Campinas, Brazil
Mello Schnorr, Lucas	UFRGS, Brazil
Meneses, Esteban	Centro Nacional de Alta Tecnología, Colaboratorio Nacional de Computación Avanzada, Costa Rica

Mocskos, Esteban	Departamento de Computación, Facultad de Ciencias Exactas y Naturales, Universidad de Buenos Aires & Centro de Simulación Computacional p/aplic Tecnológicas (CSCCONICET),Argentina
Monsalve Diaz, Jose M.	Argonne National Laboratory, USA
Montoya, Javier	Universidad de Cartagena, Instituto de Matematicas Aplicadas, Colombia
Netto, Marco	Microsoft, USA
Ocaña, Kary	Laboratório Nacional de Computação Científica, Brazil
Osthoff, Carla	Laboratório Nacional de Computação Científica, Brazil
Padoin, Edson Luiz	Regional University of the Northwest of the State of Rio Grande do Sul, Brazil
Pantoja, Maria	California Polytech, USA
Raskar, Siddhisanket	Argonne National Laboratory, USA
Rivas, Robinson	Universidad Central de Venezuela, Venezuela
Rizzi, Silvio	Argonne National Laboratory, USA
Steffenel, Luiz Angelo	Université de Reims Champagne-Ardenne, France
Wolovick, Nicolás	Universidad Nacional de Córdoba, Argentina

Reviewers

Barrios H., Carlos J.	Universidad Industrial de Santander, Colombia
Carrillo, Oscar	University of Lyon, CPE, INSA Lyon, Inria, France
Castro, Harold	Universidad de los Andes, Colombia
Cazar Ramírez, Dennis	Universidad San Francisco de Quito, Ecuador
Cortés, Ulises	Barcelona Supercomputing Center, Spain
Cristóbal-Salas, Alfredo	Universidad Veracruzana, México
Cruz Silva, Pedro	NVIDIA, Brazil
Dagostini, Jessica	University of California Santa Cruz, USA
Garcia Henao, John Anderson	Nucleus AI, Switzerland
Gitler, Isidoro	ABACUS - CINVESTVA, México
Hernandez, Benjamin	NVIDIA, USA
Hernandez, Oscar	Oak Ridge National Laboratory, USA
Hernandez, Esteban	Mercado Libre, Colombia
Herrera Guaitero, Rafael Andres	University of Delaware, USA
Iturriaga, Santiago	Universidad de la República, Uruguay
Kahira, Albert Njoroge	Jülich Supercomputing Center, Germany

Contents

High Performance Computing Applications

High Performance Computing (HPC)

Evaluation of Alternatives to Accelerate Scientific Numerical Calculations on Graphics Processing Units Using Python

Johansell Villalobos[1(✉)] and Esteban Meneses[1,2]

[1] Advanced Computing Laboratory, National High Technology Center,
San Jose, Costa Rica
{jovillalobos,emeneses}@cenat.ac.cr
[2] School of Computing, Costa Rica Institute of Technology, Cartago, Costa Rica

Abstract. In this paper, the Numba, JAX, CuPy, PyTorch, and TensorFlow Python GPU accelerated libraries were benchmarked using scientific numerical kernels on a NVIDIA V100 GPU. The benchmarks consisted of a simple Monte Carlo estimation, a particle interaction kernel, a stencil evolution of an array, and tensor operations. The benchmarking procedure included general memory consumption measurements, a statistical analysis of scalability with problem size to determine the best libraries for the benchmarks, and a productivity measurement using source lines of code (SLOC) as a metric. It was statistically determined that the Numba library outperforms the rest on the Monte Carlo, particle interaction, and stencil benchmarks. The deep learning libraries show better performance on tensor operations. The SLOC count was similar for all the libraries except Numba which presented a higher SLOC count which implies more time is needed for code development.

Keywords: Parallel Programming · Parallel Python · Graphics Processing Units

1 Introduction

Scientific computing (SC), alongside high performance computing (HPC), have revolutionized the way complex problems are approached across disciplines. With the exponential growth in computational power, problems that were once only theorized can now be solved by supercomputers. This development allows the design of simulations that are closer to reality, which sheds light on problems like weather forecasting, plasma dynamics, and oceanic current modeling.

Also, the supercomputing simulation workflows used are becoming more complex not only in their simulation process but in their pre-processing and data analysis components. Accommodating these pipelines on HPC systems currently requires a heterogeneous approach using accelerators which mainly include but

C. J. Barrios H. et al. (Eds.): CARLA 2023, CCIS 1887, pp. 3–20, 2024.
https://doi.org/10.1007/978-3-031-52186-7_1

are not limited to GPUs [18]. Currently, the GPU is the most common accelerator in HPC clusters and supercomputers, due to their high energy efficiency [9] and throughput. Referring to the Top500 supercomputer list, the heterogeneous systems are comprised mostly of NVIDIA and AMD manufactured GPUs. Intel has recently incorporated their GPU chips into the market by implementing the Aurora HPC system at Argonne National Laboratory [6].

Introducing these high performance CPU-GPU systems to the HPC world presented a faster, more energy efficient method of executing scientific software. However, it did so by introducing a different perspective on software parallelism and a change in the usual programming paradigm. This new environment presented challenges for the scientific community. CUDA, HIP, and OpenCL, although specifically designed for GPU computing, are low level programming languages that slow down productivity while prototyping and generating SC code. It is important to note that "an increasing number of scientists are using high productivity programming languages" [18], in which Python is a clear protagonist.

Computational scientists would prefer to have fast and portable code while still being able to design the software for the solution of the numerical methods [18]. Python is popular for it portrays a numerical modeling and SC high level abstraction with appropriate APIs. According to GitHub Octoverse statistics, Python is the second most used programming language as of 2022 [1]. Generally, Python code is thought of as slow due to its interpreted nature, but with the introduction of new libraries that implement just-in-time (JIT) compilation and GPU deployment with Python bindings for C/C++ code, considerable acceleration of code execution can be seen [10]. This is the main reason Python has diffused over many disciplines that are not limited to SC. For instance, the machine learning (ML) and artificial intelligence fields have been constructed on the basis of clean high-level Python APIs, such as PyTorch and TensorFlow, that implement bindings to fast compiled CUDA/C/C++ routines. These routines perform the heavy duty linear algebra and numerical computations for deep learning model distributed training, which leaves condensed, readable Python code at the high level.

In that direction, this paper aims to evaluate different Python APIs that make use of GPU architectures via JIT compilation and CUDA/C/C++ subroutines to accelerate scientific numerical calculations. This evaluation considers the use of fundamental scientific numerical methods as benchmarks, specifically Monte Carlo methods, particle interaction routines, stencil operations and linear algebra operations. Furthermore, programmability, performance and scalability of the libraries is measured. The contributions of this work include: *i*) a comparative evaluation of available parallel programming Python tools for a set of SC benchmarks; *ii*) a public GitLab repository with the implemented SC benchmarks alongside the time and memory measurement modules and results; and *iii*) an analysis of tradeoffs between the programming tools.

1.1 Related Work

Python GPU execution has been benchmarked for Python bindings to CUDA and OpenCL [8], focusing on an evaluation of performance portability and energy efficiency between GPU models. The evaluation was done using a finite volume shallow water code implemented with both of these libraries. Evidence suggests that using the Python bindings does not have an important impact on the overall performance of the code and that using Python is as computationally efficient as using C++. Using the Python APIs alongside the Jupyter Notebook environment increased development productivity.

NPBench is a set of NumPy computer programs that represent various HPC applications in different domains [20]. Python machine code compilers and NumPy-like accelerated libraries were tested and benchmarked, specifically CuPy, DaCe, DaCe GPU, Numba, and Pythran. It was determined that alternate implementations of numerical methods using other Python libraries drastically accelerate execution of code but lower productivity in most cases.

OMB-Py is a module consisting of micro benchmarks that evaluate performance of MPI libraries on HPC systems. It implements the first set of communication benchmarks suite for MPI-based parallel Python applications. This package also performs benchmarks on GPU message passing latency and library overheads for multi GPU applications [3].

A comparative evaluation of the performance of a cellular nonlinear network simulator programmed in the CuPy, Numba, PyCUDA, and NumPy Python libraries was performed in [5]. This simulator served as a benchmark for these libraries. The data collected shows that the PyCUDA implementation was the fastest out of the four libraries.

2 Background

2.1 Graphics Processing Unit (GPU) Architecture

GPUs are a core component in today's HPC systems. In the last 15 years the realm of application of GPU has expanded from gaming to the artificial intelligence and scientific computing field. The main reason being the high computing throughput that GPUs can handle due to their parallel computing architecture.

The modern GPU has as its core computational unit the streaming multiprocessor (SM). SMs are comprised of thousands of registers that can be partitioned among numerous threads of execution. This presents a single instruction multiple thread (SIMT) programming paradigm that can be taken advantage of. Even though GPUs have a slower clock speed than CPUs, the ability to handle data in parallel with the SMs gives GPUs an edge for numerical applications that involve multidimensional array operations.

The high information throughput of GPUs, which is in the order of TB/s for high performance GPU architectures, due to the SIMT programming paradigm proves beneficial for scientific computing. Figure 1 shows the general architecture of modern GPUs. GPUs like NVIDIA's Tesla V100 and Ampere A100 have been used in the acceleration of sections of computational modeling codes in fields such as lattice quantum chromodynamics, computational fluid dynamics, molecular dynamics, and climate modeling. This acceleration takes place, for instance, in the linear algebra solvers used, and domain decomposition of the system for parallel computation, or even the whole formulation of the algorithm of a simulation [13].

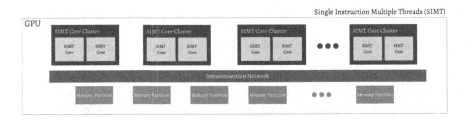

Fig. 1. Modern GPU architecture diagram.

2.2 Python Libraries for Scientific Numerical Calculations

There are a many Python tools that allow the implementation of numerical methods to solve scientific computing problems on GPU. In this paper, the CuPy, PyTorch, TensorFlow, Numba and JAX libraries were chosen for analysis. This selection was a result of a qualitative evaluation of library relevance in the scientific computing community, library development, and maintenance in the Python community.

Multidimensional Array Handling Libraries: The standard programming library for multidimensional array handling is NumPy. It is built on array objects (`ndarray`) that can handle large amounts of data in a more efficient way than native Python. The NumPy library can perform mathematical operations with these array objects mainly vectorized and broadcasted mathematical functions, linear algebra, and random number generation. It provides easy integration with other scientific computing libraries such as SciPy, Pandas, and Matplotlib.

Similarly, CuPy is a Python library oriented towards the deployment of the NumPy functionality onto NVIDIA GPUs [14]. This library is also based on `ndarray` objects, and performs most of the NumPy functions using a CUDA backend, which accelerates the execution of code. As CuPy is compatible with NumPy code, a programmer can import the library with the same alias as NumPy, usually `np`, and the code will be executed provided there is a GPU backend for it. CuPy is and active project, has regular maintenance, and a large user base. CuPy has been implemented as an accelerator simulation code [5,11].

Deep Learning Oriented Frameworks: Deep learning Python frameworks have shown potential in numerical computations for deep neural network training with large models. These libraries accelerate scientific computing tasks due to their ability to efficiently vectorize matrix multiplications on GPU.

PyTorch is a deep learning library that presents a `tensor` data structure as its core. This `tensor` data structure is similar to a `ndarray` but with support for automatic differentiation for the backpropagation phase in deep learning model training [15]. PyTorch proves beneficial for research since it executes dynamical computational graphs which implies faster debugging and prototyping of models. PyTorch is actively maintained by the Facebook/Meta group.

Comparably, TensorFlow is a deep learning library which also uses a `tensor` data structure and automatic differentiation. However, at the time of execution TensorFlow takes a more static approach to numerical computation [2]. Using the `@tf.function` decorator a compiled computational graph is built which executes faster than regular TensorFlow code. There are some caveats about this decorator. The compiled code will run faster if TensorFlow functions are used. However, when using native Python, the code may be slower. Using this decorator makes the library harder to debug and in turn makes prototyping more complex. In return speed is incremented. TensorFlow is actively maintained by Google, and is used extensively in industry applications.

Just-in-Time (JIT) Compilation Libraries: Numba is a JIT compilation library that translates Python code to optimized machine language using LLVM [10]. Numba is built to produce code that can be executed on CPU or NVIDIA GPUs. This code can be parallelized in three ways: simple multi-threading, SIMD vectorization and GPU vectorization. In this work only the GPU acceleration functionality will be explored. To execute code on the GPU, Numba presents the `@cuda.jit` decorator, which informs the compiler to build a GPU executable kernel. These kernels need to be defined completely, including the number of grid blocks and threads per block specified beforehand so the compiler can correctly execute on the GPU. Numba has been tested for code acceleration an yielded positive results in several cases [3,11,16].

JAX is a JIT compilation library that uses accelerated linear algebra (XLA) and automatic differentiation (Autograd) to compile native Python code into differentiable machine code which runs on CPU, GPU or TPU [7]. The main decorator this library presents is `@jax.jit`. This decorator allows for the XLA compilation of any snippet of code provided it satisfies a set of rules. It provides a similar API to NumPy and is highly compatible with NumPy `ndarrays`. JAX automatically vectorizes code, but manual vectorization using `vmap` and distributed parallelization using `pmap` can be used to parallelize code.

2.3   Scientific Numerical Calculation Kernels

Scientific computing applications often use similar numerical methods to solve problems. Depending on the size of the problem being handled, the solution time can scale up rather quickly. By contrasting the results of algorithms implemented with each library, insights about their advantages and drawbacks can be obtained. From this, the decision of which is the most effective tool for a specific scientific computing task can be taken.

The benchmarks designed in this work were inspired by Berkeley's 13 Dwarfs on CUDA [17]. These benchmarks fall into four of the 7 categories presented in [4] which are dense linear algebra operations, n-body methods, structured grids, and Monte Carlo methods.

Monte Carlo: Monte Carlo simulations are statistical numerical methods that can describe the dynamics of complex systems in a more detailed manner that analytical or experimental analyses would. The fundamental concept behind Monte Carlo simulations is to generate a large number of random samples from the probability distribution that describes the behavior of system being analysed. These samples can be used as initial conditions for the model being described or as parts of a coupled system.

In this case, a simple numerical calculation will be carried out. A way to calculate the irrational number π is to generate N_{samples} random pairs of numbers $\{(x,y)\,|\,x \in [0,1],\,y \in [0,1]\}$ and count the number of pairs N_{in} that satisfy the condition $r = \sqrt{x^2 + y^2} \leq 1$. The number π then can be approximated as $\pi \approx 4N_{\text{in}}/N_{\text{samples}}$.

Particle Interaction: Molecular dynamics simulations are based upon the classical interaction of particles. This technique allows the study of the behavior of complex particle systems. Simply put, the method integrates the equations of motion of all the particles or molecules that compose the system being analyzed. The equations of motion of an individual particle is given by,

$$m_i \frac{d\mathbf{r}_i}{dt} = \mathbf{F}_i = -\sum_{i=0}^{N} \nabla V(r_i); \quad V(r) = 4\varepsilon \left[\left(\frac{\sigma}{r}\right)^{12} - \left(\frac{\sigma}{r}\right)^{6} \right] \quad (1)$$

in which m_i is its mass, $\mathbf{r}_i$ is its position, and $\mathbf{F}_i$ is the total force acting on the particle. For the interatomic potential V, r is the distance between the two particles, σ is the distance at which the potential function becomes zero, and ε is the depth of the potential well.

The total force $\mathbf{F}$ is dependent on specific functions which describe the attraction and repulsion of two particles. These functions or interparticular potentials can be theoretically or experimentally constructed. The most used potential function for the study of gases is the Lennard-Jones (LJ) interatomic potential. This function describes the potential energy between two particles of the same kind taking into account the Van der Waals attraction and repulsion due to their overlapping electron clouds. Theoretically, for each individual particle the total force $\mathbf{F}_i$ is the sum of the forces caused by the interaction of the N

particles in the system, which can scale up computation time quite rapidly for large problems. Considering this issue, an approximation can be made based on the distance σ, which is to define a cutoff radius $r_{\text{cutoff}} = \sigma$ to only consider the particles that influence significantly the total force. With this approximation only $N_{\text{r}} < N$ calculations have to be made per particle.

Stencil: Partial differential equations (PDEs) are often used in scientific computing. From computational fluid dynamics to electromagnetism, the models used are always based on spatial and temporal changes of a set of variables. Given that analytical solutions are not always available, numerical methods need to be implemented to solve these problems. The finite difference method (FDM) is a simple method to implement spatial model discretization for numerical PDE solutions. The discretization process of PDEs results in an expression that describes the value of a node in a structured array-like mesh as a function of itself and neighboring nodes. This expression constitutes a computational stencil. In this work, a simple averaging stencil will be applied to a three dimensional cubic array. This operation is given by,

$$a_{ijk} = (a_{(i+1)jk} + a_{(i-1)jk} + a_{i(j+1)k} + a_{i(j-1)k} + a_{ij(k+1)} + a_{ij(k-1)} + a_{ijk})/7.$$

Tensor Operations: Tensor operations generalize concepts which are present in physics and mathematics to a high degree. In continuum mechanics, PDEs are combined with tensors to represent the change in the stress, strain, and velocity of a system. In relativity, tensors are used to compute the trajectories of particles in curved space-times using the geodesic equations. These mathematical objects are not limited to any particular field of science and are commonly used in multidimensional array handling. Simple tensor operations like outer and inner products of matrices and vectors will be used as benchmarks for the chosen Python tools. These operations are defined mathematically as,

$$\mathbf{A} : \mathbf{B} = A_{ij}B_{ij} = C \qquad \mathbf{A} \otimes \mathbf{B} = A_i B_j = C_{ij} \qquad \mathbf{AB} = A_{ij}B_{jk} = C_{ik} \qquad (2)$$

3 Kernel Design and Implementation

Each numerical method was implemented using the five libraries in a similar algorithmic structure. Naturally, some differences in the algorithms are to be expected. This section will give an overview of how the four benchmarks were implemented in the study using the libraries mentioned[1].

Monte Carlo: This benchmark had an alteration on its usual implementation which was the introduction of a loop to generate $N \times N_{\text{iter}}$ pairs of numbers for a more accurate calculation of π. The random number generation process is implemented as similar functions in each library but the pseudorandom number generators (PRNGs) used differ. The TensorFlow implementation made use of the decorator `@tf.function`. This decorator creates computational graphs to optimize functions which are called on numerous times.

---

[1] The source code of these benchmarks may be found in this repository: https://gitlab.com/CNCA_CeNAT/sc_parallelpython.

Particles: The particle codes all followed the same structure, a main loop which used a Verlet integration algorithm, a vectorized approach to obtain the particle neighbor list using distance matrices, and a vectorized evaluation of the Lennard-Jones particle force for each neighbor in the list. All this was necessary to take advantage of the accelerated linear algebra (XLA) and JIT compilation implementation characteristics of the libraries used. The exception to this is the Numba particle code implementation which differs considerably with respect to the others in its approach to calculate neighbor lists. This benchmark looped over all particles to define their neighbors instead of calculating a distance matrix.

Stencil: The stencil algorithm was implemented with the exact same structure throughout all codes. Array slicing was used for vectorized updates of the whole array. In this benchmark, JIT compilation was used to optimize the TensorFlow and JAX code. The Numba variant needed specification of thread ids for array indexing.

Tensor Operations: All tensor operations are already implemented in every library except Numba. The specific algorithms for each tensor operation had to be programmed. The matrix contraction and outer product algorithms were implemented using global thread IDs since both operations are direct, the matrix contraction algorithm was programmed to calculate the resulting matrix and then perform a sum reduction of this matrix using the `@cuda.reduce` decorator. The matrix multiplication algorithm used shared memory programming since looping directly with all threads is computationally expensive.

4   Methodology

4.1   Computational Infrastructure

The resources used for the benchmarking process are found in the Kabré Supercomputing Cluster at the Costa Rica National Center of High Technology (CeNAT). Kabré is a collection of 52 computing nodes of four different architectures that are used in four main areas: machine learning, computational science, big data, and bioinformatics. The machine learning section of the Kabré supercomputing cluster was used in this study. These nodes are composed of four NVIDIA TESLA V100, with 32 GB of GPU memory, and 24 2.40 GHz CPU cores with 2 physical threads each. The software tested in this benchmark is summarized in Table 1.

Table 1. Computer program versions

Computer tool	Version
Linux distribution	CentOS Linux 7 (Core)
Linux kernel	3.10.0-1160.81.1.el7 .x86_64
Python	3.9.0
PyTorch	1.13.0
TensorFlow	2.2.0
Numba	0.56.4
CuPy	8.3.0
JAX	0.4.10

Table 2. Benchmark problem sizes for experimental design

Benchmark	Problem sizes N
Monte Carlo	[1.0e1, 2.5e7, 5.0e7, 7.5e7, 1.0e8]
Particle Interaction	[10, 3757, 7505, 11252, 15000]
Stencil	[10, 232, 455, 677, 900]
Matrix contraction	[10, 6257, 12505, 18752, 25000]
Outer product	[10, 6257, 12505, 18752, 25000]
Matrix mult.	[10, 6257, 12505, 18752, 25000]

4.2 Experimental Design

A two stage nested design was used for the data acquisition process using 15 observations per entry. The factors in this experiment were the problem size N, and programming library, Table 2 shows the problem sizes for each benchmark. This experimental design was chosen since it allowed for a more robust data analysis [12]. Statistical difference between means can be evaluated using a parametric analysis of variance (ANOVA). If ANOVA assumptions are not satisfied, a non parametric approach using the Kruskal-Wallis median comparison can be implemented.

4.3 Benchmarking Procedure

GPU Kernel Timing: Due to asynchronous execution of kernels, the kernel timing process cannot rely on the usual timing techniques used in Python. The `time` library is the standard for measuring execution time of functions by implementing the `time.perf_counter` function. In this case, function timing was done by using the Numba library. Numba presents the `elapsed_time` function to time GPU kernel execution between two Numba `events` which implement the CUDA event structure. This function ensures GPU accurate timing. A timing module was then programmed to quantify elapsed time on the GPU. The timing was carried out only for the kernels and not the data transfer between host and device.

Memory Consumption Measurement: GPU memory usage was quantified for each kernel using the `pynvml` Python bindings for the NVIDIA management library. The measurement was done in parallel using subprocesses triggered by event structures. Using the `time` library, data was logged every 10 microseconds. Memory data was saved to `json` files for later post-processing.

Script Benchmarking: With the experimental design in mind, the data generation process started by gathering all kernels and writing scripts for function benchmarking for each library. The whole set of scripts was then modularized for easy access of the functions. Later, Python scripts were programmed for timing all functions. Each script implemented the set of all benchmarks for a specific library. This script then looped over the problem sizes specified in Table 2.

With respect to the problem size N, it varied according to the kernel being tested since each piece of code has a different memory footprint. This way, the GPU resources can be fully used, and the benchmark times can be long enough to reduce any source of randomness in the execution of the kernels.

A set of $N_{\mathrm{warmup}} = 10$ warm-up runs and $N_{\mathrm{iters}} = 10$ timed iterations were used to obtain consistent data. These scripts were then executed on a NVIDIA V100 GPU using isolated Conda environments for reproducibility. The results were then saved to disk using `json` files.

Data Analysis: The data analysis of these results was done using the NumPy, Pandas, Statsmodels, and Pingouin Python libraries. First and foremost, an ANOVA test was performed for the nested design, this way the ANOVA statistical assumptions of residuals could be tested. The linear model $y_{ijk} = \mu + \tau_i + \beta_{j(i)} + \epsilon_{(ij)k}$ was fit using ordinary least squares with the Statsmodels function `ols` to carry this out. Then, a normality test was conducted quantitively using a Shapiro-Wilk test. For data that followed the ANOVA assumptions the Tukey pairwise mean comparison test was implemented. The Kruskal-Wallis non parametric ANOVA was used for data which did not satisfy the parametric ANOVA assumptions. It was executed using the Pingouin library. After this, Dunn's pairwise comparison was used as a post hoc test to evaluate the differences between medians and quantify statistical difference. After the post hoc pairwise tests, the best performing library was chosen according to statistical difference and minimum median/mean execution time.

Productivity Measurement: Lines of code were used as a measure of library productivity. To standardize this metric, the Black Python package was employed, which applies the same format to all Python code it analyzes. After this, the Pygount tool was used to statically analyze Python scripts and get the source lines of code (SLOC) count.

5   Results

5.1   Normality Test

ANOVAs were implemented to test the statistical assumptions of the residuals of the obtained time data. The residuals showed no normality at a 95% confidence level. Data normalization was considered by implementing a Box-Cox transformation, however that did not yield positive results. Due to this, non parametric ANOVA studies were carried out for all levels. Table 3 presents the P-values for the residuals of each benchmark.

5.2   Memory Consumption

Memory consumption was measured generally for all benchmarks at the largest problem sizes shown in Table 2. Figure 2 shows the data acquired by the NVIDIA

Table 3. Normality results for each benchmark.

Benchmark	Montecarlo	Particles	Stencil	Matrix contraction	Outer product	Matrix multiplication
P-value	3.34e−32	3.85e−33	1.41e−37	7.59e−35	2.04e−35	7.72e−33
Normal?	No	No	No	No	No	No

driver software. To correctly measure memory consumption for the TensorFlow and JAX libraries memory preallocation was disabled previously. This was only performed for the memory usage benchmarking process. Differences in memory consumption for the libraries may arise due to different background processes.

Considering the Monte Carlo benchmark, Numba used the least memory out of all the libraries. This may be attributed to its lighter CUDA array object implementation.

With respect to the particle interaction benchmark, it presented variability in between libraries due to the difference in functions used to implement the same method. Some scattering modules had slight alterations on functionality.

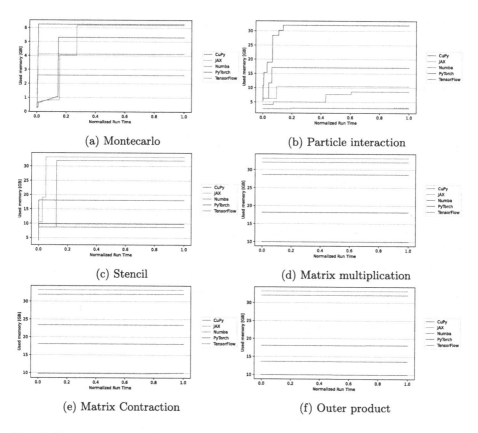

(a) Montecarlo

(b) Particle interaction

(c) Stencil

(d) Matrix multiplication

(e) Matrix Contraction

(f) Outer product

Fig. 2. Memory usage results from the execution of the GPU proposed benchmarks.

Therefore, workarounds had to be implemented. The Numba implementation used the least memory since it did not allocate a distance matrix of $N \times N$ particles as the other libraries did.

For the stencil benchmark, Numba presented the least memory consumption out of all the libraries. In this implementation threads access each array entry independently and evolve the algorithm without the need to create a view or slices. The other four libraries implement slicing which creates objects hence, higher memory consumption.

The tensor operations presented high, constant memory usage for all libraries except Numba. The matrix multiplication benchmark was implemented using shared memory programming to accelerate the computation, while the other two tensor operations were straightforward.

5.3 Scalability

Referring to Fig. 3, the Monte Carlo algorithm displays linear scalability with respect to problem size. The CuPy library presents the highest execution times for all sizes except $N = 10$. Profiling of the Monte Carlo code sheds light on the inefficiency of the `cupy.sum` function. The reduction algorithm in this module may be the cause of slow execution. Numba presents the fastest execution of all the libraries given its different memory implementation. Random numbers are generated on the device per thread and not stored in main memory which speeds up the Monte Carlo process.

Considering the particle interaction benchmark, it scales as N^2 for all libraries. JAX presents poor performance in this benchmark as its execution time is 20 times the other libraries. Profiling the code with `nvprof` highlighted a fusion kernel in which almost 70% of the time was spent. The XLA compiler fuses computations to optimize the computational graph. It is possible the fusion of some computations in this code may be reducing performance thus raising execution time.

Figure 3 clearly shows that Numba outperforms every other library in the stencil benchmark. This due to the fast thread access mentioned before. JAX starts off with a high execution time attributed to the JIT and XLA compilation of code, yet it scales like the other libraries.

Regarding tensor operations, the deep learning libraries including JAX outperformed Numba and CuPy. These libraries are optimized for N-dimensional array handling and multiplication due to the field they are applied in. These libraries present static, compiled GPU routines which surpass JIT compilcated kernels.

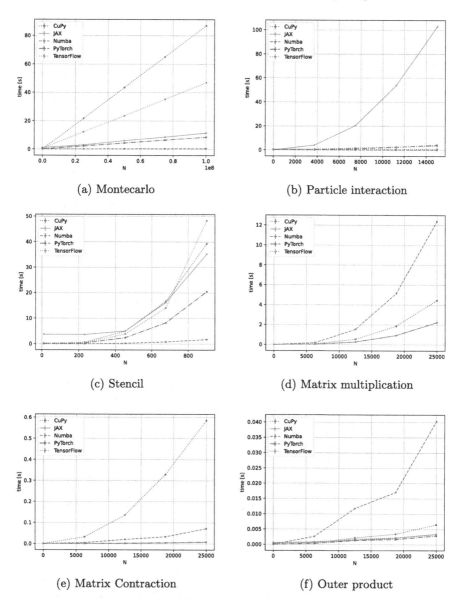

Fig. 3. Scalability results from the GPU proposed benchmarks.

After the Kruskal-Wallis non parametric ANOVAs, data was analyzed using the Dunn post-hoc test. Table 4 presents the best statistically similar results after performing post-hoc tests.

Table 4. Execution time medians [s] of the best statistically similar libraries for the benchmarks evaluation.

Benchmark	Problem Size (N)				
	N_1	N_2	N_3	N_4	N_5
Montecarlo	Numba : 0.0002	Numba : 0.1246	Numba : 0.2489	Numba : 0.3736	Numba : 0.4986
	CuPy : 0.0780	PyTorch : 2.1880	PyTorch : 4.3235	PyTorch : 6.4481	PyTorch : 8.5914
Particles	Numba : 0.0574	Numba : 0.0571	Numba : 0.0572	Numba : 0.0815	Numba : 0.0562
	JAX : 0.0576	CuPy : 0.2186	CuPy : 0.3501	CuPy : 0.5765	CuPy : 0.8917
Stencil	Numba : 0.0001	Numba : 0.0238	Numba : 0.2410	Numba : 0.8121	Numba : 1.7729
	CuPy : 0.0280	PyTorch : 0.3274	PyTorch : 1.0429	PyTorch : 3.4906	PyTorch : 11.0197
Matrix Mult.	CuPy : 0.0000	PyTorch : 0.0356	PyTorch : 0.2811	TensorFlow : 0.9431	JAX : 2.2371
	PyTorch : 0.0000	TensorFlow : 0.0356	TensorFlow : 0.2819	PyTorch : 0.9438	PyTorch : 2.2418
Matrix Contr.	CuPy : 0.0000	PyTorch : 0.0005	PyTorch : 0.0022	JAX : 0.0044	JAX : 0.0072
	PyTorch : 0.0000	JAX : 0.0009	JAX : 0.0024	PyTorch : 0.0049	TensorFlow : 0.0086
Outer Prod.	CuPy : 0.0000	PyTorch : 0.0003	PyTorch : 0.0013	PyTorch : 0.0016	PyTorch : 0.0028
	PyTorch : 0.0000	CuPy : 0.0005	JAX : 0.0014	JAX : 0.0021	JAX : 0.0033

Table 4 shows the dominance of the Numba library in terms of execution time for the Monte Carlo, particle interaction, and stencil benchmarks. The deep learning frameworks, on the other hand, achieved better performance in the tensor operations benchmarks.

5.4 Productivity

Python is heavily used for prototyping in the scientific community and it is a valuable aspect. As such, there is a need to maintain this characteristic while evolving the language towards HPC. Measuring SLOC is the main way to examine if productivity indeed is maintained. The SLOC data for each benchmark is shown in Table 5. Qualitatively, all libraries seem to have similar productivity relying only on SLOC, with the exception of Numba. Numba presents notorious differences in SLOC count. These are visible in the particle interaction, and the tensor operations benchmarks. These counts are to be expected since the CUDA functionality in Numba is of a lower level with respect to the other libraries.

Table 5. SLOC for each benchmark.

Benchmark	Library					
	CuPy	JAX	Numba	NumPy	PyTorch	TensorFlow
Monte Carlo	11	14	20	11	14	16
Particles	87	70	97	88	77	76
Stencil	15	19	21	17	18	20
Tensor Operations	9	9	49	11	10	9

6   Final Remarks

An evaluation of five GPU computing Python libraries was performed, specifically Numba, CuPy, PyTorch, TensorFlow, and JAX. This evaluation included memory consumption, scalability, and productivity analyses on a single NVIDIA V100 GPU. With respect to memory consumption, all libraries seem to handle GPU memory differently and this behavior is expected. Numba presented the least memory usage in most benchmarks.

Considering scalability results, our analysis concluded that the data needed a non parametric statistical evaluation due to non normality of residuals. Kruskal-Wallis tests with Dunn's post-hoc test were implemented to quantify the differences between the median execution times of the libraries. It was found that the Numba library performs better than the rest for the Monte Carlo, particle interaction, and stencil benchmarks. The deep learning libraries, specifically PyTorch, outperform Numba in tensor operations. This behavior is expected since these libraries implement highly optimized GPU routines. However, between these libraries the times are close so no distinction was made with the exception of CuPy which presents slightly higher computation times for linear algebra kernels.

Regarding the productivity of code, SLOC were counted and from all benchmarks the library that stands out is Numba. This library presents higher SLOC count for the particle interaction algorithm and tensor operations. From this it can be concluded that while using Numba some productivity may be sacrificed for speed depending on the nature of the problem trying to be solved. The rest of the libraries present similar SLOC count on all benchmarks.

Acknowledgments. This research was partially supported by a machine allocation on Kabré supercomputer at the Costa Rica National High Technology Center.

A   Roofline Graphs for the Algorithms Proposed

The algorithms proposed in this work were profiled with the NVIDIA Nsight Compute command line interface (CLI) using the methodology found in [19]. Roofline graphs are shown in Figs. 4 and 5.

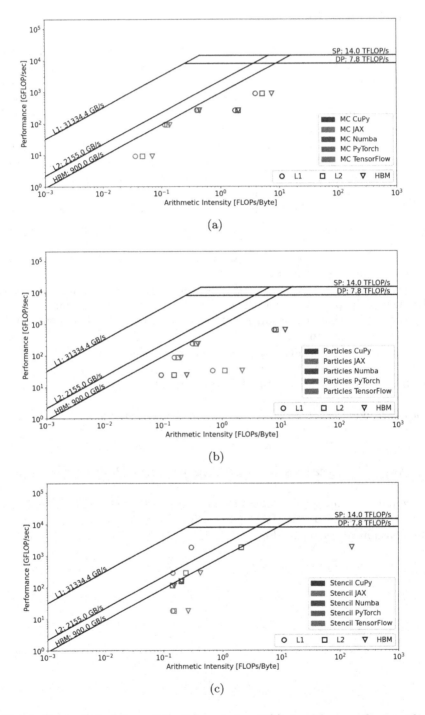

Fig. 4. Monte Carlo (a), particles (b), and stencil (c) algorithms roofline graphs.

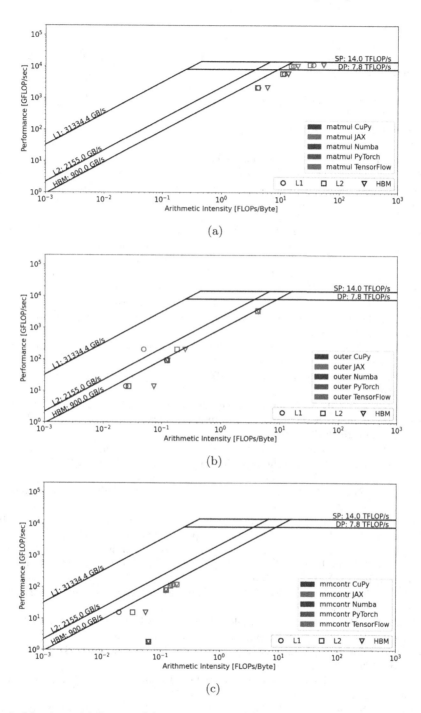

Fig. 5. Matrix multiplication (a), outer product (b), and matrix contraction (c) algorithms roofline graphs.

References

1. The top programming languages. https://octoverse.github.com/2022/top-programming-languages. Accessed 23 June 2022
2. Abadi, M., Agarwal, A., Barham, P., Brevdo, E., et al.: Tensorflow: large-scale machine learning on heterogeneous distributed systems (2016). https://arxiv.org/abs/1603.04467
3. Alnaasan, N., Jain, A., Shafi, A., Subramoni, H., Panda, D.K.: OMB-PY: Python micro-benchmarks for evaluating performance of MPI libraries on HPC systems (2021). https://arxiv.org/abs/2110.10659
4. Asanović, K., Bodik, R., Catanzaro, et al.: The landscape of parallel computing research: a view from berkeley. Technical Reports, UCB/EECS-2006-183, EECS Department, University of California, Berkeley, Dec 2006. http://www2.eecs.berkeley.edu/Pubs/TechRpts/2006/EECS-2006-183.html
5. Dogaru, R., Dogaru, I.: A Python framework for fast modelling and simulation of cellular nonlinear networks and other finite-difference time-domain systems (2021)
6. Facility, A.L.C.: Aurora. https://www.alcf.anl.gov/aurora
7. Frostig, R., Johnson, M.J., Leary, C.: Compiling machine learning programs via high-level tracing (2016). https://arxiv.org/abs/1603.04467
8. Holm, H.H., Brodtkorb, A.R., Sætra, M.L.: GPU computing with Python: Performance, energy efficiency and usability. Computation 8 (2020). https://doi.org/10.3390/computation8010004
9. Huang, S., Xiao, S., Feng, W.: On the energy efficiency of graphics processing units for scientific computing. In: 2009 IEEE International Symposium on Parallel and Distributed Processing, pp. 1–8 (2009). https://doi.org/10.1109/IPDPS.2009.5160980
10. Lam, S.K., Pitrou, A., Seibert, S.: Numba: a LLVM-based python JIT compiler, vol. 2015-January. Association for Computing Machinery (2015). https://doi.org/10.1145/2833157.2833162
11. Marowka, A.: Python accelerators for high-performance computing. J. Supercomput. 74, 1449–1460 (2018). https://doi.org/10.1007/s11227-017-2213-5
12. Montgomery, D.C.: Design and analysis of experiments (2017)
13. NVIDIA: Nvidia HPC application performance. https://developer.nvidia.com/hpc-application-performance
14. Okuta, R., Unno, Y., Nishino, D., Hido, S., Loomis, C.: Cupy: a numpy-compatible library for NVIDIA GPU calculations. https://github.com/cupy/cupy
15. Paszke, A., Gross, S., Massa, F., et al.: Pytorch: an imperative style, high-performance deep learning library (2019). https://arxiv.org/abs/1912.01703
16. Pata, J., Dutta, I., Lu, N., Vlimant, J.R., et al.: ETH library data analysis with GPU-accelerated kernels (2020). https://doi.org/10.3929/ethz-b-000484721
17. Springer, P.L.: Berkeley's dwarfs on CUDA (2012)
18. Vetter, J.S., Brightwell, R., Gokhale, M., McCormick, P., et al.: Extreme heterogeneity 2018 - productive computational science in the era of extreme heterogeneity: report for doe ASCR workshop on extreme heterogeneity (2018). https://doi.org/10.2172/1473756, https://www.osti.gov/servlets/purl/1473756/
19. Yang, C.: Hierarchical roofline analysis: how to collect data using performance tools on Intel CPUs and NVIDIA GPUs (2020)
20. Ziogas, A.N., Ben-Nun, T., Schneider, T., Hoefler, T.: NPBench: a benchmarking suite for high-performance numpy, pp. 63–74. Association for Computing Machinery (2021). https://doi.org/10.1145/3447818.3460360

Enhancing a GPU-Based Wave Propagation Application Through Loop Tiling and Loop Fission Optimizations

Gabriel Costa[✉][ID], Peterson Nogueira[ID], João Speglich[ID], and Laian Silva[ID]

Supercomputing Center for Industrial Innovation SENAI CIMATEC (CS2I),
Salvador, Bahia, Brazil
{gabriel.pinheiro,peterson.santos,joao.speglich,laian.silva}@fieb.org.br

Abstract. Graphics Processing Units (GPUs) harbor immense parallelization capabilities that can significantly accelerate the processing of large datasets. In the context of geophysical modeling, these capabilities can be harnessed to achieve faster execution times without compromising the accuracy of results. This study investigates optimization techniques implemented in a three-dimensional elastic model developed using the DEVITO tool.

DEVITO is a Domain-Specific Language for stencil computation, with a focus on seismic inversion problems. DEVITO enables the creation of geophysical models in Python through functions and classes provided by the tool. Using an internal compiler, DEVITO can translate the model written from symbolic equations in Python into a finite difference code in C/C++.

The performance of an initial naive implementation is compared against two optimized versions. One of the approaches was named Tiling, and uses the OpenACC *tile* directive to block the most relevant loop nests of the application. The other optimized approach, Sig Fission, uses the loop fission technique to divide the workload of one of the nests and then applies the *tile* directive. These optimizations have led to notable improvements, including an increased cache hit rate, enhanced GPU scheduler occupancy, a decrease in the number of registers needed to issue instructions, and a remarkable 40% reduction in execution time.

By capitalizing on the parallel computing power of GPUs, this study demonstrates the efficacy of employing optimization strategies, such as loop tiling and loop fission, in geophysical modeling targeting graphics processing units. These techniques pave the way for accelerated data processing, ultimately contributing to improved efficiency and accuracy in computational geophysics, without any loss of integrity in the results.

Keywords: GPU · loop tiling · loop fission · DEVITO

C. J. Barrios H. et al. (Eds.): CARLA 2023, CCIS 1887, pp. 21–35, 2024.
https://doi.org/10.1007/978-3-031-52186-7_2

1   Introduction

DEVITO is a Domain-Specific Language (DSL) written in Python for stencil computation, focusing on seismic inversion problems [1,2]. DEVITO enables the creation of geophysical models in Python with a high degree of abstraction, thanks to the functions and classes provided by the tool. Using an internal compiler, DEVITO can translate the model written from symbolic equations in Python into a finite difference code in C/C++, which is partially optimized for execution on the specified architecture.

In addition to running on multi-core machines, DEVITO allows code generation targeting accelerators and GPUs. Offloading the workload to the graphics unit is done through OpenACC, a programming standard implemented through a library for C/C++ and Fortran, enabling code optimization in an automated way via directives [3]. The loop tiling technique stands out among the optimizations implemented in OpenACC and is available for DEVITO. This loop transformation alters the data access pattern, so the data is no longer accessed continuously until the end of a dimension but instead accessed in blocks with dimensions specified by the programmer [4]. The goal of this technique is to take advantage of the principle of spatial locality of data, favoring the reuse of nearby stencil points [5,6].

This work focuses on the computational optimization of a DEVITO-based implementation of elastodynamic equations as described by Virieux [7]. Therefore, the objective is to develop modifications in the C++ algorithm to improve performance and mitigate bottlenecks without changing the nature of the equations and their solutions.

This work continues an ongoing effort to optimize the DEVITO tool, aiming to contribute to existing efforts with a similar goal. N. Kukreja et al. [1] provide an initial presentation of DEVITO, introducing some of the optimizations in the DSL to ensure code generation with optimization levels comparable to manually optimized code. These automated optimizations include vectorization, aligned memory allocation, parallelization through pragmas, loop blocking on CPU, and common sub-expression elimination. The work also measures performance in GFLOPS/s and arithmetic intensity in FLOPS/byte for the simulation of a three-dimensional acoustic model.

M. Louboutin et al. [8] conducted industrial-scale tests for seismic imaging of an anisotropic model using DEVITO. The authors compared the number of floating-point operations required for each grid point in two cases: without any optimization and with the optimizations implemented by DEVITO (common sub-expression elimination, factorization, and cross-iteration redundancy elimination). The difference reached values approximately 81% lower in the lowest discretization order used and around 95% lower in the highest discretization order used, both in favor of the optimized version of the code.

L. Jesus et al. [9] performed GPU tests for six visco-acoustic equations, comparing the performance of two codes for each equation: one with the advanced optimizations offered by DEVITO and another with these same optimizations plus the use of OpenACC loop tiling. The authors used the default tile shape provided by DEVITO, without tuning this parameter. In the three-dimensional models of larger magnitude, the authors were able to significantly increase cache hit rates in more than one memory level, as well as improve floating-point operation performance and arithmetic intensity.

This study aims to continue these and other efforts to optimize code generated by DEVITO, proposing an investigation into the performance achieved by well-established loop modification strategies in HPC: loop tiling (with tuned values) and loop fission.

The remaining article is divided into the following sections: the Materials, Methods, and Theory section describes the NSYS and NCU tools used for data collection and profiling, the forward operator of the elastic equation, the optimized approaches developed for the operator, and the conditions and environment in which the tests were executed; the Results section presents and discusses a series of performance-related results collected in tests with the Naive, Tiling, and Sig Fission approaches, both in single and multi GPU executions; finally, the Conclusions section summarizes the main conclusions that can be drawn from the presented results.

2   Materials, Methods, and Theory

2.1   Profiling Tools

Nsight Systems (NSYS) is a GPU profiling tool that provides a comprehensive view of the system throughout the application's life cycle. It can track calls to external APIs, system operations, and the use of other hardware, such as the CPU, as well as record bilateral memory traffic between the host and device [10]. In the present study, NSYS was used to identify which kernels were responsible for most of the computational effort involved in the application.

Nsight Compute (NCU) is a CUDA kernel profiler that provides a range of metrics for data collection and analysis. For the purpose of conducting a focused and vertical analysis exclusively on kernels, this tool is highly recommended as it provides statistical insights, isolated information, and facilitates performance comparisons among different versions of the same kernel [11].

2.2   The Elastic Wave Equation

The propagation of seismic waves in heterogeneous, isotropic, elastic earth media can be expressed by the elastodynamic equations [7].

$$\begin{cases} \rho\dfrac{\partial v_x}{\partial t} - \left(\dfrac{\partial \sigma_{xx}}{\partial x} + \dfrac{\partial \sigma_{xy}}{\partial y} + \dfrac{\partial \sigma_{xz}}{\partial z}\right) = 0, \\[2mm] \rho\dfrac{\partial v_y}{\partial t} - \left(\dfrac{\partial \sigma_{yx}}{\partial x} + \dfrac{\partial \sigma_{yy}}{\partial y} + \dfrac{\partial \sigma_{yz}}{\partial z}\right) = 0, \\[2mm] \rho\dfrac{\partial v_z}{\partial t} - \left(\dfrac{\partial \sigma_{zx}}{\partial x} + \dfrac{\partial \sigma_{zy}}{\partial y} + \dfrac{\partial \sigma_{zz}}{\partial z}\right) = 0, \\[2mm] \dfrac{\partial \sigma_{xx}}{\partial t} - (\lambda+2\mu)\dfrac{\partial v_x}{\partial x} - \lambda\left(\dfrac{\partial v_y}{\partial y} + \dfrac{\partial v_z}{\partial z}\right) = f_{xx}, \\[2mm] \dfrac{\partial \sigma_{yy}}{\partial t} - (\lambda+2\mu)\dfrac{\partial v_y}{\partial y} - \lambda\left(\dfrac{\partial v_x}{\partial x} + \dfrac{\partial v_z}{\partial z}\right) = f_{yy}, \\[2mm] \dfrac{\partial \sigma_{zz}}{\partial t} - (\lambda+2\mu)\dfrac{\partial v_z}{\partial z} - \lambda\left(\dfrac{\partial v_x}{\partial x} + \dfrac{\partial v_y}{\partial y}\right) = f_{zz}, \\[2mm] \dfrac{\partial \sigma_{yz}}{\partial t} - \mu\left(\dfrac{\partial v_z}{\partial y} + \dfrac{\partial v_y}{\partial z}\right) = 0, \\[2mm] \dfrac{\partial \sigma_{zx}}{\partial t} - \mu\left(\dfrac{\partial v_x}{\partial z} + \dfrac{\partial v_z}{\partial x}\right) = 0, \\[2mm] \dfrac{\partial \sigma_{xy}}{\partial t} - \mu\left(\dfrac{\partial v_x}{\partial y} + \dfrac{\partial v_y}{\partial x}\right) = 0. \end{cases} \tag{1}$$

v_x, v_y, v_z are the horizontal and vertical particle velocity fields, $\sigma_{xx}, \sigma_{yy}, \sigma_{zz}$, $\sigma_{yz}, \sigma_{zx}, \sigma_{xy}$ are the stress fields, f_{xx}, f_{yy}, f_{zz} are the source terms, ρ is density, λ and μ are the Lamé parameters. These coefficients describe the spatially variable property of the earth, and are related to the seismic P-wave and S-wave velocities via $\lambda + 2\mu = \rho V_p^2$ and $\mu = \rho V_s^2$.

2.3 Approaches

Analyses performed with the NSYS profiler on the generated C++ code showed that 98.3% of the computational effort employed in the total execution of the application is concentrated in just two kernels: V (53.2%) and Sig (45.1%). These kernels are responsible for calculating the particle velocity fields (V) and the stress fields (Sig), as shown in Eq. 1. Therefore, optimization efforts focused on extracting performance from these two kernels. The present work compares the results obtained from the standard version of the operator generated by DEVITO with two new approaches developed for performance extraction, as described below:

– **Naive:** the DEVITO default approach, in which the main optimization is the use of the *collapse* clause to transform a three-dimensional nesting into a one-dimensional iteration loop.
– **Tiling:** an approach that replaces the *collapse* clause by the *tile* clause in the V and Sig kernels, with tuned values. The V kernel uses tiles with dimensions of (32, 4, 4), while the Sig kernel uses dimensions of (16, 4, 4).

– **Sig Fission:** an approach that combines the techniques of loop tiling and loop fission. In this approach, the V kernel maintains the tile dimensions of (32, 4, 4). The loop fission technique divides the workload of a nesting into two or more nests of smaller workload but with the same iteration space [12]. It was applied to the Sig kernel by separating the cross-derivatives into one nest, and the derivatives taken in the same dimension into another nest, with these two new kernels being computed sequentially. The *tile* clause is applied again to these two new nests, maintaining the (32, 4, 4) dimension applied in the V nest.

The tile dimensions of each of the kernels were determined empirically, always choosing the ones that achieved the best performance. A limitation to be taken into account in this process is that the product of the tile dimensions should not exceed the maximum limit of threads per block on the GPU. Since the limit of the utilized device is 1024 threads per block, the product of the dimensions must be less than or equal to this value, as shown in Eq. 2, where the $D_{\text{size}(i)}$ represents the size of dimension i, and n is the number of dimensions in the tile.

$$\prod_{i=1}^{n} D_{\text{size}(i)} \leq 1024 \tag{2}$$

Algorithms 1, 2, and 3 illustrate the pseudocodes of the Naive, Tiling, and Sig Fission approaches, respectively.

Algorithm 1. Naive Approach

```
 1: procedure COMPUTE V
 2:     pragma acc parallel loop collapse(3)
 3:     for x... do
 4:         for y... do
 5:             for z... do
 6:                 Compute vx, vy, vz
 7:             end for
 8:         end for
 9:     end for
10: end procedure
11: ...
12: procedure COMPUTE SIG
13:     pragma acc parallel loop collapse(3)
14:     for x... do
15:         for y... do
16:             for z... do
17:                 Compute σxx, σyy, σzz,
    σyz, σzx, σxy
18:             end for
19:         end for
20:     end for
21: end procedure
```

Algorithm 2. Tiling Approach

```
 1: procedure COMPUTE V
 2:     pragma acc parallel loop tile(32,4,4)
 3:     for x... do
 4:         for y... do
 5:             for z... do
 6:                 Compute vx, vy, vz
 7:             end for
 8:         end for
 9:     end for
10: end procedure
11: ...
12: procedure COMPUTE SIG
13:     pragma acc parallel loop tile(16,4,4)
14:     for x... do
15:         for y... do
16:             for z... do
17:                 Compute σxx, σyy, σzz,
    σyz, σzx, σxy
18:             end for
19:         end for
20:     end for
21: end procedure
```

Algorithm 3. Sig Fission Approach

```
1: procedure COMPUTE V
2:     pragma acc parallel loop tile(32,4,4) ...
3:     for x... do
4:         for y... do
5:             for z... do
6:                 Compute vx, vy, vz
7:             end for
8:         end for
9:     end for
10: end procedure
11: ...
12: procedure COMPUTE SIG SAME DIM.
13:     pragma acc parallel loop tile(32,4,4) ...
14:     for x... do
15:         for y... do
16:             for z... do
17:                 Compute σxx, σyy, σzz
18:             end for
19:         end for
20:     end for
21: end procedure
22: ...
23: procedure COMPUTE SIG CROSSED
24:     pragma acc parallel loop tile(32,4,4) ...
25:     for x... do
26:         for y... do
27:             for z... do
28:                 Compute σyz, σzx, σxy
29:             end for
30:         end for
31:     end for
32: end procedure
```

It is important to note that three-dimensional tile shapes do not necessarily translate to CUDA blocks of the same shape. The tile shapes (32,4,4) and (16,4,4) resulted in CUDA blocks of (512,1,1) and (256,1,1) formats, respectively.

2.4   Environment and Parameters

All tests were performed on a Nvidia© Tesla© V100 SXM2 32 GB card, with dedicated access to the hardware, eliminating any potential interference from other applications. The runtime results presented in this study are averaged over five runs conducted under identical conditions and parameters.

The simulations were performed on a three-dimensional model with 400 elements in each dimension and a simulation time of 1000 milliseconds. A simple three-dimensional layered model was used, with a horizontal, longitudinal, and depth extent of 4 km, and a velocity variation ranging from 1.5 km/s in the top layer to 3.5 km/s in the bottom layer. A more detailed overview of the execution parameters can be found in Table 1.

Table 1. Simulation parameters.

Parameter	Description	Value
nx	Number of points in X	400
ny	Number of points in Y	400
nz	Number of points in Z	400
dx	Spacing in X	10 m
dy	Spacing in Y	10 m
dz	Spacing in Z	10 m
tn	Simulation time	1000 ms
dt	Discretization timestep size	1.414 ms
nbl	Number of boundary layers	40
so	Space order	16

3 Results

3.1 Single GPU

Table 2 presents the average execution times in seconds for the three approaches and the respective saved time percentage of the optimized approaches compared to the time obtained by the Naive version. The number of cycles required to execute the two main kernels in each approach is shown in Table 3. For better visualization and ease of comparison, all data collected from the two additional kernels generated in Sig Fission will be presented in a combined manner through a weighted average (taken according to the workload of the kernels), as if they continued to be a single kernel. Considering that, according to NCU reports, computing same direction derivatives represents 42% of the original Sig kernel workload, and cross-derivatives make up the remaining 58%, the results of the two new kernels are weighted, summed, and then divided by 100 to yield the final combined outcome.

The results shown in both tables reveal that the optimized approaches were able to reduce the number of cycles required for processing the two kernels and, consequently, significantly reduce the execution time of the application.

Table 2. Elapsed time and saved time percentage (regarding Naive time).

Approach	Elapsed Time	Saved
Naive	85.87 s	–
Tiling	58.48 s	33%
Sig Fission	52.22 s	40%

Table 3. Cycles spent in kernel V and kernel Sig.

Approach	V Cycles	Sig Cycles
Naive	56,741,131	67,458,321
Tiling	31,355,925	51,141,142
Sig Fission	31,289,283	41,885,863

Tables 4 and 5 present the computational performance and arithmetic intensity of each approach in the V and Sig kernels, respectively. Computational performance is a metric that measures the number of floating-point operations per second (FLOP/s), and arithmetic intensity is the number of floating-point operations per byte (FLOP/byte).

Compared to the Naive version, the use of loop tiling in the V kernel in the two optimized approaches was able to increase both computational performance and arithmetic intensity, which exceeded twice the value obtained by the Naive approach. In the Sig kernel, the two optimized approaches allowed performance gains in both analyzed metrics. Both the Tiling and Sig Fission approaches come close to doubling the arithmetic intensity values obtained by the Naive version and show substantial performance improvements, with the Sig Fission approach achieving the best results.

Table 4. Performance and Arithmetic Intensity on kernel V.

Approach	Performance (FLOP/s)	Arith. Intensity (FLOP/byte)
Naive	$0.469 \cdot 10^{12}$	0.72
Tiling	$0.834 \cdot 10^{12}$	1.63
Sig Fission	$0.834 \cdot 10^{12}$	1.63

Table 5. Performance and Arithmetic Intensity on kernel Sig.

Approach	Performance (FLOP/s)	Arith. Intensity (FLOP/byte)
Naive	$0.618 \cdot 10^{12}$	1.07
Tiling	$0.799 \cdot 10^{12}$	2.10
Sig Fission	$0.965 \cdot 10^{12}$	1.99

For the V kernel, the L1 cache hit rate has increased with the application of loop tiling in the Tiling and Sig Fission approaches, and the L2 hit rate in both optimized approaches remained very close to that obtained by the Naive version, as shown in the graph of Fig. 1(a). The graph in Fig. 1(b) shows that the Sig kernel presented improvements in L1 cache hit rates, both with the isolated application of loop tiling in the Tiling approach and with loop fission combined with tiling in the Sig Fission approach. In L2, the Naive version obtained the highest hit rate in this kernel, but with very little difference compared to the two optimized versions.

The cache hit values obtained by the two optimized approaches on both kernels converge with the previous results. The increase in cache hit rates allows for more efficient use of data, reducing processing bottlenecks and allowing the application to increase the use of the available processing power (increasing FLOP/s performance and arithmetic intensity).

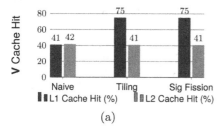 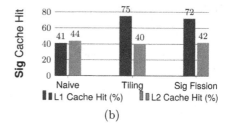

(a)   (b)

Fig. 1. L1 and L2 cache hit rates on kernels V (a) and Sig (b).

Other essential metrics for performance analysis of an application are the warp issue rate and the number of registers required for a thread to issue an instruction. A GPU has multiple microprocessors called Stream Multiprocessors (SM), and each SM has a set of schedulers responsible for managing and issuing groups of threads carrying instructions. These groups of threads are called warps. The warp issue rate, therefore, refers to the average number of warps issued per scheduler in a certain number of cycles. Nevertheless, each thread requires a certain amount of hardware registers to issue an instruction, so the heavier the workload, the more registers will be required, leading to increased competition for available hardware resources, which can reduce the scheduler issue rate.

Figure 2(a) shows that the use of loop tiling in the Tiling and Sig Fission versions for the V kernel was able to substantially increase the warp emission rate in this fraction of the operator, surpassing twice the value obtained in the Naive version. The number of registers required for a warp to be issued also showed similar behavior, dropping to just over half with the application of loop tiling in the two developed approaches.

In the Sig kernel, the Tiling approach slightly increased the number of issued warps compared to the Naive approach. In contrast, the application of loop tiling after the fission process in the Sig Fission approach achieved a significant increase in the issued rate, surpassing twice that obtained by the Naive version, which proves that the fission process led to an optimization in the use of schedulers. Compared to the Naive version the utilization of loop tiling in the Sig kernel, as employed in the Tiling approach, resulted in minimal variations in register requirements, as depicted in the graph illustrated in Fig. 2(b). The Sig Fission approach exhibited a significant reduction in register usage, nearly halving the original count, as expected. This occurred because the original workload was divided into two new workloads of similar magnitudes.

Tables 6 and 7 present the warp occupancy per SM achieved in each of the approaches for the kernels V and Sig, respectively. It is noteworthy that the occupancy profile in both kernels resembles the profile of issued warps observed in Fig. 2, and also follows the trend of register reduction. The decrease in the number of registers required per thread, observed in the Tiling and Sig Fission approaches for kernel V and in the Sig Fission approach for kernel Sig, is one of the factors that allow an increase in the occupancy of the SM's schedulers.

Table 6. SM occupancy (Warps/ SM) in kernel V.

Approach	Occupancy
Naive	7.88
Tiling	15.29
Sig Fission	15.33

Table 7. SM occupancy (Warps/SM) in kernel Sig.

Approach	Occupancy
Naive	7.93
Tiling	7.89
Sig Fission	15.26

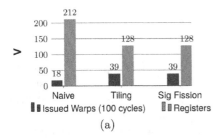

(a)

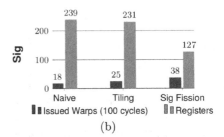

(b)

Fig. 2. Rate of issued warps every 100 cycles and amount of registers needed on kernels V (a) and Sig (b).

The main advantage of the two optimized approaches in the V kernel was reducing the cache miss rate, allowing more efficient use of data, and decreasing the need for expensive memory accesses since the necessary data for processing are now more frequently found in the cache memory. The reduction of waiting bottlenecks caused by accesses to main memory allowed for better use of available computational resources, increasing performance and arithmetic intensity. These gains explain the superior performance of the Tiling and Sig Fission approaches in this kernel if compared to the Naive approach, which obtained significantly lower cache hit rates.

In the Sig kernel, the reduction in cache miss rate is also the main factor responsible for the positive results of the Tiling and Sig Fission approaches. Once again, the more efficient use of data and the reduced need for costly memory accesses allowed for better utilization of the hardware computational power. However, the Sig Fission approach proved to be more efficient in reducing the number of registers required per thread, which led to a higher rate of issued warps. This higher emission of warps also contributes to even better utilization of the processing power offered by the hardware, making the application of loop fission deliver superior results, even though the two optimized approaches achieved very similar cache hit rates in both levels of cache.

3.2   Multi GPU

In order to validate the scalability of the presented solutions, the tests were replicated with increased spatial dimensions and domain decomposition across four Nvidia© Tesla© V100 SXM2 32 GB devices, using MPI and with *NVLink* disabled. The runtime results presented in this section are averaged over five runs conducted under identical conditions and parameters. The tests were conducted in the same three-dimensional model with 820 elements in each dimension. Each execution applied a simulation time of 6000 ms and a space order of 16 elements. The values are summarized in Table 8.

Table 8. Parameters for multi GPU executions.

Parameter	Description	Value
nx	Number of points in X	820
ny	Number of points in Y	820
nz	Number of points in Z	820
dx	Spacing in X	10 m
dy	Spacing in Y	10 m
dz	Spacing in Z	10 m
tn	Simulation time	6000 ms
dt	Discretization timestep size	1.414 ms
nbl	Number of boundary layers	40
so	Space order	16

The execution times of each approach and their respective percentage gains compared to the Naive version can be found in Table 9. Once again, similar to the tests on a single GPU, the optimized approaches achieved gains compared to the Naive version, with a stronger emphasis on the Sig Fission approach, which achieves the most significant performance increase. This maintenance of the performance gain can be interpreted positively, as it indicates that the communication overhead and other computational costs of domain decomposition are small compared to the effort employed to compute the workload. Thus, there is an indication that the developed optimizations remain effective in more robust models, with larger stencil size, longer simulation time, and domain shared across multiple devices.

Table 9. Elapsed times for each version running on 4 GPUs. nx 820, ny 820, nz 820, tn 6000, so 16.

Approach	Elapsed Time	Saved
Naive	1206.35 s	–
Tiling	761.75 s	37%
Sig Fission	698.88 s	42%

3.3 SEG/EAGE 3D Salt Model

In order to emphasize the robustness of the presented solutions, multi-GPU tests were also performed using another geological model.

The SEG/EAGE 3D Salt model was constructed by the SEG and EAGE research committee as part of a computational technological advancement initiative. This model exhibits similarity to the Gulf of Mexico Basin, featuring a salt body with high-velocity contrast in the central region, various types of faults distributed throughout the model, and lenses and sandstone bodies [13]. Figure 3 shows the wave P velocity model, with velocity values ranging from 1.5 km/s to 4.8 km/s. Its spatial parameters are 7.9 km in the horizontal and longitudinal directions, with a depth of 4 km. The S velocity and Density models were calculated using empirical formulas.

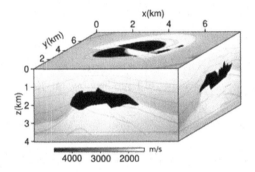

Fig. 3. SEG/EAGE 3D Salt model: P-wave velocity models.

Table 10 presents the most relevant parameters used in modeling the tests conducted in this work. Synthetic seismograms were generated with a Ricker source placed at the center of the model. The receivers were positioned on the surface for the pressure field, while for particle velocity seismograms, the receivers were placed on the seafloor (OBN geometry). The tests were conducted using a distributed computing approach facilitated by MPI, enabling domain decomposition across four Nvidia© Tesla© V100 SXM2 32 GB devices, with *NVLink* disabled. The runtime results presented in this section are again averaged over five runs conducted under identical conditions and parameters.

The approaches underwent a new tuning process to ensure that optimal tile sizes were used in each of the kernels for this model. The dimension (16,4,4) was used for the V kernel in both approaches, and the dimension (32,4,4) was used for the Sig kernel in the Tiling approach as well as for the two new kernels generated by the fission process in the Sig Fission approach.

Table 11 compares the execution times of the three tested approaches. The results indicate a reduction in the total execution time of the operator in the two optimized approaches, which were once again able to achieve performance gains when compared to the Naive version.

Table 10. SEG/EAGE 3D Salt model parameters for multi GPU executions.

Parameter	Description	Value
nx	Number of points in X	400
ny	Number of points in Y	400
nz	Number of points in Z	505
dx	Spacing in X	19.87 m
dy	Spacing in Y	19.87 m
dz	Spacing in Z	7.96 m
tn	Simulation time	4000 ms
dt	Discretization timestep size	1.025 ms
nbl	Number of boundary layers	50
so	Space order	16

The significantly lower gains compared to those obtained in the multi-GPU execution of Table 9 can be partially explained by the size of the computational mesh used in both experiments. The experiments with the SEG/EAGE 3D Salt model used smaller values in all three dimensions compared to the experiment in Table 9. This reduction in the stencil size naturally leads to a reduced workload, which can mitigate the efficiency of the proposed solutions. Additionally, this reduction in the spatial dimensions leads to a lower resource occupancy rate on the devices. Consequently, the communication overhead between devices becomes a more significant fraction of the total processing employed in the execution.

Profile reports obtained from NSYS indicate that the multi-GPU execution of Sect. 3.2 incurred a 5.1% processing overhead due to device-to-device communication facilitated by a dedicated CUDA stream. However, in the tests conducted in this section using the SEG/EAGE 3D Salt model, the percentage of communication overhead between devices was 13.4%, significantly higher than that observed in the test with 820 elements in each dimension. This increased communication overhead limits the potential performance gains, as more time is spent on non-kernel processing, reducing the sensitivity of the final results to positive changes made within these loop nests.

Nevertheless, the Tiling and Sig Fission approaches demonstrated their capacity to harness performance gains compared to the Naive version without compromising the integrity of the solution. This result corroborates the validity of the proposed solutions and reaffirms the potential gains of the implemented modifications.

Table 11. Elapsed times for each approach running on 4 GPUs. *nx* 400, *ny* 400, *nz* 505, *tn* 4000, *so* 16.

Approach	Elapsed Time	Saved
Naive	137.88 s	–
Tiling	112.52 s	18%
Sig Fission	117.42 s	15%

4   Conclusions

Based on the results collected by the NCU profiler, as well as the average execution times obtained, it is possible to assert that the two developed approaches were able to overcome some of the limitations of the Naive approach and deliver positive results. Both loop transformation techniques used positively impacted the application, with loop tiling taking advantage of the data locality principle and making better use of cache memory, and loop fission increasing computational performance in the Sig kernel.

The Sig Fission approach is the one that achieves the best results by combining the strategies that obtained the most expressive results in the two main kernels of the operator: using loop tiling of dimensions (32, 4, 4) in the V kernel and using loop fission separating the cross derivatives followed by the use of loop tiling of dimensions (32, 4, 4) in the Sig kernels.

The replicated tests on multiple GPUs maintained a similar gain pattern as those conducted on a single GPU, demonstrating the scalability of the proposed solutions. The sustained performance gains in the experiments with the SEG/EAGE 3D Salt model, albeit to a lesser extent, also emphasize the effectiveness of the developed work in achieving improved performance, despite variations in the computational mesh format and the utilized model.

Acknowledgements. This work was developed in partnership between SENAI CIMATEC and PETROBRAS. The authors acknowledge PETROLEO BRASILEIRO S.A and the Agência Nacional de Petróleo, Gás Natural e Biocombustível (ANP), for their support and investment in research and development.

References

1. Kukreja, N., Louboutin, M., Vieira, F., Luporini, F., Lange, M., Gorman, G.: Devito: automated fast finite difference computation. In: 2016 Sixth International Workshop on Domain-Specific Languages and High-Level Frameworks for High Performance Computing (WOLFHPC), pp. 11–19. IEEE (2016)
2. Lange, M., et al.: Devito: towards a generic finite difference DSL using symbolic python. In: 2016 6th Workshop on Python for High-Performance and Scientific Computing (PyHPC), pp. 67–75. IEEE (2016)

3. OpenACC. OpenACC Programming and Best Practices Guide (2022). https://www.openacc.org/sites/default/files/inline-files/openacc-guide.pdf
4. Jeffers, J., Reinders, J.: High Performance Parallelism Pearls Volume Two: Multicore and Many-Core Programming Approaches. Morgan Kaufmann, Burlington (2015)
5. McKinley, K.S., Carr, S., Tseng, C.-W.: Improving data locality with loop transformations. ACM Trans. Program. Lang. Syst. (TOPLAS) 18(4), 424–453 (1996)
6. Kandemir, M., Ramanujam, J., Choudhary, A.: Improving cache locality by a combination of loop and data transformations. IEEE Trans. Comput. 48(2), 159–167 (1999)
7. Virieux, J.: P-SV wave propagation in heterogeneous media: velocity-stress finite-difference method. Geophysics 51(4), 889–901 (1986)
8. Louboutin, M., et al.: Scaling through abstractions-high-performance vectorial wave simulations for seismic inversion with devito. arXiv preprint arXiv:2004.10519 (2020)
9. Jesus, L., Nogueira, P., Speglich, J., Boratto, M.: GPU performance analysis for viscoacoustic wave equations using fast stencil computation from the symbolic specification. J. Supercomput. 1–16 (2023)
10. Nvidia. Nsight Systems: Developer Tools Documantation (2023). https://docs.nvidia.com/nsight-systems/UserGuide/index.html
11. Nvidia. Nsight Compute: Developer Tools Documantation (2023). https://docs.nvidia.com/nsight-compute/NsightCompute/index.html
12. Cardoso, J.M.P., de Figueired Coutinho, J.G., Diniz, P.C.: Embedded Computing for High Performance: Efficient Mapping of Computations Using Customization, Code Transformations and Compilation, pp. 137–183. Morgan Kaufmann, Burlington (2017)
13. Aminzadeh, F., Burkhard, N., Long, J., Kunz, T., Duclos, P.: Three dimensional SEG/EAEG models-an update. Leading Edge 15(2), 131–134 (1996)

Acceleration of High-Dimensional Quantum Computing Simulator QuantumSkynet

Hernán M. Zuluaga-Bucheli[1,2]([✉]) [iD], Andres Giraldo Carvajal[1] [iD],
and Jose A. Jaramillo-Villegas[1,2] [iD]

[1] Universidad Tecnologica de Pereira, Pereira, Colombia
herzulu@utp.edu.co
[2] Laboratory for Research in Complex Systems, Menlo Park, CA, USA

Abstract. This paper focuses on the acceleration of QuantumSkynet, a high-dimensional quantum computing simulator. QuantumSkynet enables operations with qudits (generalized quantum bits), by executing quantum circuits, which are fundamentally based on tensor products and Kronecker operations. However, these integral functions within the simulator are currently not optimized. The proposed acceleration method involves a combination of hardware and software enhancements. Hardware acceleration will be achieved through the use of graphical processing units (GPUs) and multicore processing units, while software acceleration will be implemented via the Eigen library. These enhancements can significantly improve the performance of QuantumSkynet, with speedups of up to 100x. This makes it possible to simulate larger quantum systems and algorithms, which is essential for the development of practical quantum computing applications. For example, the proposed method could be used to accelerate the simulation of quantum systems with many qubits, or quantum algorithms with numerous steps. The results of this study suggest that the proposed method can be used to accelerate the performance of future high-dimensional quantum computing simulators and to enable the development of practical quantum computing applications.

Keywords: QuantumSkynet · high-dimensional Quantum Computing simulator · Qudit operations · Quantum circuits · Tensor products · Kronecker operations · Hardware acceleration · Software acceleration · Graphical Processing Units (GPUs) · Multicore processing units · Hyperthreading · CPU processors · Performance optimization

1 Introduction

High-dimensional quantum computing presents a promising frontier in the computational world, with the potential to address problems of a complexity that classical computers cannot handle [4]. In this arena, quantum simulators play

Supported by Universidad Tecnologica de Pereira.

C. J. Barrios H. et al. (Eds.): CARLA 2023, CCIS 1887, pp. 36–49, 2024.
https://doi.org/10.1007/978-3-031-52186-7_3

a pivotal role, enabling researchers to model and investigate quantum systems. One such quantum computing simulator is QuantumSkynet [5]. It allows for operations with qudits and executes quantum circuits based on tensor products and Kronecker operations. Notably, QuantumSkynet has been instrumental in the classification of quantum measurements with qudits [14].

However, a significant challenge lies in the fact that QuantumSkynet has not been fully optimized to harness the computational power of existing hardware and software tools. This has imposed restrictions on its efficiency and the scale of simulations it can handle.

In response to this, we present an approach to optimize QuantumSkynet through hardware and software enhancements. On the software side, leveraging the Eigen framework, a robust C++ library for linear algebra, we have accelerated the processing in QuantumSkynet [2]. On the hardware side, we have utilized Graphics Processing Units (GPUs) for parallel computing tasks and multicore processing units with Hyperthreading technology to create virtual computing units and allow shared unused functional units between processes [6–8, 15, 16].

In response to this, we present an approach to optimize QuantumSkynet through hardware and software enhancements. Leveraging the Eigen framework, a robust C++ library for linear algebra, we have accelerated the processing in QuantumSkynet [2]. On the hardware side, we have exploited the capabilities of Graphics Processing Units (GPU) processing units [6–8, 15, 16]. Concurrently, on the software side, we have utilized Amazon Web Services (AWS) instances for additional computational resources.

The objective of these enhancements is to markedly reduce the runtimes of QuantumSkynet's functions, thereby augmenting the efficiency of the quantum computing simulator. This is expected to make QuantumSkynet more robust and faster, capable of handling larger and more complex quantum simulations.

In the subsequent sections, we detail our acceleration methodology, present the performance test results of the optimized QuantumSkynet, and discuss these findings. We believe this optimization of QuantumSkynet holds significant implications for future advancements in quantum computing research.

2   Quantum Computing Simulator

A quantum computing simulation system is a computer program that simulates the behavior of quantum systems and the execution of quantum algorithms on a classical computer [1]. These systems are valuable because current quantum computers have limited processing capabilities and are prone to errors. Hence, simulations on a classical computer provide an effective means of testing and developing algorithms before implementing them on a quantum computer. In addition, simulation systems enable experimentation with various configurations and parameters to optimize performance and accelerate the development of new quantum applications.

High-dimensional quantum computing, extends the traditional 2-dimensional quantum computing (qubits) to a complex d-dimensional Hilbert space. This higher dimensionality allows more information to be encoded into each quantum state and can potentially offer computational advantages over standard qubit systems.

Key elements of quantum computing include:

- **Outer Product:** This operation measures the interaction between two quantum states. The computational complexity associated with this function within a high-dimensional quantum computing simulator is related to the number of nested iteration cycles, in this case it has two cycles, so the total number of operations to be performed is 2^n where n is each element of the matrix (1).

$$|\Psi\rangle \langle \Phi| = \begin{pmatrix} a \\ b \end{pmatrix} \begin{pmatrix} c^* & d^* \end{pmatrix} = \begin{pmatrix} ac^* & ad^* \\ bc^* & bd^* \end{pmatrix}. \tag{1}$$

- **Tensor Product:** This operation is used to measure the interaction between two or more high-dimensional quantum states (2).

$$\begin{bmatrix} a \\ b \end{bmatrix} \otimes \begin{bmatrix} d \\ e \end{bmatrix} = \begin{bmatrix} ad \\ ae \\ bd \\ be \end{bmatrix}, \tag{2}$$

- **Pauli Matrices and Their Generalizations:** The Pauli matrices can be generalized to high dimensions using the Weyl adjoint operator (3). This allows for the generalization of the Pauli X, Y, and Z gates to high dimensions (4).

$$W_{q,p}^\dagger = \sum_{k=0}^{d-1} \omega^{kq} |k \oplus p\rangle \langle k|, \tag{3}$$

Thus, obtaining the generalization of the gates (4):

$$I^m = W_{0,0}^\dagger$$
$$X^m = W_{0,m}^\dagger$$
$$Z^m = W_{m,0}^\dagger \tag{4}$$
$$Y^m = i^{(m\%d)} W_{m,m}^\dagger.$$

$$x$$

- **High-Dimensional Quantum Gates:** Quantum gates for high dimensions, such as the Generalized Pauli gates (5), (6), (7), the Generalized Quantum Fourier Transform, and the Generalized Controlled Gate are crucial in high-dimensional quantum computing.

- **Generalized Pauli matrix X** To find the Generalized Pauli matrix X, we must replace the variables q, p by 0, m in the Weyl adjoint operator Eq. (5):

$$X^m = W^\dagger_{0,m} \tag{5}$$

The code associated with this operation has a complexity $O(n^3 + n^2)$ where n is the number of dimensions.

- **Generalized Pauli matrix Z** To find the Generalized Pauli Z matrix, we can replace the variables q, p by m, 0 in the Weyl adjoint operator Eq. (6):

$$Z^m = W^\dagger_{m,0} = \sum_{k=0}^{d-1} \omega^{km} P_k \tag{6}$$

The code associated with this gate has a complexity $O(n^3 + 2n^2)$.

- **Generalized Pauli matrix Y** To find the Generalized Pauli Y matrix, the variables q, p must be replaced by m, m in the Weyl adjoint operator equation, and it must also be multiplied by a global cyclic phase of $i^{m\%b}$ (7).

$$Y^m = i^{(m\%d)} W^\dagger_{m,m} \tag{7}$$

In summary, the 4 generalized gates within the high-dimensional computing simulator are the most important feature, since they clearly show the relationship between Weyl matrices and Pauli gates. Generating a solid base to make quantum circuits where gates are applied in high dimensions.

- **Generalized Quantum Fourier Transform** It is part of the set of gates that are applied to a qubit and is implemented in the simulator as the generalized quantum Fourier transform (GQFT).

  The code associated with this function considers the order, whether direct or inverse, which generates a quadratic complexity given by: $O(n^2)$ where n is the number of dimensions.

- **CNOT** the CNOT gate creates a qubit that controls another qubit, this means that if the control qubit is equal to one, the controlled qubit will be negated. The matrix associated with the CNOT gate is defined by a 4×4 matrix, like this (8):

$$CNOT(|1\rangle \otimes |0\rangle) = \begin{bmatrix} 1 & 0 & 0 & 0 \\ 0 & 1 & 0 & 0 \\ 0 & 0 & 0 & 1 \\ 0 & 0 & 1 & 0 \end{bmatrix} \times \begin{bmatrix} 0 \\ 0 \\ 1 \\ 0 \end{bmatrix} = \begin{bmatrix} 0 \\ 0 \\ 0 \\ 1 \end{bmatrix} \tag{8}$$

- **Generalized Controlled Gate** The quantum control gate for two dimensions (CNOT) can be applied to more than one qubit through modular addition. For example, if you have two qubits $|x\rangle$ and $|y\rangle$, where the control qubit is $|x\rangle$, the result would be equal to the following multiplication (9):

$$CNOT\,|x\rangle\,|y\rangle = |x\rangle\,|x \oplus y\rangle, \tag{9}$$

- **SWAP** To exchange the content of two qubits, the SWAP gate can be used, whose associated matrix is as follows (10):

$$SWAP = \begin{bmatrix} 1 & 0 & 0 & 0 \\ 0 & 0 & 1 & 0 \\ 0 & 1 & 0 & 0 \\ 0 & 0 & 0 & 1 \end{bmatrix}, \tag{10}$$

Up to this point, a summary of the different quantum gates was presented, these are presented to perform the optimization of the compendium of gates supported by the simulator.

3 Acceleration Methodology

The acceleration methodology for the high-dimensional QuantumSkynet quantum computing simulator is meticulously designed to make effective use of the Eigen library, multithreading, and CUDA [3,11]. The Eigen library, renowned for its efficient matrix and vector operations, introduces concepts such as Lazy Evaluation, Vectorization, and Broadcasting. Lazy Evaluation minimizes unnecessary computations by intelligently determining the need for temporary variables at compile time. Vectorization optimizes the simulator by transforming it from a Single Instruction, Single Data (SISD) to a Single Instruction, Multiple Data (SIMD) paradigm, effectively utilizing the SIMD capabilities of modern CPUs for enhanced performance. Broadcasting, on the other hand, allows for operations between matrices of different dimensions by conceptually expanding the smaller matrix, thereby ensuring smooth and efficient computations.

In addition to the Eigen library, the methodology also incorporates multithreading to exploit the multicore architectures of modern CPUs. This enables the simultaneous computation of multiple quantum states, thereby significantly improving the scalability and performance of QuantumSkynet. Furthermore, the integration of CUDA allows the simulator to leverage the computational power of NVIDIA GPUs for highly parallel tasks such as large matrix and vector operations [9,10]. Although the CUDA memory management model presents unique challenges, careful design and optimization of the QuantumSkynet simulator can result in substantial performance gains.

Overall, this combination of techniques constitutes a comprehensive acceleration methodology that significantly enhances the computational efficiency of high-dimensional quantum computing simulations in QuantumSkynet, making it a powerful tool for exploring the complex world of quantum computing.

3.1   Lazy Evaluation

Eigen has an intelligent model based on the compile time, evaluating for each sub-expression if it is necessary to use temporary variables, which represent processing time and additional storage space. Eigen automatically determines, using an Expression-Templates-Based template, which stores different models of expressions and their storage needs, according to their underlying operations, these templates work on sub-expressions, this model allows a considerable acceleration.

3.2   Vectorization

This concept comes from converting a program that by default is $SISD$ salary implemented to a SIMD vector implementation. In general, most computers today have vector implementations that allow them to optimize the resources available to them.

To execute these SIMD-type functions, computational systems have sets of subroutines that describe operations external to the processor with the aim of sending the same operation to the different processing units within the CPUs, but each unit operates with different data so that tries to use as little single-threaded processing as possible.

3.3   Broadcasting

When operating with matrices, their dimensions might be different, so operating them conceptually is impossible. To solve this issue, the concept of Array Broadcast arises, which is based on increasing the dimension of the lower matrix to have the possibility of operating them, Eigen has implemented this concept within its library to give developers fluidity.

3.4   Introduction to the Experiments

In the process of developing and implementing efficient and accelerated algorithms for complex operations, a rigorous empirical evaluation is essential to compare the performance and effectiveness of different versions of the algorithms. The experimental methodology presented in this section addresses two key stages:

1. **Creation of Accelerated Algorithms**: The first stage involved the design and implementation of new accelerated algorithms, applying optimizations at both the hardware and software levels.
2. **Evaluation Through Test Functions**: The second stage consisted of developing specific test functions to evaluate both the standard and accelerated versions of the algorithms. Tests were conducted using vectors of varying dimensions, allowing for a detailed and realistic comparison. For example, while tests of the standard version of the base vector algorithm

were performed with dimensions ranging from 50 to 260000000, the accelerated versions allowed for testing with even larger dimensions, reaching up to 570000000.

The primary goal of these experiments was to ascertain the effectiveness of the proposed enhancements, analyzing performance and limitations under different scenarios and conditions. The subsequent sections will detail the design, procedure, measurement, and analysis of these experiments, offering a comprehensive perspective on the adopted methodology and the results obtained.

3.5   Experimental Design

Hardware Configuration. The experiments were conducted on two specific cloud-based architectures, G4ad and G4dn instances, both configured with 1 GPU, 4 vCPUs, and 16 GB of RAM to ensure equality in the testing environment.

- **G4ad Instances**: Utilizing AMD Radeon Pro V520 GPUs and AMD EPYC second-generation processors, these instances were configured with 1 GPU, 4 vCPUs, and 16 GB of RAM. They are suitable for various graphical applications and provide 25 Gbps networks and 2.4 TB of NVMe-based local SSD storage.
- **G4dn Instances**: Employing NVIDIA Tesla GPUs, these instances were also configured with 1 GPU, 4 vCPUs, and 16 GB of RAM. They feature high-bandwidth networking and robust floating-point capabilities, with each GPU having 16 GiB of GDDR6 memory.

The identical configuration of these instances was integral to providing a robust and consistent platform for running the algorithms, ensuring accurate and comparable results across the different versions and dimensions tested. Utilizing these specific cloud-based architectures allowed for flexibility and scalability in conducting the experiments, accommodating the extensive range of vector dimensions that were assessed.

4   Results

This section presents a comparative analysis of the performance of the accelerated version of the QuantumSkynet simulator on two different hardware architectures: Intel and AMD. The analysis focuses on the speedup rates achieved in various operations that are critical to the simulator due to their substantial impact on its overall computational complexity. Speedup rates provide a measure of performance improvement obtained with the accelerated version compared to a non-accelerated one. A detailed examination of these rates can reveal how effectively the accelerated simulator performs computations faster and, in certain instances, extends its storage capacity on different hardware architectures. The specific results and discussions of speedup rates for each operation tested on Intel and AMD architectures will be detailed in the following sections.

Acceleration of High-Dimensional Quantum Computing Simulator

Sum of Probabilities. The test set that was generated for both versions is the same, although the accelerated version was able to trade up to 90% more data. In the case of the sum of probabilities without accelerating, the dimension interval ranges from a vector of size 1 to 12000. In the case of the accelerated version, the dimension range grows exponentially from 1 dimension to 12000000, which represents an increase of 1 to 10. The maximum number of dimensions it can support the normal version is 12000, with a time of 41 seconds. The total throughput considering the maximum amount of each test and time is 99% more for the accelerated version on Intel and AMD architecture with GPU.

Sum of Probabilities: The speedup rates for both Intel and AMD are significantly higher compared to other operations, especially for Intel. However, the variability in speedup rates is also much higher, as indicated by the very long box in the Intel (see Fig. 1).

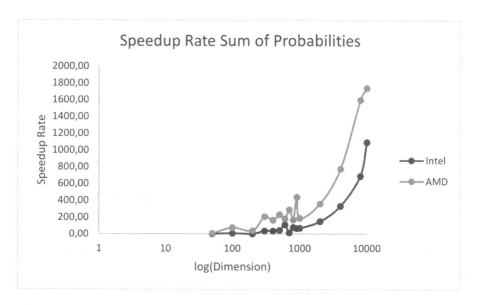

Fig. 1. Comparison of speedup rates for the Sum of Probabilities using different vector dimensions on Intel (blue) and AMD (orange) architectures. The x-axis represents the logarithmic scale of dimensions, ranging from 50 to 12000, while the y-axis shows the corresponding speedup rates. The graph offers insights into the relative performance between the two architectures for this specific function. (Color figure online)

Vector Base. This function in its normal form has a linear complexity $O(n)$, where n is the number of dimensions. For the tests, this function achieved a mark of 8 seconds to generate vectors of 26000000 dimensions. In contrast, the accelerated version reached a maximum amount of 57 million in dimensions in a time of 8 s. This means that the accelerated version doubles the number of dimensions with which it can operate. This represents an acceleration and performance improvement of 46%.

Speedup Rate Base Vector: The speedup rates for Intel are generally lower than for AMD, and there's a large variability in the Intel speedup rates, as indicated by the long box in the figure (see Fig. 2).

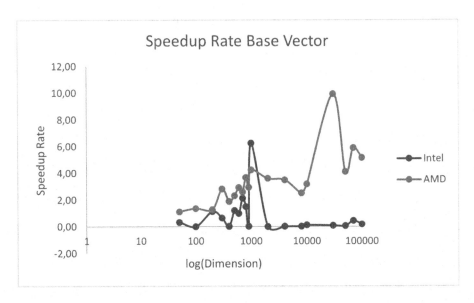

Fig. 2. Comparison of speedup rates for vector-based calculations across various dimensions (logarithmic scale) using Intel and AMD architectures. The x-axis represents the vector dimensions in a logarithmic scale, ranging from 50 to 100000, allowing for direct comparison across a wide range of sizes. The y-axis indicates the speedup rate, with the blue line depicting the performance for Intel and the orange line for AMD. The graph illustrates the relative efficiencies of these architectures in handling vector calculations. (Color figure online)

Product $Vector \times Matrix$. This test was developed to measure the processing capacity for the product function between a vector and a matrix. The test was performed in principle for the version without accelerating, with a set of matrices where the maximum processing capacity was from the operation of vectors and matrices of dimension 1 to 120. Each dimension is represented in vector form of size n and matrix with size $n \times n$. The same dataset was used for accelerated version testing. In this version, it could be evidenced that you can trade with a higher number of dimensions, compared to the non-accelerated version, which had a maximum dimension of 120, which had a runtime of 0.05 s. As for the accelerated version, it allowed trading a maximum number of 15000 dimensions, with a time of 4.84 s. This represents a yield improvement of 117%.

***Matrix* × *Matrix* Product.** The product function of an array by an array in general terms allows operating arrays of dimensions of size $n \times n$. In the case of not accelerated and the accelerated this size is proportional, so that the dimension of the test matrices goes from 2 to 1592, this allows us to assert that this function is constant in the number of dimensions. Now, the difference lies in the amount of time it takes each to operate. In the case of the non-accelerated function, it obtained a score of 122 s. In contrast, the accelerated version obtained a time of 62 s. This evidence allows verifying the improvement in time of the accelerated version, which was of 30%.

Matrix × *Matrix* *Product:* The speedup rates for both Intel and AMD are relatively low compared to other operations, and the variability in speedup rates is also relatively low, as indicated by the short boxes in the figure (see Fig. 3).

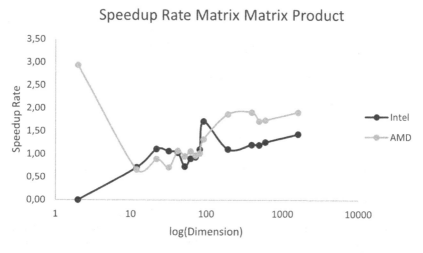

Fig. 3. Comparison of speedup rates for the Matrix-Matrix Product operation using different matrix dimensions on Intel (blue) and AMD (orange) architectures. The x-axis represents the logarithmic scale of matrix dimensions, ranging from 2 to 1592, while the y-axis depicts the corresponding speedup rates. The graph illustrates the behavior of the function, shedding light on the efficiency and performance characteristics of both architectures for this particular computation. (Color figure online)

External Product. The external product is an operation that is applied between two arrays of dimension $n \times n$, where each represents, in the Dirac notation, it BRA $\langle \phi |$ and its KET $| \psi \rangle$. In the tests carried out, the accelerated version was examined with a set of arrays of dimensions of 2×2 up to 15092×15092. The amount of time it took to trade was 25 s. As for the accelerated version, it allowed us to exceed the maximum number of dimensions, since it made it possible to evaluate arrays of dimension 2×2 up to 20092×20092, implying a storage improvement of 24%. As for how long it took you to solve, this is 15 s. In general, the acceleration of this matrix allows achieving two specific goals which are performance improvement regarding time and space.

External Product: The speedup rates for Intel are generally higher than for AMD, but there's a large variability in the Intel speedup rates, as indicated by the height of the box in the figure (see Fig. 4).

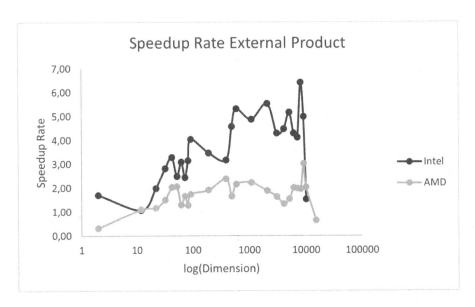

Fig. 4. Comparison of speedup rates for the External Product operation using different vector dimensions on Intel (blue) and AMD (orange) architectures. The x-axis represents the logarithmic scale of vector dimensions, ranging from 2 to 15092, while the y-axis highlights the corresponding speedup rates. The graph demonstrates the comparative performance of both architectures, illuminating the complex relationships between dimensionality and computation efficiency in the context of External Product calculations. (Color figure online)

Kronecker Product. Testing for the Kronecker product [12], was performed for the non-accelerated version with dimension arrays from 5×5 to 125×125, with a maximum time of 22 s. In the accelerated version, it was possible to expand the maximum size of the dimensions, from 5 × 5 to 150 × 150, with a time for the last one of 8 s. The performance improvement that was obtained regarding space is 17% and the time improvement is 36%. This represents 218% of the total acceleration obtained by the accelerated version in an Intel architecture with GPU.

Kronecker Product: The speedup rates for Intel are generally higher than for AMD, with a larger variability in the Intel speedup rates, as indicated by the long box in the figure (see Fig. 5).

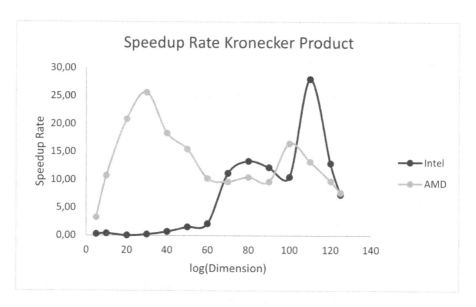

Fig. 5. Comparison of speedup rates for the Kronecker Product operation using Intel (blue) and AMD (orange) architectures across different vector dimensions. The x-axis illustrates the logarithmic scale of vector dimensions, ranging from 5 to 125, while the y-axis delineates the associated speedup rates. This representation offers an insightful analysis of the behavior and efficiency of both architectures in Kronecker Product computations, accentuating the interplay between dimensionality and performance. (Color figure online)

5   Conclusions and Future Work

This paper aimed to accelerate the high-dimensional quantum computing simulator that would allow scientists to evaluate, analyze and fine-tune high-dimensional quantum algorithms.

The main contribution of this project can be divided into two main aspects, on the one hand, the acceleration of the high-dimensional quantum gates included in the simulator as a result of the research carried out on this subject and the other, the acceleration of quantum gates and other high-dimensional functions that finally allowed a functional and stable version of the simulator.

This confirms the initial hypothesis that it is possible to improve the performance of the high-dimensional quantum computing simulator using CPU acceleration, GPU.

- Apply parallelization techniques by CPU and GPU, to accelerate the processing of gates or functions that demand greater memory capacity and greater runtime.
- Using dense matrix processing techniques, with the Eigen framework, provides better performance results in terms of time and space used to perform calculations.
- Using GPU to accelerate algorithms is a technique that, as far as the problem of dense arrays is concerned, generates a reduction in computational complexity.
- There is a relationship between the number of dimensions and the number of qubits, where it is better to grow in number of dimensions than in place of qubits.

5.1   Future Work

Several lines of research remain open that can extend the scope of this project, for example in areas such as high-performance computing, quantum computing, high-dimensional quantum machine learning, drug discovery using quantum algorithms, among others. Some work based on QuantumSkynet that could be carried out in the future are:

- Take advantage of simulator acceleration to test different quantum algorithms or subroutines associated with high-dimensional quantum computing applications.
- Add a support module to make the distinction between pure and mixed states, in addition to the simulation of different levels of quantum decoherence, to provide results more similar to those of a physical quantum computer.
- Add a module that allows noise simulation in quantum circuits.
- Analysis and incorporation of new acceleration techniques through reconfigurable computer systems.

References

1. André, T., Sjöqvist, E.: Dark path holonomic qudit computation. Phys. Rev. A **106**(6), 062402 (2022). https://journals.aps.org/pra/abstract/10.1103/PhysRevA.106.062402
2. Avramouli, M., Savvas, I.K., Vasilaki, A., Garani, G.: Unlocking the potential of quantum machine learning to advance drug discovery. Electronics (Switzerland) **12**(11), 2402 (2023). Multidisciplinary Digital Publishing Institute. https://www.mdpi.com/2079-9292/12/11/2402
3. Criado-Ramón, D., Ruiz, L.B.G., Pegalajar, M.C.: CUDA-bigPSF: an optimized version of bigPSF accelerated with graphics processing Unit. Expert Syst. Appl. **230**, 120661 (2023). https://doi.org/10.1016/j.eswa.2023.120661
4. Daley, A.J., et al.: Practical quantum advantage in quantum simulation. Nature **607**(7920), 667–676 (2022). https://www.nature.com/articles/s41586-022-04940-6

5. Giraldo-Carvajal, A., Jaramillo-Villegas, J.A.: QuantumSkynet: a high-dimensional quantum computing simulator. In: Optics InfoBase Conference Papers (2020)
6. Intel Corporation. (n.d.). Tecnología Hyper-Threading Intel®. https://www.intel.la/content/www/xl/es/architecture-and-technology/hyper-threading/hyper-threading-technology.html
7. Hall, M.: Intel - History, Products, & Facts - Britannica (2021). https://www.britannica.com/topic/Intel
8. INTEL. ¿Que es Hyper-Threading? - Intel (2020). https://www.intel.la/content/www/xl/es/gaming/resources/hyper-threading.html
9. Kang, D.K., Kim, C.W., Yang, H.I.: GPU-based parallel computation for structural dynamic response analysis with CUDA. J. Mech. Sci. Technol. **28**(10), 4155–4162 (2014). https://link.springer.com/article/10.1007/s12206-014-0928-2
10. Kim, C.W.: Use of distributed-memory parallel processing in computing the dynamic response of the passenger-car system. Proc. Inst. Mech. Eng. Part D J. Automobile Eng. **220**(10), 1373–1381 (2006). https://doi.org/10.1243/09544070JAUTO286
11. Manathunga, M., Aktulga, H.M., Götz, A.W., Merz, K.M.: Quantum mechanics/molecular mechanics simulations on NVIDIA and AMD graphics processing units. J. Chem. Inf. Model. **63**(3), 711–717 (2023). https://pubs.acs.org/doi/abs/10.1021/acs.jcim.2c01505
12. Poltronieri Vargas, J.: Productos de Kronecker. Revista de Matematica: Teoria y Aplicaciones **3**(1), 45–60 (1996)
13. Givi, P., et al.: Quantum speedup for aeroscience and engineering. AIAA J. **58**(8), 3715–3727 (2020)
14. Useche, D.H., Giraldo-Carvajal, A., Zuluaga-Bucheli, H
15. Seen, W.M., Gobithaasan, R.U., Miura, K.T.: GPU acceleration of Runge Kutta-Fehlberg and its comparison with Dormand-Prince method. AIP Conf. Proc. **1605**, 16–21 (2014)
16. Intel Corporation. (n.d.). Tecnologia Hyper-Threading Intel®. https://www.intel.la/content/www/xl/es/architecture-and-technology/hyper-threading/hyper-threading-technology.html

Multi-objective Analysis of Power Consumption and Quality of Service in Datacenters for Effective Demand Response

Jonathan Muraña[(✉)] and Sergio Nesmachnow

Universidad de la República, Montevideo, Uruguay
{jmurana,sergion}@fing.edu.uy

Abstract. This article presents a multi-objective optimization approach aimed at minimizing the power consumption while mitigating the quality of service degradation in datacenter operations. The study holds significant relevance for datacenter and supercomputing facilities to effectively participate in the electricity market, especially in demand response events. The research explores an on/off energy-aware strategy combined with five list scheduling heuristics, comparing their efficacy to solve the proposed operation problem. The obtained results demonstrate that the proposed approach provides decision-makers a diverse set of options tailored to their specific business needs in different situations. The comparative analysis reveals that strategies that prioritize recently arrived tasks with a high probability of being completed on time, computed better solutions in scenarios where larger power consumption reductions are requested. The proposed heuristics are useful methods to assist datacenter operators for participating in demand response programs.

Keywords: Green computing · High performance Computing · Datacenter operation · Quality of service · Multi-objective analysis

1 Introduction

With the increasing popularity of demand response programs, large consumers face the challenge of adopting intelligent planning strategies to effectively leverage the new business opportunities presented in the electricity market [14,24]. However, the integration into the electricity market can introduce complexities if the potential impacts on normal operations are not carefully considered. In this context, conducting a comprehensive multi-objective analysis becomes crucial for both automated decision-making and post-evaluation processes.

Multi-objective scheduling plays a crucial role in maximizing the computing capabilities of computing infrastructures while simultaneously meeting business needs. Multi-objective scheduling has been extensively studied in the literature [6,11,13,20]. By leveraging the concept of the Pareto front, it becomes possible to

C. J. Barrios H. et al. (Eds.): CARLA 2023, CCIS 1887, pp. 50–65, 2024.
https://doi.org/10.1007/978-3-031-52186-7_4

narrow down the solution space to high-quality solutions. This enables effective comparison of various techniques and facilitates accurate trade-off decisions.

This article focuses on the challenge of minimizing two objectives in datacenter operation: the power consumption and the quality of service (QoS) degradation. Considering the inherent conflict between these objectives, the solution to this problem is a Pareto front that encompasses a range of trade-off values. To solve the considered problem, the proposed approach combines an on-off energy-aware scheduling strategy with efficient greedy list-scheduling heuristics [9,12,21].

The manuscript is organized as follows: Sect. 2 provides a detailed description of the multi-objective problem addressed in this study. Subsequently, Sect. 3 presents a review of related work in the field. Section 4 outlines the methodology employed to resolve the problem. The experimental evaluation of the proposed methodology is discussed in Sect. 5. Finally, Sect. 6 concludes the article by summarizing the key findings and outlining potential directions for future research.

2 Power Consumption and QoS Degradation Reduction Problem in Datacenters for Demand Response

This section described the addressed problem and presents its mathematical formulation.

2.1 Multi-objective Energy Management in Demand Response

Demand response refers to the practice of consumers to adapt their electricity consumption in response to either a rise in electricity prices or incentives provided to encourage lower or higher electricity usage [1,24]. The paradigm is applicable to small (i.e., residential) consumers, but it is more relevant when large consumers are included as active agents in demand response events. Datacenters are a specific case of large electricity consumer that are able to participate in demand response events by providing the service of managing and adjusting electricity consumption to given signals by the electricity market operator/provider. Datacenters can also incorporate and manage the generation and use of renewable energy sources [23]. When reductions are requested, datacenters can manage electricity consumption by deferring tasks or turning off non-essential computational infrastructure during the demand response (peak) event. This reduction results in a reduction in the processing capacity of the computational infrastructure and an eventual QoS degradation. After the peak period finishes, the datacenter returns to normal operation, resuming the regular energy usage, turning on servers, and executing deferred tasks.

Datacenters usually evaluate their potential participation in demand response events by employing a one-dimensional utility function. This utility function considers the gains received from the electricity provider and the monetary losses incurred as a result of service level agreements violations with their clients [2–4,30]. The utility function provides a simple manner to assess the benefits of the datacenter participation in the response event. A better option for characterizing the datacenter participation in the response event is via multi-criteria analysis. Applying multi-objective (Pareto) comparison provides a more comprehensive perspective of the interplay and trade-offs between monetary gains and provided QoS, which can severely affect the reputation and have a severe negative implications for the business.

The multi-objective analysis presented in this article provides decision-makers with a broad range of trade-off levels between power reduction and quality of service, in order to meet their specific business needs in different situations. Furthermore, the analysis allows for the consideration of several relevant factors such as: i) *datacenter reputation*, since having knowledge about the impact on QoS helps to prevent the image of the datacenter from being affected, ii) *sustainability*, allowing ecological goal to be weighted and even prioritized over monetary incomes (profit), and iii) *emergency situations*, where reducing power consumption is mandatory to guarantee a proper electricity supply for other critical facilities.

Our previous work addressed the problem of demand response in multi-tenant datacenters that operate in colocation mode [16, 19]. The analysis were conducted at two levels. On the higher level, the datacenter negotiates with its tenants to achieve the best price for power consumption reduction. On the lower level, tenants offered a price based on their convenience in terms of their profits, applying single-objective optimization evaluated through simulation.

This article focuses on the optimization performed by a tenant that owns its own computational infrastructure and serves multiple clients, following the enterprise datacenter model [25]. Instead of applying a single-objective approach (only considering profit), a multi-objective analysis is developed. The multi-objective analysis takes into account the power consumption reduction and the degradation of service quality as objective function. The next subsection defines the specific problem addressed in this article.

2.2   Problem Overview

During demand response events, datacenters must reduce their power consumption while simultaneously meeting the computing requirements of their clients. On one hand, a datacenter operates with a defined set of tasks that must be completed within a specific scheduling horizon. Each task is associated with a deadline and penalty cost, which represents the financial compensation that the datacenter must pay to clients (task owners) in the event of failing to meet the agreed-upon completion time. On the other hand, the datacenter is also mandated by the electricity provider to reduce its power consumption within a specific interval during the scheduling horizon.

Figure 1 shows a comparison of the power consumption curve in two different situations: business-as-usual operation and a demand response event. The power curve was obtained using a datacenter simulator specifically designed for demand response studies, introduced in our previous article [19]. In both business-as-usual and demand response situation, the same set of tasks is considered.

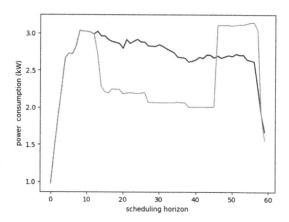

Fig. 1. Comparison of datacenter power consumption curves between business-as-usual operation (blue curve) and a participation in a demand response event (orange curve). (Color figure online)

Figure 1 illustrates significant changes in the power consumption curve during the demand response event, compared to the standard business-as-usual operation. Specifically, within the reduction interval [15, 45] the power consumption is effectively reduced by 0.7 kW in the demand response situation. As a consequence of this reduction, certain tasks experience delays in their execution. The observed peak at the end of the reduction interval is a result of the execution of delayed tasks.

2.3   Formulation

Formally, the problem is defined as a bi-objective optimization, considering the following elements and objective functions:

- Let T be a set of time steps, $T = \{t_i\}$, for $i = 1 \dots M$. The interval $[0, t_M]$ defines the scheduling horizon of the problem.
- Let $I \subseteq [0, t_M]$ be the interval where the power consumption must be reduced (i.e., the demand response interval)
- Let J be the set of tasks to be executed in $[0, t_M]$, $J = 1, \dots, N$
- Let d_j be the deadline of the task j
- Let c_j be the penalty cost of the task j.
- Let f_j be the completion time of the task j in a task schedule S. If task j is not completed in $[0, t_M]$ (because it is delayed in the computed schedule), then $f_j = \infty$.
- Let $p(t_i)$ be the power consumption in the time step t_i, for a task schedule S.

The bi-objective optimization problem proposes the simultaneous optimization of two objective functions that evaluate the penalty cost and the power consumption of the datacenter:

$$[\text{penalty cost}] \quad \min \sum_{j=1}^{N} \mathbb{1}_{f_j > d_j} c_j \tag{1}$$

$$[\text{power consumption}] \quad \min \max_{t_i \in I} \{p(t_i)\} \tag{2}$$

The first objective function is presented in Eq. 1; it aims at minimizing the penalty cost. This cost corresponds to the summation of the penalty costs of the tasks that finish after their deadlines. The second objective function, as described in Eq. 2, aims at minimizing the maximum power consumption considering all timesteps within the reduction interval. The function $p(t)$ is computed using the power consumption model in our previous article [18]. This model depends on two key factors: the number of tasks being executed on the server and the type of tasks, which can be categorized as either memory-intensive tasks, CPU-intensive tasks, or a combination of both.

3   Related Work

Several articles have proposed energy-aware scheduling methods, including heuristics, classical optimization strategies, and game theory methods for planning in datacenters and other high performance and distributed computing platforms, under the smart grid paradigm.

Meng and Zeng [15] applied game theory to simulate the interaction between an electricity retailer and its residential customers. The objective was to optimize pricing for the electricity company while allowing customers to manage their power consumption. The applied methods were a genetic algorithm for profit maximization of the electricity company, and a linear programming model for minimizing customers costs. Experiments conducted on a neighborhood with 1000 customers showed that customers using the proposed smart grid planning scheme were able to reduce their energy bills compared to those using a business-as-usual operation. A similar non-competitive method was presented by Dai et al. [7], studying real-time pricing schemes for demand response to reduce user and grid operating costs. Multiple retailers and residential users were considered and modeled the coordination problem among users as an evolutionary game with private information. The algorithms were validated on a small scenario with two retailers and five users. Results showed the convergence of the proposed algorithms and the effectiveness of the demand response model in reducing costs for residential users.

The model for demand response in cloud computing datacenters by Wang et al. [29] shifts computation loads to use cheaper electricity or renewable sources. The interaction is modeled by game theory and heuristics were proposed for time-ahead pricing and resource allocation. Results showed that the model was effective in improving profit and reducing the risk of power system overflow. In the model by Chen et al. [4], the operator negotiates with tenants to reduce their power consumption, while tenants aim to maximize their profits. An iterative evaluation of a supply function mechanism is used, offering monetary incentives per power unit reduced to all tenants equally until the target reduction is achieved. The monetary penalty function on tenants is defining according to queuing theory. The model was proven to achieve optimal solutions under certain assumptions. A small case study with three tenants showed that the proposed mechanism achieved solutions close to optimal. In the approach by Tran et al. [28] tenants are encouraged to reduce their electricity consumption. The model combines game theory, exact and heuristic optimization methods, and a theoretical supply function. The model considered a theoretical quadratic cost function to model the use of other energy generation sources.

Regarding multi-objective analysis, Tchernykh et al. [27] studied several online scheduling heuristics in cloud computing to optimize the provider income, related to the server level agreement (and therefore to QoS degradation), and power consumption. The best results, according to the Pareto dominance analysis, were achieved by the strategy of allocating task to servers with the minimum power consumption among the available options. Stavrinides et al. [26] proposed an energy-efficient and QoS-aware scheduling approach for cloud computing. The strategy is based on Dynamic Voltage and Frequency Scaling (DVFS) to minimize power consumption. The approach solely considered the number of jobs that fail to meet their deadlines. The proposed strategy outperformed an early deadline first heuristic across all conducted experiments.

Our previous articles [17,19] studied the participation of datacenters in demand response programs, applying a two-level planning approach that estimated the power consumption of tasks execution and the cooling system. The model was extended by considering multiple power reduction targets during a demand response event and bio-inspired metaheuristic algorithms for optimization [10].

4   Resolution Method

An energy-aware heuristic strategy is proposed to minimize power consumption and minimize the QoS degradation. The strategy applies an on/off approach, aimed at reducing power consumption, in combination with greedy list scheduling, aimed at minimizing QoS degradation. The on/off model is simple, effective, and widely used approach in demand response schemes to encourage customers to reduce power consumption during peak periods. In this model, consumers are supposed to be noticed ahead of peak periods, to turn off consuming devices for a given period of time. In the addressed case study, the devices to turn off are the served owned by tenants.

Algorithm 1 outlines the proposed energy-QoS aware scheduling heuristics. The heuristic receives as input a list of tasks to be scheduled for execution in the available computing infrastructure within the considering scheduling horizon and a list of processing thresholds. Each processing threshold is a percentage of the total available computing cores, which bounds the number of cores in on state allowed to be used within the reduction interval. Cores not included within the threshold are considered in idle state. Two output vectors are returned, each one containing the corresponding value of the two objective functions (penalty cost and power consumption) for the considered processing thresholds.

Algorithm 1. Proposed energy-QoS-aware heuristic for task scheduling

---

Input: task_list, processing_thresholds
Output: penalty_cost ($\vec{C}$) and power_consumption ($\vec{P}$)
1: **for** each processing_threshold k **do**
2:     sorted_task_list ← `sort_by_criterion`(task_list)
3:     (F, Q) ← `scheduling`(sorted_task_list, k)
4:     $\vec{C}[k] \leftarrow \sum_{j=1}^{N} \mathbb{1}_{f_j > d_j} c_j$
5:     $\vec{P}[k] \leftarrow \max_{t_i \in I} \{p(t_i)\}$
6: **end for**
7: **return** $(\vec{C}, \vec{P})$

In Algorithm 1, function `sort_by_criterion`(task_list) (line 2) orders the task list based on a chosen priority criterion. The sorting determines the priority of the pending task queue, i.e., which pending task is selected first to be assigned to a suitable computing resource, as long as they are available, in a given scheduling step. The following criteria are considered:

- First Come First Served (FCFS): tasks are ordered by arrival time, in ascending order.
- Last In First Out (LIFO): tasks are ordered by arrival time, in descending order.
- Early deadline first (EDF): tasks are ordered by deadline, in ascending order.
- High penalty first (HDF): tasks are ordered by penalty cost, in descending order.
- Late deadline first (LDF): tasks are ordered by deadline, in ascending order.

After ordering, `scheduling`(sorted_task_list, k) performs the scheduling for the ordered task list. The scheduling is performed via simulation using the datacenter simulator introduced in our previous work [19], specifically designed for modeling demand response events. The simulator includes power consumption modeling of servers and a set of QoS metrics, among other features.

The schedule is computed considering the processing threshold. It determines the completion time of each task $F = [f_1, f_2, ..f_j..f_N]$, as well as the power consumption ($Q = [p(t_1), p(t_2), ..p(t_i)..p(t_M)]$) for each timestep of the schedule.

5 Experimental Multi-objective Analysis

This section describes the experimental evaluation of the proposed multi-objective approach for datacenter participation in demand response programs.

5.1 Methodology of the Experimental Evaluation

The evaluation methodology analyzed three key aspects of the proposed multi-objective approach for realistic problem scenarios that model different datacenter dimensions. First, the values of relevant multi-objective optimization metrics are reported and evaluated for each scheduling heuristic. Then, the computed Pareto fronts are reported and analyzed. Finally, three special solutions are considered to analyze and compare important solutions provided to decision-makers:

- the *best trade-off solution*, defined as the closest point to the ideal vector, which represents a decision based on equally weighting both objectives. The ideal vector is a non-realistic solution with the best values for power consumption and penalty cost, computed from the extreme values of the global Pareto front. The trade-off solution is defined by $\arg\min_{p_i \in P} ||p_i - \vec{id}||$, where $\vec{id}$ is the ideal vector and P is the set of non-dominated solutions computed for all heuristics, both normalized to equally weigh both objectives. The ideal vector is different for each problem scenario solved.
- the *best power consumption* solution, i.e., the computed solution with the minimum power consumption.
- the *best penalty cost* solution, i.e., the computed solution with the minimum penalty cost.

The experimental analysis was performed on the high performance computing platform of National Supercomputing Center (Cluster-UY), Uruguay [22]. The reported results correspond to representative independent executions of the proposed scheduling strategies for the considered problem scenarios. For the comparative analysis, the results computed using the FCFS heuristic are used as a reference baseline, since it represents the most simple and traditional method for scheduling in datacenters under a business-as-usual scenario.

5.2 Description of the Scenarios and Problem Instances

The experiments were performed on three representative problem scenarios: a small scenario (considering 20 servers and 4544 tasks), a medium scenario (considering 50 servers and 7666 tasks), and a large scenario (considering 75 servers and 14598 tasks). The servers have of 24 computing cores, each one capable of processing 3000 million instructions per second. Task characteristics were generated based on real workloads from the Parallel Workloads Archive [8]. To compute the power consumption, each task is classified as either CPU-bound or memory-bound, based on the memory usage information obtained from the PWA workload. If the memory usage of a task is equal to or greater than 200

MB, it is considered memory-bound; otherwise, it is considered CPU-bound. The power consumption of a server at a certain timestep is computed using the power consumption model presented in our previous article [18]. The penalty cost for a task is randomly selected from a Poisson distribution with $\lambda = 3$. A complete description of the procedure applied for generating the problem scenarios is presented in our previous work [10].

5.3   Multi-objective Optimization Metrics

The multi-objective comparison of the proposed scheduling strategies was based on computing the following relevant multi-objective optimization metrics:

- Overall Non-dominated Vector Generation (ONVG): quantifies the number of non-dominated solutions in the computed Pareto front approximation.
- Error Ratio (ER): indicates the percentage of computed non-dominated solutions that are not members of the true Pareto front. Lower values of the metric correspond to better results.
- Generational Distance (GD): evaluates the distance between the set of computed non-dominated solutions and the true Pareto front. GD is defined in Eq. 3, where $|P|$ is the number of computed non-dominated solutions and d is the Euclidean distance from the i-th solution in the computed Pareto front (p_i) to the nearest solution in the true Pareto front.

$$GD(P, PF) = \frac{1}{|P|} \sqrt{\sum_{p_i \in P} d^2(p_i, PF)}, \qquad (3)$$

The ideal value of GD is 0, when all computed non-dominated solutions are in the true Pareto front. Lower values of GD correspond to better results.

Since the true Pareto front of the problem is unknown, all metrics were calculated considering the global Pareto front, built by gathering all the non-dominated solutions found in all independent executions performed for each scheduling strategy. This is a common approach for evaluating multi-objective optimization metrics for real world problems [5].

Metrics were calculate using the `pfevaluator` library (https://pypi.org/project/pfevaluator/). This library contains a useful set of tools for evaluating multi-objective optimization algorithms.

5.4   Results and Discussion

This subsection reports and analyzes the results of the proposed heuristics. The analysis focuses on the comparison of the studied multi-objective optimization metrics to identify the usefulness of each heuristic on different situations.

Multiobjective Optimization Metrics. Table 1 presents the numerical values of the multi-objective metrics for the three studied scenarios. Columns Δ_{ONVG}, Δ_{ER}, and Δ_{GD} are the relative improvements over FCFS. The best results for each metric and the best improvements are indicated in bold.

Table 1. Results of the multiobjetive optimization metrics

scenario	strategy	ONVG	ER	GD	Δ_{ONVG}	Δ_{ER}	Δ_{GD}
small	FCFS	75	0.987	0.030	0.000	0.000	0.000
	LIFO	**79**	**0.316**	**0.002**	**0.053**	**−0.680**	**−0.933**
	EDF	75	0.789	0.027	0.000	−0.201	−0.100
	HPF	77	0.987	0.005	0.027	0.000	−0.833
	LDF	**79**	1.013	0.007	**0.053**	0.026	−0.767
medium	FCFS	62	0.908	0.036	0.000	0.000	0.000
	LIFO	**70**	0.605	**0.009**	**0.129**	−0.334	**−0.750**
	EDF	62	**0.395**	0.021	0.000	**−0.565**	−0.417
	HPF	**70**	0.684	0.010	**0.129**	−0.247	−0.722
	LDF	**70**	0.895	0.018	**0.129**	−0.014	−0.500
large	FCFS	**56**	0.836	0.080	**0.000**	0.000	0.000
	LIFO	55	**0.090**	**0.002**	−0.018	**−0.892**	**−0.975**
	EDF	**56**	0.731	0.059	**0.000**	−0.126	−0.263
	HPF	55	0.731	0.010	−0.018	−0.126	−0.875
	LDF	**56**	0.761	0.016	**0.000**	−0.090	−0.800

According to Table 1, LIFO was the best heuristic regarding ER and GD, except for ER in the medium scenario, where EDF was the best. However, the reason LIFO outperforms EDF in GD despite having less coverage of the global Pareto front is that LIFO solutions are closely aligned with the global Pareto front, whereas EDF solutions tend to deviate in other areas. HPF was the second-best heuristic regarding GD, indicating that close solutions to the Pareto front were computed. Regarding ONVG metric, all strategies obtained similar values.

Analysis of Pareto Fronts. Figure 2 presents the Pareto fronts computed by each proposed strategy for the small scenario. The blue line indicates the global Pareto front and the black cross is the ideal vector.

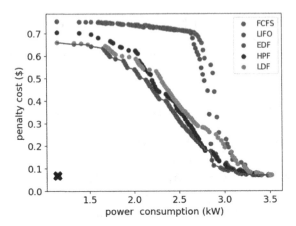

Fig. 2. Computed Pareto fronts for the small scenario (Color figure online)

Figure 2 reveals that the solutions obtained by FCFS and EDF are farther away from the ideal vector compared to other heuristics, especially at medium and low power consumption. However, as the power consumption values increase and the penalty costs decrease accordingly, FCFS and EDF solutions gradually approach to the global Pareto front. EDF solutions outperformed the other heuristics in solutions close to 3 kW of consumption. This behavior is due to FCFS and EDF prioritize tasks with long wait times in the pending queue. Thus, only a few tasks are completed within the specified deadlines when computing resources are scarce. FCFS and EDF are optimistic in the sense that they assume that tasks that have been waiting longer can still be executed on time, even if they are already delayed. Pessimistic heuristics (LIFO and LDF) prioritize recently arrived tasks with a high probability of being completed on time, meeting their deadlines. The pessimistic approach is more favorable for meeting deadlines of certain tasks when there computing resources are scarce due to power consumption restrictions. However, it must be considered that some clients may be adversely affected by long waiting times. The HPF strategy, which prioritize tasks with high penalty cost, properly balanced solutions that outperformed pessimistic strategies at low power consumption and outperformed optimistic strategies at high power consumption.

Figure 3 presents the Pareto fronts computed by each proposed scheduling strategy for the medium scenario.

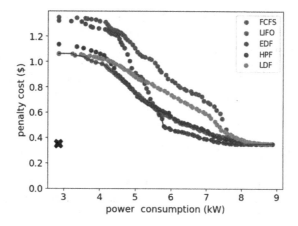

Fig. 3. Computed Pareto fronts for the medium scenario

Similar to the small scenario, Fig. 3 shows that optimistic strategies computed better results at low power consumption levels. EDF outperformed the other strategies at medium power consumption levels, in contrast to the results in the small scenarios. FCFS also had better results than in the small scenario at medium power consumption levels. The differences with results computed in the small scenario are because the load on the computing infrastructure is lower. In the medium scenario the task-to-server ratio is 153, whereas in the small scenario is 227. Considering that the tasks and servers have similar characteristics in both scenarios and the time horizon is the same, the observed improvement for optimistic strategies is explained by the difference in the task-to-server ratio.

Figure 4 shows the Pareto fronts computed by each proposed heuristic for the large scenario. The behavior was similar to the small scenario, where optimistic heuristic solutions were better than other heuristics at low and medium power consumption levels. EDF solutions are better at high power consumption levels.

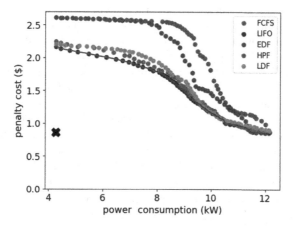

Fig. 4. Computed Pareto fronts for the large scenario

Analysis of Relevant Solutions. Table 2 reports the trade-off, best power consumption and best penalty cost solution for the three scenarios. The column p is the power consumption and the column c is the penalty cost, and the relative improvement over the power consumption and penalty cost of FCFS are columns Δ_p and Δ_c respectively. The best results for each column are indicated in bold.

Table 2. Trade-off, best power consumption and best penalty cost solutions

scenario	strategy	trade-off				best power				best cost			
		p	c	Δ_p	Δ_c	p	c	Δ_p	Δ_c	p	c	Δ_p	Δ_c
small	FCFS	3.09	**0.14**	0.00	0.00	1.14	0.75	0.0	0.00	**3.47**	0.07	**0.00**	0.0
	LIFO	2.75	0.20	−0.11	0.43	1.14	**0.66**	0.0	−0.12	3.53	0.07	0.02	0.0
	EDF	2.86	**0.14**	−0.07	−0.02	1.14	0.75	0.0	0.00	3.51	0.07	0.01	0.0
	HPF	2.78	0.18	−0.10	0.29	1.14	0.70	0.0	−0.06	3.53	0.07	0.01	0.0
	LDF	**2.71**	0.29	−0.12	1.09	1.14	**0.66**	0.0	−0.12	3.53	0.07	0.02	0.0
medium	FCFS	6.26	0.80	0.00	0.00	2.85	1.35	0.0	0.00	8.70	0.35	0.0	0.0
	LIFO	**5.66**	0.59	−0.10	−0.26	2.85	**1.06**	0.0	−0.21	8.84	0.35	0.02	0.0
	EDF	5.80	**0.49**	−0.07	−0.39	2.85	1.32	0.0	−0.02	**8.20**	0.35	−0.06	0.0
	HPF	5.67	0.62	−0.10	−0.22	2.85	1.14	0.0	−0.16	8.87	0.35	0.02	0.0
	LDF	6.27	0.69	0.00	−0.13	2.85	1.07	0.0	−0.21	8.81	0.35	0.01	0.0
large	FCFS	10.60	**1.25**	0.00	**0.0**	4.27	2.61	0.0	0.00	**12.13**	0.85	**0.00**	0.0
	LIFO	**9.24**	1.38	−0.13	0.10	4.27	**2.17**	0.0	−0.17	12.17	0.85	**0.00**	0.0
	EDF	9.41	1.57	−0.11	0.25	4.27	2.61	0.0	0.00	**12.13**	0.85	**0.00**	0.0
	HPF	9.49	1.35	−0.10	0.07	4.27	2.25	0.0	−0.14	12.25	0.85	0.01	0.0
	LDF	9.62	1.28	−0.09	0.02	4.27	2.21	0.0	−0.16	12.14	0.85	**0.00**	0.0

Results in Table 2 indicate that LIFO obtained the best value of power consumption for trade-off solutions in medium and large scenarios, and was the second-best heuristic in the small scenario. Additionally, LIFO achieved acceptable values of penalty cost for trade-off solutions in all scenarios. FCFS obtained the best values of penalty cost for trade-off solutions in small and large scenarios, but with high power consumption in all scenarios. Regarding the best power consumption solutions, all strategies obtained the same value on power consumption but LIFO and LDF obtained the best penalty cost in all scenarios, outperforming FCFS in 12% in the small scenario, 21% in the medium scenario, and 17% in the large scenario. Relative improvements show that pessimistic heuristics obtained better results than the other heuristics at low power consumption levels. Regarding the best penalty cost solutions, no significant differences were observed among the computed solutions, except for the EDF heuristic in the medium scenario (EDF improved 6% over FCFS). This improvement that EDF presents indicates that the EDF heuristic, in situations of low load of the computing infrastructure, manages to obtain solutions with the same penalty cost as the other heuristics while using 6% less energy than FCFS, which is the strategy that achieves the second-best penalty cost value.

The notebook with the complete Python code used for computing the studied metrics and elaborating the figures is publicly available at https://colab.research.google.com/drive/1lrkHP8u9aWaPdgmRIIf0LJ2aPbM99Rpc?usp=sharing.

6   Conclusions and Future Work

This article presented a multi-objective analysis of heuristic methods for minimizing power consumption and quality of service degradation in datacenter operation for participating in demand response programs An on/off energy-aware strategy in combination with five list scheduling heuristics are studied and compared for realistic problem scenarios.

The experimental evaluation showed that the proposed heuristics were able to compute accurate results. Heuristics obtained Pareto fronts that allows decision makers to have a wide range of scheduling options, accounting for different trade-offs between the considered problem objectives. The comparative analysis demonstrated that, when power consumption is restricted and computing resources are limited, pessimistic heuristics (e.g., LIFO) computed better solutions than optimistic ones, achieving improvements of up to 21% in quality of service while maintaining the same power consumption. Conversely, when there is a high availability of computing resources, optimistic strategies computed better results than pessimistic heuristics, achieving improvements of up to 6% in power consumption for the same quality of service.

The main outcomes of the multi-objective analysis demonstrated that using rather simple heuristics has a significant impact on reducing both power consumption and quality of service degradation. Therefore, it is promising to direct future research towards the design of more complex strategies that incorporate more specific domain knowledge. The main directions for future work include implementing strategies that simultaneously consider multiple criteria, such as prioritizing high-cost and recently arrived tasks together. Additionally, incorporating strategies that focus on power consumption reduction through task consolidation, taking into account the different types of tasks.

References

1. Assad, U., et al.: Smart grid, demand response and optimization: a critical review of computational methods. Energies **15**(6) (2022)
2. Bahrami, S., Wong, V., Huang, J.: Data center demand response in deregulated electricity markets. IEEE Trans. Smart Grid **10**(3), 2820–2832 (2019)
3. Cao, X., Zhang, J., Poor, V.: Data center demand response with on-site renewable generation: a bargaining approach. IEEE/ACM Trans. Network. **26**(6), 2707–2720 (2018)
4. Chen, N., Ren, X., Ren, S., Wierman, A.: Greening multi-tenant data center demand response. Perform. Eval. **91**, 229–254 (2015)
5. Coello, C., Van Veldhuizen, D., Lamont, G.: Evolutionary Algorithms for Solving Multi-objective Problems. Kluwer Academic, New York (2002)

6. Cui, Y., Geng, Z., Zhu, Q., Han, Y.: Review: multi-objective optimization methods and application in energy saving. Energy **125**, 681–704 (2017)
7. Dai, Y., Gao, Y., Gao, H., Zhu, H.: Real-time pricing scheme based on Stackelberg game in smart grid with multiple power retailers. Neurocomputing **260**, 149–156 (2017)
8. Feitelson, D., Tsafrir, D., Krakov, D.: Experience with using the parallel workloads archive. J. Parallel Distrib. Comput. **74**(10), 2967–2982 (2014)
9. Guo, C., Luo, F., Cai, Z., Dong, Z.: Integrated energy systems of data centers and smart grids: state-of-the-art and future opportunities. Appl. Energy **301** (2021)
10. Iturriaga, S., Muraña, J., Nesmachnow, S.: Bio-inspired negotiation approach for smart-grid colocation datacenter operation. Math. Biosci. Eng. **19**(3), 2403–2423 (2022)
11. Iturriaga, S., Dorronsoro, B., Nesmachnow, S.: Multiobjective evolutionary algorithms for energy and service level scheduling in a federation of distributed datacenters. Int. Trans. Oper. Res. **24**(1–2), 199–228 (2016)
12. Iturriaga, S., García, S., Nesmachnow, S.: An empirical study of the robustness of energy-aware schedulers for high performance computing systems under uncertainty. Commun. Comput. Inf. Sci. 143–157 (2014)
13. Iturriaga, S., Nesmachnow, S., Dorronsoro, B., Bouvry, P.: Energy efficient scheduling in heterogeneous systems with a parallel multiobjective local search. Comput. Inform. **32**(2), 273–294 (2013)
14. Lu, X., Li, K., Xu, H., Wang, F., Zhou, Z., Zhang, Y.: Fundamentals and business model for resource aggregator of demand response in electricity markets. Energy **204**, 117885 (2020)
15. Meng, F.L., Zeng, X.J.: A Stackelberg game-theoretic approach to optimal real-time pricing for the smart grid. Soft. Comput. **17**(12), 2365–2380 (2013)
16. Muraña, J., Nesmachnow, S., Iturriaga, S., Montes de Oca, S., Belcredi, G., Monzón, P., Tchernykh, A.: Two level demand response planning for retail multi-tenant datacenters. In: 18th International Conference on High Performance Computing and Simulation, pp. 1–8 (2021)
17. Muraña, J., Nesmachnow, S., Iturriaga, S., Montes de Oca, S., Belcredi, G., Monzón, P., Shepelev, V., Tchernykh, A.: Negotiation approach for the participation of datacenters and supercomputing facilities in smart electricity markets. Program. Comput. Softw. **46**, 636–651 (2020)
18. Muraña, J., Nesmachnow, S., Armenta, F., Tchernykh, A.: Characterization, modeling and scheduling of power consumption of scientific computing applications in multicores. Clust. Comput. **22**(3), 839–859 (2019)
19. Muraña, J., Nesmachnow, S.: Simulation and evaluation of multicriteria planning heuristics for demand response in datacenters. SIMULATION **99**(3), 291–310 (2021)
20. Nesmachnow, S.: Parallel multiobjective evolutionary algorithms for batch scheduling in heterogeneous computing and grid systems. Comput. Optim. Appl. **55**(2), 515–544 (2013)
21. Nesmachnow, S., Dorronsoro, B., Pecero, J., Bouvry, P.: Energy-aware scheduling on multicore heterogeneous grid computing systems. J. Grid Comput. **11**(4), 653–680 (2013)
22. Nesmachnow, S., Iturriaga, S.: Cluster-UY: collaborative scientific high performance computing in Uruguay. In: Torres, M., Klapp, J. (eds.) ISUM 2019. CCIS, vol. 1151, pp. 188–202. Springer, Cham (2019). https://doi.org/10.1007/978-3-030-38043-4_16

23. Nesmachnow, S., Perfumo, C., Goiri, Í.: Holistic multiobjective planning of data-centers powered by renewable energy. Clust. Comput. **18**(4), 1379–1397 (2015)
24. Porteiro, R., Nesmachnow, S., Moreno-Bernal, P., Torres-Aguilar, C.: Computational intelligence for residential electricity consumption assessment: detecting air conditioner use in households. Sustain. Energy Technol. Assess. **58**, 103319 (2023)
25. Snevely, R.: Enterprise Data Center Design and Methodology. Pearson, London (2002)
26. Stavrinides, G., Karatza, H.: An energy-efficient, QoS-aware and cost-effective scheduling approach for real-time workflow applications in cloud computing systems utilizing DVFS and approximate computations. Futur. Gener. Comput. Syst. **96**, 216–226 (2019)
27. Tchernykh, A., Lozano, L., Schwiegelshohn, U., Bouvry, P., Pecero, J., Nesmachnow, S.: Bi-objective online scheduling with quality of service for IAAS clouds. In: IEEE 3rd International Conference on Cloud Networking, pp. 307–312 (2014)
28. Tran, N., Pham, C., Ren, S., Han, Z., Hong, C.: Coordinated power reduction in multi-tenant colocation datacenter: an emergency demand response study. In: IEEE International Conference on Communications, pp. 1–6 (2016)
29. Wang, Y., Lin, X., Pedram, M.: A Stackelberg game-based optimization framework of the smart grid with distributed PV power generations and data centers. IEEE Trans. Energy Convers. **29**(4), 978–987 (2014)
30. Zhang, Y., Paschalidis, I., Coskun, A.: Data center participation in demand response programs with quality-of-service guarantees. In: Proceedings of the 10th ACM International Conference on Future Energy Systems (2019)

Enhancing the Sparse Matrix Storage Using Reordering Techniques

Manuel Freire[1]($\boxtimes$), Raul Marichal[1], Sanderson L. Gonzaga de Oliveira[2], Ernesto Dufrechou[1], and Pablo Ezzatti[1]

[1] Instituto de Computación, INCO, Facultad de Ingeniería, Universidad de la República, Montevideo, Uruguay
{mfreire,rmarichal,edufrechou,pezzatti}@fing.edu.uy
[2] ICT-Unifesp, Universidade Federal de São Paulo, São José dos Campos, Brazil

Abstract. Sparse linear algebra kernels are memory-bound routines, and their performance varies significantly according to the non-null pattern of the sparse matrix operands. The impressive computing power and memory bandwidth of modern massively parallel computing devices encourage researchers to develop sparse linear algebra kernels that can exploit these platforms efficiently. In this sense, a main line of work improves the storage of matrices, aiming to optimize the communication between the memory and the cores. In previous work, the use of a strategy consisting of a delta-encoding with matrix reorderings compressed the indexing data of the matrix, saving storage and communications. This work presents an algorithm to improve the reordering strategy and the resulting compression of the indexing data. The results show that this strategy leads to important storage savings, which can also reduce data movements between the main memory and processors.

Keywords: sparse matrices · storage · memory access · reordering technique

1 Introduction

Sparse linear algebra is an important and rapidly evolving field, where researchers invest much effort in improving the basic operations, frequently the performance bottleneck of many scientific problems. Unlike the dense counterpart, in sparse matrix problems, the performance of these routines is conditioned by the particularities of the matrix nonzero pattern. These characteristics make it difficult the use of a one-fits-all strategy.

One of the most dominant sparse linear algebra operations is the product of a sparse matrix and a dense vector, known as SpMV. This operation is the core of many iterative methods to solve sparse linear systems of equations. Due to the importance of the SpMV, the literature contains several proposals to improve this operation in diverse hardware platforms [8,9,14]. Naturally, sparse matrix research, and scientific computation in general, have accompanied the evolution of high-performance computing hardware, which now includes devices that integrate many lightweight cores and have high memory bandwidths like GPUs or FPGAs. Since the appearance of CUDA in 2007, the GPUs have dominated the HPC landscape for numerical linear algebra problems.

The SpMV is a typical memory-bound problem due to its low arithmetic intensity, i.e., the number of floating-point operations performed for each byte of data loaded from memory. Besides that, the performance of sparse codes in GPU is also affected by the load imbalance (the variation of non-null entries processed by each core), low data locality, and data indirection (indexing data structures to access the floating-point values). Even considering the above, the GPU generally offers interesting throughput due to its superior memory bandwidth. To exploit this feature of GPUs, much of the effort on sparse kernels seeks to improve the storage of matrices, aiming to optimize the communication between the memory and the cores.

In a previous effort [10], we tried to identify the benefit offered by using compression strategies to store the matrix index data. In particular, we revisited the use of delta encoding to store the matrix indices with and without the application of the Reverse Cuthill-Mckee (RCM) method [11]. The study exposed the significant benefits reached when the strategy uses the techniques complementarily.

This work deepens our previous effort, focusing on improving the reordering strategy. In more detail, we design a light heuristic procedure specially tailored to enhance the delta encoding technique. The experimental evaluation over a subset of real-world matrices extracted from the SuiteSparse Matrix Collection [7] demonstrates an important saving in storage (and, therefore, data movements between the memory and processors) offered by the new idea.

The rest of this article is structured as follows. We describe the main ideas behind the sparse matrices storage, and the matrix reordering techniques, in Sect. 2. We propose the new strategy in Sect. 3. In Sect. 4, we show the experimental evaluation of the novel scheme. Finally, the concluding remarks, as well as lines of the future work, are presented in Sect. 5.

2   Background

This section briefly introduces basic concepts such as sparse matrix storage formats, the Reverse Cuthill-Mckee algorithm for reordering, and the index compression technique known as delta encoding.

2.1   Sparse Matrices Storage Formats

Sparse matrices storage formats are strategies that avoid storing void information of the sparse matrices (i.e., null coefficients usually represented by zeros) by using underlying structures which hold information to recover the position of the non-null elements.

The most straightforward idea (in the static context) is to store only the non-null elements in a vector and store their row and column indices separately. This format is known as Elementary or Coordinate (COO) [2].

One of the most popular formats to store matrices is the Compressed Sparse Row (CSR) [21]. This format is similar to COO because it holds only the non-null values and their indices. CSR goes further in the compression, ordering the non-null elements row-wise in the values vector and storing the index where each row starts. If one keeps elements column-wise, the same idea gives place to the Compressed Sparse Column (CSC) format.

In both cases, each floating-point value needs extra information storage to recover its position in the matrix. In COO, the memory overhead is $8B$ per element and in CSR is $4B$ per element plus $4B$ per row. In general, indices occupy a big part of the memory used to store the matrices, so many formats focus on reducing that overhead.

Some sparse formats admit the storage of some zeros to mitigate the irregularity in the memory accesses, which damages the performance of sparse routines in massively parallel processors like GPUs. A typical example is the ELLPACK storage format [3] which represents the sparse matrix as two dense matrices of size $n \times m$, where n is the number of rows in the matrix, and m is the number of non-null of the longest row. One of these matrices stores the non-null coefficients plus the zero padding, and the other stores the column index corresponding to each coefficient.

If the matrix has its non-null elements grouped in clusters, a sparse format could store just one pair of coordinates for each cluster (or block) and calculate the rest. The set of layouts that use this strategy are known as blocked formats, and one of the most popular is the Blocked CSR (BCSR) [15] which divides the matrix into dense blocks of fixed size, treating it as a matrix of blocks and applying CSR to index the blocks. The efficiency of a blocked format depends on the sparsity pattern of the matrix it is storing. Other examples of arrangements that use blocking techniques are bmSparse, Sliced ELL (SELL-C), or Column Diagonal Storage [1,4,5,13,24].

In recent years much effort has been directed to reducing the weight of index storage. In that line of work, Tang et al. proposed a family of efficient compression schemes called bit-representation optimized (BRO) [22]. They introduced two techniques, BRO-ELL and BRO-COO, based on ELL and COO formats. In addition, they presented BRO-HYB, which is analogous to HYB because it stores the regular part in BRO-ELL and the irregular on BRO-COO.

2.2   Reverse Cuthill-Mckee (RCM)

The Reverse Cuthill-Mckee method [11] is the most popular reordering algorithm to reduce the bandwidth and profile of a matrix. This heuristic improves the original Cuthill-Mckee (CM) algorithm [6] by reversing the numbering obtained from CM. RCM has been found to produce matrices with the same bandwidth as CM but usually with a lower profile. The CM method is a greedy variation of the breadth-first search procedure, which numbers each vertex in an adjacency list in ascending degree order. Concretely, it interprets the sparse matrix as the adjacency matrix of a graph and perform Bread-First Search (BFS) on the graph associated. The algorithm finds the unvisited nodes in each iteration of the BFS, starting in an arbitrary root node labeled level 0. The original CM traverses adjacent nodes to a visited node from low to high degrees.

Since the results of the reductions depend on the node selected as the starting vertex, researchers have proposed many algorithms to choose the starting vertex. Extensive experiments among these pseudoperipheral vertex finders showed that the George-Liu algorithm [12] remains in the state of the practice to provide pseudoperipheral vertices to the Reverse Cuthill-McKee method when applied to matrices with symmetric sparsity patterns [19].

2.3 Delta Encoding

An interesting idea to reduce the memory used to store indices in sparse matrices is to compress them by storing the distance to the previous element of the row instead of the column index itself. This technique is known as *delta encoding* [23].

In the worst case, the bits needed to store a distance can be as much as those used for the index (i.e., the index is the distance from the element $(r, 0)$). On the other hand, in many cases, the coefficients in a row are considerably closer, and we can store them in smaller data types, such as int_{16} or int_8 (instead of int_{32}).

The main advantage is that this strategy is not related (or opposed) to any particular storage format. For example, CSR can use delta encoding to store the column indices, while CSC could do so with row indices. Other layouts such as ELL or COO can also use this strategy to arrange their column indices (or, in COO, the row index if one uses column-major ordering).

The idea of applying delta encoding and other related techniques to compress the indexes of sparse matrices, accelerating the performance of the SpMV in shared memory processors and GPUs was explored in [16,17].

3   Proposal

Considering the time spent fetching sparse matrix indexing data from memory in kernels such as the SpMV, it is reasonable to expect a performance benefit from storing these indices with only the necessary number of bits. The standard integer size is 4 bytes, but, for example, one can store indices lower than 2^{16} with a `uint16` data type. Even when we can keep only a part of the matrix indices with fewer bytes, one can store entire matrix rows with the smaller data types. In that case, we could use a sparse format that stores rows using different integer sizes. As the processing of rows is independent in kernels such as the SpMV, this could improve the processing performance for the part of the matrix stored with a smaller integer size.

In [10] we analyzed the minimum integer size needed to store the matrix indices for a large set of symmetric sparse matrices. We also evaluated the number of rows in each matrix that needs 8, 16, or 32 bits for their indices. We used delta encoding to replace the column index in the CSR sparse format by the delta to the next non-null in the row and studied the impact of reordering the matrix on that strategy. The results showed that using the Reverse Cuthill-Mckee (RCM) reordering heuristic in conjunction with delta encoding, a significant number of matrices passed from the 32 bits category (those matrices with at least one row that needs 32 bits) to 16 bits category, and from the 16 bits category to 8 bits category. Of all the 1407 matrices studied, only 56 matrices ended in the 32 bits category after applying RCM and delta encoding.

RCM has proven to be a good heuristic to reduce the bandwidth of a matrix, but, on the other hand, in doing so, sometimes it extends the distance of two contiguous elements in the rows that end up with more bandwidth. The problem is that RCM is not designed to reduce the distance between consecutive elements but reduces bandwidth. Reducing the bandwidth of the matrix brings non-null elements closer to each other. Thus, we can expect a collateral improvement in the delta. However, there are many cases where reducing the bandwidth increases the deltas (e.g., TSOPF/TSOPF_FS_b300_c3) and many more where RCM improves the deltas, but other strategies yield better results. In particular, other authors have replaced the RCM with other heuristics for an specific purposes, see as an example [18] where the objective is the number of diagonals.

Considering the above, we centered the effort on designing a strategy that enhances the reordering returned by RCM. The proposal relies on a light search strategy focused on improving the ordering of matrices that stayed in the 32 bits category after applying RCM. In a previous study [20], the authors employed similar ideas for bandwidth reduction.

The algorithm uses a random search in conjunction with a local search to improve the permutation produced by RCM. To guide the search, we define a metric of how much away the matrix is to be able to be stored in 16 bits. The fitness function is defined as follows:

$$f(p) = \sum_{r \in rows} \#away16_r \tag{1}$$

where $\#away16_r$ is the number of elements of row r that are more than 2^{16} positions away from the previous one (or from zero if it is the first element of the row).

The proposal consists of two stages. In the first stage, the algorithm performs several random steps, and in the second stage, it makes directed steps towards improving the solution. The random steps consist of a permutation of n rows chosen randomly, allowing the routine not to get stuck in a local optimum. We fixed a boundary α for the deterioration of f to prevent the random steps from worsening the solution too much.

The second stage is to improve the solution given by the first one. Ideally, the improvement in this stage outweighs the other's deterioration (if any). This stage focuses on fixing the matrix's "worst" problem by finding the element further away from the previous coefficient. Once found, the procedure tries to make a permutation that moves it to a distance less than $2^{16} - 1$, making it possible to store the column index in 16 bits.

Naturally, this change can have an overall negative effect because it can enlarge distances between other elements. The procedure evaluates if the change worsens the solution and discards it in that case. If the algorithm does not use a permutation, it tries with other permutations that make that delta storable in 16 bits. If none of the experimented permutations works, the procedure applies a fixed permutation that makes the delta equal to one.

4   Experimental Evaluation

In this section, we present the evaluation of our novel heuristic. For this work, we chose a subset of the five matrices that, after applying RCM and delta encoding, still cannot be stored using deltas of 16 bits. We took this set of symmetric matrices from the Suite Sparse Matrix Collection [7]. Table 1 shows the main characteristics of the testing set.

Table 1. Matrices used for the experimental evaluation with their principal characteristics.

Id	Name	Dim	Number of non-zeros (NNZ)
1	ASIC_100k	99340	940,621
2	preferentialAttachment	100,000	999,970
3	boyd1	93,279	1,211,231
4	lp1	534,388	1,643,420
5	c-big	345,241	2,340,859

As the primary goal of our heuristic is to increase the number of rows that uses less than 32 bits for the studied matrices, Table 2 presents the number of rows and deltas (i.e., particular elements) that require 32 bits for their storage. These characteristics can be considered the baseline with which we compare the performance of the new heuristic. The table presents these metrics for the original matrices and after applying the permutation given by RCM.

Even if the most important metric is the number of rows that need int_{32}, because it directly impacts the memory requirements of the matrix, the number of deltas gives a more precise idea of the problem (at least considering our search strategy). The table shows that applying RCM has an overall positive impact on

Table 2. Number of rows and deltas representable only in 32 bits for the original matrices (right) and after applying RCM (left).

	With RCM		Without RCM	
Id	N_{rows}	N_{deltas}	N_{rows}	N_{deltas}
1	6.11E+03	6.11E+03	6.98E+03	6.98E+03
2	1.11E+03	1.12E+03	2.47E+03	2.47E+03
3	2.62E+04	2.62E+04	2.77E+04	2.77E+04
4	5.34E+05	7.20E+05	2.26E+05	2.32E+05
5	2.98E+05	3.78E+08	3.45E+05	4.54E+05

both metrics. The only exception was the matrix $lp1$. In this case, the number of rows that require int_{32} grew significantly.

In the first experiment, we executed RCM and applied the proposed heuristic to the permutations that resulted from the method. In these tests, we fixed the number of iterations in $n = 6000$. Furthermore, we used the boundary α as a parameter that grows with the iterations to avoid getting trapped in a local optimum. Since α grows with the number of iterations, the random step can severely deteriorate the candidate solution after many iterations. For this reason, each iteration stores the best solution until that point.

Table 3 shows the number of rows and deltas that still require 32 bits after applying our heuristic method. The results show that for two of the matrices ($ASIC\_100k$ and $boyd1$), the proposed heuristic gets N_{rows} to zero, which means that we can store the entire matrices with a smaller data type. On the other hand, for the other three, where there are still rows that require int_{32}, we get a sizeable reduction in the number of rows that require this data type.

Table 3. Number of rows and deltas representable only in 32 bits after applying the heuristic

Id	Rows 32	Deltas 32
1	0	0
2	763	763
3	0	0
4	462,690	462,690
5	252,980	254,240

Another analysis we have performed in our previous work is the distribution of the rows between categories depending on the data type needed to represent its deltas. Tables 4 and 5 present the numbers of rows that belong to each classification.

Table 4. Number of rows that need 32, 16 and 8 bits to store its indices after the RCM.

Id	Rows 32	Rows 16	Rows 8
1	6.11E+03	9.31E+04	8.90E+01
2	1.11E+03	9.89E+04	2.90E+01
3	2.62E+04	6.70E+04	5.60E+01
4	5.34E+05	2.00E+01	8.00E+00
5	2.98E+05	4.71E+04	4.21E+02

Table 5. Number of rows that need 32, 16 and 8 bits to store it indices after the application of the heuristic.

Id	Rows 32	Rows 16	Rows 8
1	0.00E+00	9.93E+04	4.60E+01
2	7.63E+02	9.92E+04	1.00E+00
3	0.00E+00	9.33E+04	1.90E+01
4	4.63E+05	7.09E+04	8.48E+02
5	2.53E+05	9.20E+04	2.21E+02

Concerning the 8 bits categories, the results are diverse, with the number of 8-bit rows decreasing in some matrices but growing in others. In general, the percentage of rows in that category is small with respect to the total. The primary contribution of our heuristic is that it replaces rows from the 32 bits category to the 16 bits one. Figure 1 presents the same results in percentages comparing the matrices before and after applying the heuristic proposed. In all matrices, the first bar represents the results with only RCM and the second after the heuristic proposed.

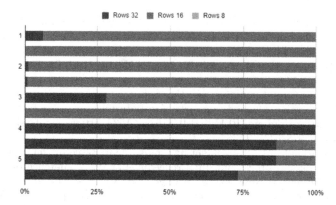

Fig. 1. Percentage of rows in each category for the evaluated matrices before and after the application of the proposed heuristic.

5   Conclusions and Future Work

The performance of sparse linear algebra kernels suffers from the cost of accessing the memory. A significant part of this memory access is dedicated to indexing data to compute the position of the non-null coefficients in the matrix. As the cost of the computations is much less than the cost of memory accesses, it can payoff to compress this data and add some work to decompress it once it reaches the cores.

In this work, we continued our previous efforts using reordering strategies that enhance the sparse matrix index compressing based on delta encoding, focusing on improving the reordering for this purpose. We used a random search in conjunction with a local search to define a novel heuristic that improves the results of RCM, reaching a higher compression in the evaluated matrices.

The heuristic proposed in this study reduced the number of rows that required the higher data type (int_{32}) in all test cases. For two of the test cases, the resulting matrix can be stored entirely in int_{16}, while for the rest, the new procedure significantly reduced the rows that require int_{32}.

In future work, we plan to follow different lines:

- Extending our approach to tackle the int_{16} to int_8 transformation.
- Designing a storage format using a mixed-integer size strategy, storing the matrix in various submatrices with different index sizes depending on the maximum delta in the row.
- Developing sparse kernels that can take advantage of the new format.

Acknowledgments. This work is partially funded by the UDELAR CSIC-INI project *CompactDisp: Formatos dispersos eficientes para arquitecturas de hardware modernas.* The authors also thank PEDECIBA Informática and the University of the Republic, Uruguay.

References

1. Monakov, A., Lokhmotov, A., Avetisyan, A.: Automatically tuning sparse matrix-vector multiplication for GPU architectures. In: Patt, Y.N., Foglia, P., Duesterwald, E., Faraboschi, P., Martorell, X. (eds.) HiPEAC 2010. LNCS, vol. 5952, pp. 111–125. Springer, Heidelberg (2010). https://doi.org/10.1007/978-3-642-11515-8_10
2. Barrett, R., et al.: Templates for the Solution of Linear Systems: Building Blocks for Iterative Methods. Society for Industrial and Applied Mathematics (1994). https://doi.org/10.1137/1.9781611971538, https://epubs.siam.org/doi/abs/10.1137/1.9781611971538
3. Bell, N., Garland, M.: Implementing sparse matrix-vector multiplication on throughput-oriented processors. In: Proceedings of the Conference on High Performance Computing Networking, Storage and Analysis, SC 2009. Association for Computing Machinery, New York, NY, USA (2009). https://doi.org/10.1145/1654059.1654078

4. Berger, G., Freire, M., Marini, R., Dufrechou, E., Ezzatti, P.: Unleashing the performance of bmSparse for the sparse matrix multiplication in GPUs. In: Proceedings of the 2021 12th Workshop on Latest Advances in Scalable Algorithms for Large-Scale Systems (ScalA), pp. 19–26, November 2021

5. Berger, G., Freire, M., Marini, R., Dufrechou, E., Ezzatti, P.: Advancing on an efficient sparse matrix multiplication kernel for modern GPUs. Concurr. Comput. Pract. Experience **35**, e7271 (2022). https://doi.org/10.1002/cpe.7271, https://onlinelibrary.wiley.com/doi/abs/10.1002/cpe.7271

6. Cuthill, E., McKee, J.: Reducing the bandwidth of sparse symmetric matrices. In: Proceedings of the 1969 24th National Conference, pp. 157–172. ACM Press (1969). https://doi.org/10.1145/800195.805928

7. Davis, T.A., Hu, Y.: The university of Florida sparse matrix collection. ACM Trans. Math. Softw. **38**(1), 1–25 (2011). https://doi.org/10.1145/2049662.2049663

8. Dufrechou, E., Ezzatti, P., Quintana-Ortí, E.S.: Selecting optimal SPMV realizations for GPUs via machine learning. Int. J. High Perform. Comput. Appl. **35**(3), 254–267 (2021). https://doi.org/10.1177/1094342021990738

9. Favaro, F., Oliver, J.P., Ezzatti, P.: Unleashing the computational power of FPGAs to efficiently perform SPMV operation. In: 40th International Conference of the Chilean Computer Science Society, SCCC 2021, La Serena, Chile, 15–19 November 2021, pp. 1–8. IEEE (2021). https://doi.org/10.1109/SCCC54552.2021.9650418

10. Freire, M., Marichal, R., Dufrechou, E., Ezzatti, P.: Towards reducing communications in sparse matrix kernels. In: Naiouf, M., Rucci, E., Chichizola, F., De Giusti, L. (eds.) Cloud Computing, Big Data & Emerging Topics, JCC-BD&ET 2023. CCIS, vol. 1828, pp. 17–30. Springer, Cham (2023). https://doi.org/10.1007/978-3-031-40942-4_2

11. George, A.: Computer implementation of the finite element method. Ph.D. thesis, Computer Science Department, School of Humanities and Sciences, Stanford University, CA, USA (1971)

12. George, J.A., Liu, J.W.: Computer Solution of Large Sparse Positive Definite Systems. Prentice-Hall, Englewood Cliffs (1981)

13. Godwin, J., Holewinski, J., Sadayappan, P.: High-performance sparse matrix-vector multiplication on GPUs for structured grid computations. In: The 5th Annual Workshop on General Purpose Processing with Graphics Processing Units, GPGPU-5, London, United Kingdom, 3 March 2012, pp. 47–56. ACM (2012)

14. Gómez, C., Mantovani, F., Focht, E., Casas, M.: Efficiently running SPMV on long vector architectures. In: Proceedings of the 26th ACM SIGPLAN Symposium on Principles and Practice of Parallel Programming, PPoPP 2021, pp. 292–303. Association for Computing Machinery, New York, NY, USA (2021). https://doi.org/10.1145/3437801.3441592

15. Choi, J.W., Singh, A., Vuduc, R.W.: Model-driven autotuning of sparse matrix-vector multiply on GPUs. In: Proceedings of the 15th ACM SIGPLAN Symposium on Principles and Practice of Parallel Programming (15th PPOPP 2010), pp. 115–125. ACM SIGPLAN, Bangalore, India, January 2010

16. Karakasis, V., Gkountouvas, T., Kourtis, K., Goumas, G.I., Koziris, N.: An extended compression format for the optimization of sparse matrix-vector multiplication. IEEE Trans. Parallel Distributed Syst. **24**(10), 1930–1940 (2013). https://doi.org/10.1109/TPDS.2012.290, https://doi.org/10.1109/TPDS.2012.290

17. Kourtis, K., Goumas, G.I., Koziris, N.: Optimizing sparse matrix-vector multiplication using index and value compression. In: Ramírez, A., Bilardi, G., Gschwind, M. (eds.) Proceedings of the 5th Conference on Computing Frontiers, 2008, Ischia, Italy, 5–7 May 2008, pp. 87–96. ACM (2008). https://doi.org/10.1145/1366230. 1366244

18. Marichal, R., Dufrechou, E., Ezzatti, P.: Optimizing sparse matrix storage for the big data era. In: Naiouf, M., Rucci, E., Chichizola, F., De Giusti, L. (eds.) Cloud Computing, Big Data & Emerging Topics - 9th Conference, JCC-BD&ET, La Plata, Argentina, 22–25 June 2021, Proceedings. Communications in Computer and Information Science, vol. 1444, pp. 121–135. Springer, Cham (2021). https://doi.org/10.1007/978-3-030-84825-5_9

19. de Oliveira, S.L.G., de Abreu, A.A.A.M.: An evaluation of pseudoperipheral vertex finders for the reverse Cuthill-McKee method for bandwidth and profile reductions of symmetric matrices. In: 37th International Conference of the Chilean Computer Science Society, SCCC 2018, Santiago, Chile, 5–9 November 2018, pp. 1–9. IEEE (2018). https://doi.org/10.1109/SCCC.2018.8705263

20. de Oliveira, S.L.G., Silva, L.M.: Low-cost heuristics for matrix bandwidth reduction combined with a hill-climbing strategy. RAIRO Oper. Res. **55**(4), 2247–2264 (2021). https://doi.org/10.1051/ro/2021102

21. Saad, Y.: Iterative Methods for Sparse Linear Systems, 2nd edn. Society for Industrial and Applied Mathematics (SIAM), Philadelphia (2003)

22. Tang, W.T., et al.: Accelerating sparse matrix-vector multiplication on GPUs using bit-representation-optimized schemes. In: Proceedings of the International Conference on High Performance Computing, Networking, Storage and Analysis. ACM, November 2013. https://doi.org/10.1145/2503210.2503234

23. Willcock, J., Lumsdaine, A.: Accelerating sparse matrix computations via data compression. In: Proceedings of the 20th Annual International Conference on Supercomputing, ICS 2006, pp. 307–316. Association for Computing Machinery, New York, NY, USA (2006). https://doi.org/10.1145/1183401.1183444

24. Zhang, J., Gruenwald, L.: Regularizing irregularity: bitmap-based and portable sparse matrix multiplication for graph data on GPUs. In: Proceedings of the 1st ACM SIGMOD Joint International Workshop on Graph Data Management Experiences & Systems (GRADES) and Network Data Analytics (NDA), GRADES-NDA 2018. Association for Computing Machinery, New York, NY, USA (2018). https://doi.org/10.1145/3210259.3210263

Towards Fault Tolerance and Resilience in the Sequential Codelet Model

Diego A. Roa Perdomo[1,2]($\boxtimes$), Rafael A. Herrera Guaitero[2], Dawson Fox[1,2],
Hervé Yviquel[3], Siddhisanket Raskar[1], Xiaoming Li[2],
and Jose M. Monsalve Diaz[1]

[1] Argonne National Laboratory, Lemont, IL, USA
diegor@udel.edu
[2] University of Delaware, Newark, DE, USA
[3] University of Campinas, Campinas, Brazil

Abstract. Failure or disruption in High-Performance Computer Systems can have a significant impact on human life, the environment, or the economy. Critical applications refer to software systems or functionalities that are essential for the safety, security, or continuity of critical infrastructure, services, or operations. Considering that semiconductor devices are susceptible to errors and failure, providing error detection and correction mechanisms in such systems is imperative. However, the main challenge for achieving fault tolerance and resiliency is compartmentalizing the causes and the consequences of error, in both hardware and software. Moreover, today's extreme-scale parallel HPC systems necessitate fundamentally non-deterministic executions, making compartmentalization an even bigger challenge. To address these challenges, this paper proposes leveraging the Sequential Codelet Model (SCM), which facilitates parallel execution of programs expressed sequentially and hierarchically. We propose to exploit SCM's encapsulation of semantics and data to compartmentalize faults transparently and efficiently. We present multiple techniques that can be implemented in the Sequential Codelet Model to include fault-tolerant and resiliency mechanisms. We implement already-known solutions by extending a functional emulator for the Sequential Codelet Model.

Keywords: Codelet Model · Program Execution Model · Fault Tolerance · Resiliency

1 Introduction

Computers and embedded systems play a significant role in the daily functioning of critical infrastructure and systems in a variety of sectors, including

This research used resources at the Argonne Leadership Computing Facility, a DOE Office of Science User Facility supported under Contract DE-AC02-06CH11357. This research was also supported by the Exascale Computing Project (17-SC-20-SC), a collaborative effort of the U.S. Department of Energy Office of Science and the National Nuclear Security Administration. This work was partially supported by the National Science Foundation, under award SHF-1763654, and by Petrobras, under grant 2018/00347-4.

C. J. Barrios H. et al. (Eds.): CARLA 2023, CCIS 1887, pp. 77–94, 2024.
https://doi.org/10.1007/978-3-031-52186-7_6

healthcare, transportation, finance, industry, and defense. In all these sectors, the disruption or failure of essential services in such areas can result in far-reaching consequences, including endangering human life, impacting the environment, or even destabilizing the economy.

Supporting fault tolerance and resiliency in critical HPC systems has been extensively studied [12, 20, 32, 33]. Fault compartmentalization is one of the main challenges that apply to both the cause and the impact of faults. When the cause is compartmentalized, the abnormal components can be isolated and corrective actions can be taken based on their overall error history. When the impact is well defined and compartmentalized, the system can recover from faults with only minimum redo. In traditional von Neumann computational models, compartmentalizing usually requires domain-specific analysis and user involvement to segregate portions of computation and monitor execution. The main reason is that large-scale HPC applications usually entangle computation, data management, and parallelism management without much distinction. Coupling that with the non-deterministic execution of threads magnified in scale, compartmentalization can hardly be done in an effective, efficient, and user-transparent way. Implementing resiliency in parallel and distributed programs often involves complex multi-layered system interactions, spanning across the operating system, runtime, application, and workload manager. In High-Performance computing, this kind of resiliency is often done through checkpointing, which helps prevent the loss of computation progress in case of failure [5, 12, 26].

A program execution model (PXM) refers to the governing set of rules or conceptual framework that dictates the execution of a computer program by a computing system [8, 30]. It defines the behaviors and interactions between the various system components involved in executing a program, including the processor, memory, operating system, and other system resources. Among various PXMs, the Codelet PXM [16, 37] describes computation based on a hybrid between dataflow and von Neumann computation models. Codelets are units of computation that can be executed when their dependencies are satisfied. Each codelet can be seen as a task, defined by a collection of instructions tailored to a particular architecture. Unlike other more widely-used task models (e.g., OpenMP, OmpSs, Legion, etc.), codelets are pure functions whose outputs only depend on their inputs. To support more complex programs, codelets interconnect with each other forming codelet dependence graphs (CDG) that represent the data and control dependencies between them. The creation of this graph is inspired by the theory of dataflow. An evolution of the Codelet model is the Sequential Codelet Model (SCM) [9, 10, 25]. SCM describes the CDG through sequential program semantics, and it uses techniques inspired by instruction-level parallelism to achieve heterogeneous, parallel, and distributed execution of programs. The SCM is based on a hierarchical view of the system. Each level separates scheduling and orchestration, execution components, and memory management interfaces.

In this paper, we argue that the Codelet Program Execution Model naturally provides an effective foundation for compartmentalization and fault tolerance. It derives from the explicit encapsulation of computation and data in the Codelet Model. This paper presents mechanisms that leverage PXM behavior to provide fault tolerance and resiliency while adapting to changing conditions or failures. We highlight fault tolerance/resiliency mechanisms that can be implemented as hardware, software, or both beyond traditional checkpointing.

In particular, we demonstrate how well-defined PXMs facilitate the compartmentalization of faults and resiliency into system components. To do so, we implement some resiliency techniques within an emulated Sequential Codelet Model, namely SCMUlate [2], running on commodity hardware. In the area of resiliency for critical applications running on computing systems, our paper contributes the following:

- classification and adaptation of existing state-of-the-art resiliency techniques for integration within the Codelet PXM,
- demonstration of the implementation of a subset of these resilience techniques within an emulated Codelet Model, highlighting their real-world applicability,
- and, examination of the performance and resiliency implications of these adapted techniques, offering data-driven insights into their effects.

2   Sequential Codelet Model

The Sequential Codelet Model (SCM) [9,10,14,25], is a hierarchical PXM that leverages sequential computer architectures for parallel computation. It integrates the advantages of having sequentially defined programs while providing flexibility for parallel execution. The SCM defines a structured and flexible approach to implementing reliability and fault tolerance mechanisms, using modularity, compartmentalization, and scalability to enhance system robustness. The following subsections describe the main elements of the SCM that are considered in the definition of the aforementioned mechanisms.

2.1   Sequential Codelet Model Abstract Machine

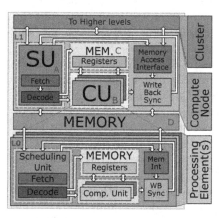

Fig. 1. Two levels of the sequential Codelet Model Abstract Machine. Each level as a 5-stage pipeline.

The SCM Abstract Machine (SCM-AM) (Fig. 1) is a theoretical definition of the hierarchical architecture that does not detail the implementation. This abstract machine is similar to the traditional 5 stages pipeline architectures: *Fetch*, *Decode*, *Execute*, *Memory* and *Write Back*. Each level is organized in these stages. The Scheduling Unit (SU) is directly related to the *Fetch* and *Decode* stages. The SU orchestrates program execution (e.g., codelet scheduling, and control flow decisions). The *Execute* phase is representative of the execution of codelets, performed by the Compute Unit (CU).

The hierarchical organization of the SCM machine comes from two aspects. First, a CU of a given level is a complete machine in the level below. Input and output data dependencies (i.e., operands) are stored in the register file of the level that schedules the codelet into a CU. Second, memory operations from the level below interface with the registers of the level above. Hence the name Memory/Register in Fig. 1. This latter property guarantees that memory operations are bounded in latency between two levels, providing performance guarantees for code executing at a given level. Notice that the higher the level in the hierarchy, the larger the footprint of the system is, resulting in larger memory sizes and increased latency, therefore translating into larger codelets. The hierarchy in the organization is broken whenever at a particular level, a Compute Unit is represented in a particular architecture (e.g., GPGPUs, CPUs, or FGPAs) representing a leaf of the architecture tree. This allows for support for heterogeneous execution of the Sequential Codelet Model, as presented in [10] in commodity hardware.

2.2   Operational Semantics of the SCM Abstract Machine

Operational Semantics for the SCM-AM describe the system's expected behavior and how programs are interpreted as sequences of computational steps. Analogous to the architecture, programs are hierarchically structured in the SCM model. A *SCM program* for a given level is represented as a stream of instructions to be mapped and interpreted by the five stages of that level. Instructions are fetched in order according to the *SCM program* of that level. Instructions can be of 3 types: control flow and basic arithmetic, compute codelets, and memory codelets. The SU (i.e., fetch+decode phases) executes control flow and basic arithmetic instructions that enable the construction of the Codelet Dataflow Dependence Graph. These basic instructions are the building blocks for conditional branches and jumps and are used to construct loops and manage dependencies discovered at runtime.

At a given level, memory is organized into regions that are effectively named registers. The higher the level, the larger the size of the registers. Memory codelets [15] orchestrate memory management between the level above and the current level. Memory codelets allow for data prefetching, data movement, and data recoding [13] (e.g., near-memory compute).

Compute codelets are assigned to the Compute Units of the *Execute* phase. Compute codelets are collections of instructions that match the execution model of a CU of a given level. For example, a CPU Codelet is a sequential excerpt of instructions written in traditional CPU architectures (e.g., RISC-V, X86, or ARM) that interact with the operand registers of the codelet. Notice that memory operations of a compute codelet are directly mapped to its register operands in the level above. Parallelism in the SCM model is achieved through techniques inspired by instruction-level parallelism [27]. In particular, out-of-order architectures allow for discovering dataflow dependence graphs within a window of instructions. Therefore, the sequential description of codelet graphs leverages this behavior, allowing the SCM program to be parallelized. Thus, the Scheduler Unit removes false dependencies (Write After Read and Write After Write) and respects true dependencies (Read After Write) based on the register names.

Finally, the *Write Back* phase of the 5 stages pipeline manages synchronization, notifying the SU that a given Codelet has finished execution and triggering the activation of other Codelets.

2.3 Application Programming Interface of the SCM

```
1   LDIMM  R64B_1, 0; //Vect A Base Addr
2   LDIMM  R64B_2, 52428800;// B Base Addr
3   LDIMM  R64B_3, 104857600;// C Base Addr
4   LDIMM  R64B_4, 0; // iteration variable
5   LDIMM  R64B_5, 0; // offset
6   LDIMM  R64B_6, 400; // num of iterations
7   loop:
8   BREQ   R64B_4, R64B_6, 8; // R64B_4=400? jmp 8
9   LDOFF  R2048L_1, R64B_1, R64B_5;
10  LDOFF  R2048L_2, R64B_2, R64B_5;
11  COD    vecAdd_2048L R2048L_3, R2048L_1,
                        R2048L_2;
12  STOFF  R2048L_3, R64B_3, R64B_5;
13  ADD    R64B_4, R64B_4, 1;
14  ADD    R64B_5, R64B_5, 131072; // Next TILE
15  JMPLBL loop;
16  COMMIT;
```

Listing 1.1. An SCM program that performs a vector addition

```
1   IMPLEMENT_CODELET(vecAdd_2048L,
2       double *A = GET_OP<2,double*>();
3       double *B = GET_OP<3,double*>();
4       double *C = GET_OP<1,double*>();
5
6
7       for(uint64_t i = 0; i < TILE; i++){
8           C[i] = A[i] + B[i];
9       }
10  );
```

Listing 1.2. Implementation of the L0 Codelet VecAdd_2048L used in Listing 1.1

The SCM also provides an Application Programming Interface (API). A codelet is a scheduling quantum of an SCM program at a given level. Codelets are non-preemptive, atomically scheduled, and represented as pure functions. As previously mentioned SCM programs are composed of 3 types of instructions: control and basic arithmetic, compute codelets, and memory codelets. Thus, the SCM program is expressed sequentially based on the three instruction types. Each codelet must also be defined in the programming interface of the level below. Listing 1.1 shows an example of an SCM program that performs a simple vector addition for the level L1 of Fig. 1. Listing 1.2 shows the definition of the codelet *vecAdd_2048L* written for the level L0. Notice that *vecAdd_2048L* is used as a single instruction in Listing 1.1 (line 11). A complete reference for the programs used in this paper can be found in [9,25].

The SCM program in Listing 1.1 calculates a vector addition in the form $A[N] = B[N] + C[N]$, where A, B, and C contain doubles and $N = 400 * 2048 * 64bytes = 52.42MB$ for a total of 6553600 items. It is important to note that although these values are hardcoded in this example, they may also come from memory. Codelets of L0 use registers of fixed size. R2048L_X refers to a register of size $2048 \times cache\_line$ (e.g., 128 KB for 64 Bytes cache lines).

3 Mechanisms for Resiliency and Fault Tolerance

A Program Execution Model such as SCM can be implemented as a combination of hardware [10] and software [37]. Particularly, the hierarchical view of the Sequential Codelet Model allows for a combination of software and hardware techniques at different levels. Figure 2 shows the 4 different components or *Functional Units* that are used to define *containment zones* at different parts of the system. Table 1 presents different fault tolerance and resilience mechanisms in the context of the Sequential Codelet Model presented in Sect. 2. The afore-mentioned table includes information about the type of implementation: in the PXM or as part of the program, static: fixed resources; dynamic: resources are assigned on-demand; hybrid: a combination of static-dynamic is possible. Mechanisms are analyzed qualitatively in terms of overhead cost: hardware, runtime, time, or storage.

Table 1. Mechanisms for Resiliency and Fault Tolerance

Functional Unit	Method	Implementation		Type			Overhead / Cost			
		PXM	Program	Static	Dynamic	Hybrid	Hardware	Runtime	Time	Storage
A) SU	N-of-M Voting (Cd R.)	X		X	X	X		X	X	X
	Dynamic Voting (Cd R.)	X			X	X		X	X	X
	Lockstep (SU R.)	X		X			X	X		
	Voting (SU R.)	X		X	X		X	X	X	X
	Main-Backup (SU R.)	X		X	X	X	X	X		
	Watchdog (SU M.)	X			X		X	X		
B) CU	Lockstep (CU R.)	X		X			X	X		
	Voting (CU R.)	X		X	X		X	X	X	X
	Main-Backup (CU R.)	X		X	X	X	X	X		
	Watchdog (CU M.)	X			X		X	X		
C) Memory	Redundant Inputs	X		X						X
	Register Duplication	X		X	X	X				X
	Memory Checkpointing	X	X	X	X	X		X		X
D) CDG	Algorithm based FT		X	X				X		X
	Supervisory System	X			X			X		

As we will observe in this section, SCM resiliency takes advantage of two fundamental properties of the Codelet Model: 1) Codelets are pure functions with no side effects beyond their registers. 2) It is possible to compartmentalize codelet execution owing to their explicit data dependencies. It also takes advantage of the division of roles in the SCM-AM. The objective of this section is not to provide a conclusive list of techniques that can be used, but rather to demonstrate the advantages of using them in the Sequential Codelet Model as well as provide some guidelines for future implementations of the Program Execution Model.

3.1   A) Scheduling Unit Resiliency

While modularity enables compartmentalization, the intrinsic hierarchical organization between the SU and the CU enables codelet nesting, storing fine-grain codelets within coarse-grain codelets. Replicating an SU also replicates the program and codelets assigned to that SU, and replicating a CU of a given level intrinsically replicates the SU of the level below. However, the fault tolerance mechanisms used in each level may target different requirements. In this section, we focus on mechanisms managed by the scheduler unit, a central piece in the

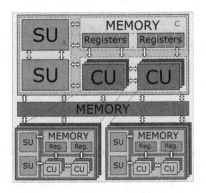

Fig. 2. Extended SCM-AM

coordination of the system. Scheduling of codelets for fault tolerance, resiliency, and self-adaptation has been previously studied [23,31]. Likewise, [35] proposes a symptom based detection and diagnosis for faults in multicore architectures.

N-of-M Voting and N-Modular Systems (Codelet Replication). Voting techniques can be applied in different forms. An N-of-M system creates M duplicates of a component and requires up to N of these components to agree to be functional.

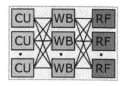

Fig. 3. NMR

Figure 3 shows the architecture of an N-Modular redundant architecture that presents the execute and writeback stages of the SCM. In this case, codelets are replicated via the scheduler unit, and voting occurs in the writeback stage. By decoupling these roles it is possible to: 1) maintain the compute units free for more work to be scheduled, and 2) decouple possible sources of errors when environmental conditions affect the two stages differently. The reader is reminded that the higher the level in the SCM abstract machine, the larger the footprint of the system is expected. Therefore, each stage may be at different environmental conditions.

It may not be necessary to replicate all codelets. Codelet metadata can specify the desired level of redundancy for a specific codelet, increasing the flexibility of this mechanism and granting some control over the consequent overhead. Such metadata is to be interpreted by the SU. However, it is important to note that high error rates tend to reduce the overall system reliability of N-of-M systems, as explained in [22]; hence, it should only be used in systems with higher reliability.

In the context of Listing 1.1, the Codelet VectAdd_2048L and its operands are duplicated. Line 11 would be executed M times, each with different input parameters. Register renaming is used for operand replication. Register replication is optional, but duplication of Write and Read/Write operands is mandatory, as they could result in scrambled output. Notice that compute codelet replication is straightforward because their input/output operands are well-defined in the form of a register and their execution is side-effect free. Additionally, codelet duplication allows for heterogeneous execution where multiple replicas are implemented by different architectures. This process is achieved by using multiple variants of the codelet that represent the same mathematical operation. On the other hand, memory codelet duplication is more challenging as it must include the side effect of communication with the memory subsystem in the level above.

A similar technique is proposed in [39], a coarse-grained dataflow system is augmented with redundant execution and thread-level recovery techniques, leveraging the inherent features of the dataflow execution model like side-effect free execution and single-assignment semantics. They demonstrate that redundant execution of dataflow threads can increase the utilization of underutilized resources in a multi-core system while maintaining tolerable overhead in a fully utilized system. [4] also investigates the scheduling of parallel applications for message-passing multi-computers via job duplication.

Dynamic Voting (Codelet Replication). Replication does not have to be static (e.g., always replicating M times as in the N-of-M system). Dynamic voting (Fig. 4) allows the number of codelet replicas to be controlled based on system conditions. The triggering mechanism for replication can be tailored to the specific system. There is a tradeoff between fault detection and recovery that the system designer must balance. An example of dynamic voting starts with only one replica of the codelet. The system compares the outputs of the original and the replica. If there are discrepancies more codelets can be scheduled. This process can be performed until a majority is reached.

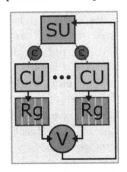

The Scheduler Unit can make decisions regarding the destination compute unit based on the system's state. For example, [31] uses error history to change scheduling decisions. The maximum number of replicas before an unrecoverable error occurs can be specified by the system or metadata in the SCM program. This method minimizes overall task overhead, but it might take longer to reach a consensus in some cases, as it spawns additional codelets on demand.

Fig. 4. Cd Rep.

SU Replication. SU replication focuses on the resiliency of control flow instructions and arithmetic operations performed by the SU that determine codelet scheduling. SU replication implies redundant execution of these instructions, but it does not mean codelet replication. In the example in Listing 1.1, SU replication will be centered around the control flow instructions (i.e., lines 8 and 15) and the simple arithmetic instructions (i.e., lines 13 and 14), concerning only the checking of the Level 1 program and its control.

Ravishankar et al. [19] describe similar techniques applied to single-core architectures. In particular, the Preemptive control-flow-checking technique tracks the program's execution and guarantees that the execution corresponds to a correct execution flow. In general, SU resiliency is centered around the consistency of the program execution and control flow (Figs. 5 and 6).

Lockstep Mode: In Lockstep mode, equivalent SUs execute the same set of operations simultaneously. Lockstep execution requires the replicated SUs to be tightly coupled physically (e.g., same clock domain), allowing fast communication between the devices. Multiple recovery methods could be used, each with different costs associated. Some examples are 1) copying the processor state from the unfaulty SU or 2) decommissioning the faulty unit by disabling or isolating the device. In SU lockstep replication, the resiliency system performs a one-to-one comparison of the scheduling decisions performed by each SU at every step of the execution.

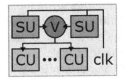

Fig. 5. SU Lockstep

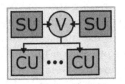

Fig. 6. SU Voting

Decoupled Replication and Voting: The Scheduling Unit is replicated. Error detection and correction work correspondingly, but the execution of each replica is completely independent from the others. The voting mechanism compares scheduler outputs and decides based on the majority. Voting only occurs after control instructions are executed and does not require the processors to be tightly coupled, loosening the physical proximity requirement. There are multiple mechanisms for comparison, allowing diverse implementations with different tradeoffs. A costly solution could compare the output of each functional unit that makes up the SU in hardware (i.e., fetch, decode, and out-of-order mechanisms). A more modest option is to only compare the program counter register of each SU, as it directly relates to the control flow decisions (Fig. 7).

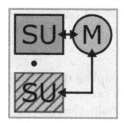

Fig. 7. SU M-B

Dynamic Redundancy and Main-Backup: SU replication can also provide dynamic redundancy in a main-backup configuration. Another SU can be placed in a location that can track the current program counter and keep track of the state of the overall machine. In this configuration, the second SU does not perform system orchestration decisions unless the first SU goes offline. The redundant SU only keeps a copy of the system's current state. Upon detection of an error, the second SU can take over control, allowing execution to continue. The Main-Backup approach allows for the backup unit to be used for other tasks until a fault occurs, or to increase hardware lifetime by decreasing utilization of the backup unit. Hot-swap techniques can be used to reduce downtime: the main unit can be replaced as the backup operates, normalizing the system's state without interruptions (Fig. 8).

Fig. 8. SU Wd

Watchdog and Monitoring: Two directions can be considered for watchdog mechanisms. First, a horizontal watchdog implementation could allow an SU to communicate with another SU. This mechanism can be used in the Dynamic Redundancy example in the section above. This would allow an SU to keep track of its peers at the same level and coordinate resiliency decisions across them. Second, a vertical watchdog implementation would involve the SU constantly checking its CUs (downwards) and communicating its state to the SU of the upper level. Based on this information, active action can be taken by an SU to avoid more programs being assigned to it or to migrate work to a horizontal SU peer. Therefore, SU resiliency provides some flexibility in how an SU is monitored by a watchdog mechanism and how it might be replaced in case of failure. Moreover, it is possible to implement a heartbeat mechanism horizontally and vertically that can range from a simple clock signal to a checksum or integrity check.

3.2 B) Computational Unit Resiliency

CU resiliency is directly connected to SU resiliency as described in Subsect. 3.1. Here we highlight elements that are most important for CU resiliency.

CU Replication. The commodity SCM-AM already includes Compute Unit (CU) replication used to achieve parallelism. Thus, a system can take advantage of already existing parallelism for resiliency while maintaining a low time overhead. This level of redundancy can be taken advantage of by the Scheduler unit by changing scheduling decisions across CUs. Additionally, notice that for a given level above L1, replicating a Computational Unit implicitly replicates the SU of the level below. Therefore, SU replication complements the mechanisms presented in Sect. 3.1. Multiple operation modes are defined based on previous work [6,17], targeting error detection and correction, system availability, and transparency to the user and application.

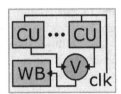

Fig. 9. CU LS

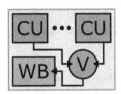

Fig. 10. CU Voting

Lockstep vs Decoupled: The level of coupling during the execution of codelets in replicated CUs can be controlled in the design. A lockstep (Fig. 9) would closely compare the state of each computation as presented in [29]. Memory operations performed within the Codelet must undergo a majority vote as they access the register file. A similar lockstep technique, along with checkpointing, roll-back, and roll-forward mechanisms, is proposed in [21].

However, the execution of each CU replica can be completely independent of one another (Fig. 10). The voting system only occurs after the Codelet is executed and does not require the processors to be tightly coupled, loosening the physical proximity requirement. This voting technique was previously described in Fig. 3.

A similar technique is proposed in [40], where a coarse-grained dataflow system is augmented with redundant execution and thread-level recovery techniques, leveraging the side-effect free execution and single-assignment semantics of the dataflow execution model. They demonstrate that redundant execution of dataflow threads can increase the utilization of underutilized resources in a multi-core system while maintaining tolerable overhead in a fully utilized system (Figs. 11 and 12).

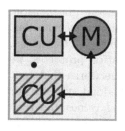

Fig. 11. CU M-B

Fig. 12. CU Wd

Dynamic Redundancy, Main-Backup, and Watchdog: Previously we described these mechanisms in the context of SUs. However, from the perspective of a CU, these mechanisms can be thought of as properties of the unit, rather than as mechanisms in the SU. The CU can still be seen as a closed unit while dynamic redundancy, main backup, and watchdog systems are built around them. Other work has also demonstrated that CUs can be used as watchdogs [28], enabling automatic anomaly detection and decision-making. These mechanisms can also be used as heartbeats [3] that inform another CU or the SU directly of the state of the processor, or as a checksum that contains further information about the program's state.

3.3 C) and D) Memory and IO, Resiliency and Fault Tolerance

Memory often presents challenges for resiliency. In general, the whole state of a program in SCM can be described as the current state of the register file, the program counter, and the memory in the levels above associated with the current execution. Regarding memory and IO, multiple mechanisms can provide fault tolerance and resiliency. Our scheme is centered around using Memory Codelets [15] for resiliency. Unlike Compute Codelets, memory codelets interact with outside systems, so they must consider possible side effects of replication.

Register File Resiliency. As described in several mechanisms above, the register file can play an important role in resiliency. First, Codelet duplication uses register renaming techniques to allow for full Codelet duplication. Furthermore, the N-Modular system in Fig. 3 demonstrates a possible configuration that also provides replication of the register file.

Registers are also named locations that can be replicated upon scheduling a Codelet. The reader may be familiar with the reservation tables in Tomasulo's algorithm [38]. In this case, registers are duplicated in the register file and possibly in multiple reservation tables. Likewise, the duplication of Codelets in multiple CUs can allow for the duplication of registers across different CUs. In particular, distributed CU systems can allow the replication of registers into each CU's local memory. Upon errors in each CU, the register file can be recovered using the original copy near the SU.

Redundant Inputs/Outputs and Reliable Communication. Redundant inputs target the problem of reliability in data acquisition. This is particularly important in the context of signal or data acquisition from external sources. The concept of Input/Output is previously described in [25] in the context of a hierarchical von Neumann view of the system. Therefore, the arrival and transmission of data from external sources directly relate to the memory interface.

Most computational systems rely on networks that transmit information; more often than not such networks have redundancy or resiliency mechanisms. For example, the TCP protocol provides a reliable connection between two nodes. While there might be some overlap with existing communication protocols, we extend the description of I/O redundancy to non-TCP/IP networks that may work as an interconnect to the outside of the system. Embedded systems, for example, may rely on electronic signals interpreted as digital values and then transmitted over cables or networks. These signals may be acquired redundantly and handled by the PXM transparently. The SCM-PXM can have a hardware implementation, relieving the CUs and the Operating System of the responsibility of network communication management and memory operations that can be handled directly by the PXM. A direct link to SmartNICs for virtual network function privatization is a possible candidate [24]. However, due to space limitations, we leave this discussion outside of the scope of this paper.

Another property of the SCM is its ability to be event-driven. Redundant signals can be used as event-driven inputs for duplicated Codelets. The application may mark these Codelets and associate them with the I/O protocol. Using multiple inputs combined with other FT&R techniques like algorithm-based fault tolerance can significantly increase the reliability of a system, targeting different levels where a fault may occur. [11] proposes QORE, a fault tolerant Network-on-Chip (NoC) architecture using reversible channel buffers. Other redundancy mechanisms used in automated design and control of critical systems can be considered as candidates for the I/O problem in SCM [18,32].

Memory Access Interface Resiliency. In general, the compartmentalization of local memory (i.e., data dependencies) and Memory Codelets allows SCM to provide resiliency mechanisms in the memory access interface strategically (Fig. 13).

Memory Checkpointing: Memory checkpointing is a method employed in computational workloads that usually require a long execution time. Memory Codelets orchestrate memory operations between the register file and the upper level. Therefore, Memory Codelets are a natural location to take advantage of checkpointing. Checkpointing often requires the application to determine the state of the program that is representative of the next checkpoint. Thanks to the strategic location of Memory Codelets, duplication can be transparently achieved for the Memory Codelets that are part of the checkpoint. Imagine, for example, the memory instruction in line 12 of Listing 1.1. This memory operation is to be executed by the memory access interface. If this Codelet represents a checkpoint, the memory access interface can write to both non-volatile and volatile memory at the same time.

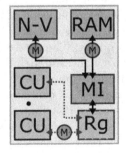

Fig. 13. Checkpoint

The additional latency overhead of the non-volatile memory access can be hidden by allowing the program to continue once the volatile memory is written. While Memory Codelets are the mechanism that performs the fine-grain memory stores for the checkpoint, the SU will have the ability to mark a specific state of the non-volatile memory as a complete checkpoint. Allowing the SU to save the state of the machine next to the checkpoint means that the recovery process is equivalent to a context switch of the system: 1) load the memory of the program from non-volatile to volatile memory and 2) load the program counter and the register file into the particular level that is being recovered.

On the other hand, the Memory Access Interface could be leveraged with recoding and compute capabilities, as described in [15]. Thus, it is possible to take advantage of algorithm-specific data integrity mechanisms. For instance, a system knows that values must not be negative. A Memory Codelet could perform additional checks on the data as it is copied back to the memory. Furthermore, Error Correction Codes can be part of the Memory Codelet interface. Although DRAM modules already support these, more general architectures (e.g., distributed systems) may still be able to take advantage of the flexibility in SCM.

To avoid silent and fail-stop errors, [36] suggests partial task replication and checkpointing for task-parallel HPC systems. Checkpointing with rollback recovery is a well-known approach for coping with transient faults. In this mechanism, an application is rolled back to the most recent consistent state using checkpoint data. A low-overhead two-state checkpointing (TsCp) approach for fault-tolerant hard real-time systems is presented in [34]. Compared to prior studies, this technique greatly reduces the number of checkpoints (62% on average), resulting in a 14% and 13% reduction in execution time and energy usage, respectively. HPC systems often face I/O bottlenecks when using global checkpointing to external storage. To address this, a technique was introduced in [26] that combines performance modeling and lightweight monitoring. This approach enables informed decisions on utilizing local storage devices, dynamically adapting to background flushes, and reducing checkpointing overhead based on their results.

3.4   Algorithm-Based Fault Tolerance in the Codelet Graph

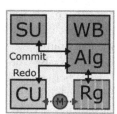

Fig. 14.   Algorithm-Based   Mechanism

Algorithm-based fault tolerance integrates error detection/correction mechanisms into the application itself. Codelets can be assigned additional metadata that refers to algorithm-based checking mechanisms. For example, to guarantee that the result of a codelet is correct, an additional segment of code could be added to the description of the Codelet. Such additional code does not need to be executed by the CU necessarily. For example, additional hardware in the writeback stage or the SU can provide a hardware-assisted interface to perform resiliency operations on output registers quickly. These mechanisms may also take advantage of domain-specific features embedded in the application (e.g., values can be checked to be within an acceptable range). Algorithm-based fault tolerance [7] can be attached as metadata of the Codelet for error detection and correction.

4 Evaluation

In order to demonstrate some of the approaches mentioned in Sect. 3 we have modified SCMUlate, an emulator of the Sequential Codelet Model previously used in [10]. SCMUlate is a functional emulator for the first level of the Sequential Codelet Model. It leverages commodity hardware found in current systems to be used as compute units of Level 1. Codelets are executed in real hardware compute units while the rest of the machine is emulated in software. As a result, the mechanism for fetch, decode, memory, writeback, and the register file for Level 1 are fully emulated. On the application side, SCMUlate interprets and executes the programs written in the assembly language of Level 1. This assembly program uses the same syntax used in Listing 1.1. Parallelization is achieved through Out-of-Order execution [9].

SCMUlate was extended to allow for SU-driven codelet duplication, performing the necessary register duplication and renaming to achieve N-replicas of the same codelet. Furthermore, a perfect voting mechanism was included that would compare all replicas in order to perform fault detection. In the presence of a recoverable error, the SU performs the necessary actions to recover computation. Finally, a fault injection mechanism is included that implements codelet fault injection based on two fault models: Poisson (i.e., constant error rate), and Weibull. The fault injection mechanism used is an implementation of the simulation strategy presented in [22].

Our evaluation includes the implementation of three resiliency mechanisms: a 2-of-3 system, a 3-of-5 system, and a dynamic M-of-N system with a maximum N of 10 duplications. As a baseline, we use a system that has no resiliency mechanism but is prone to failures based on the specific statistical model of the fault injection mechanism (i.e., Poisson vs Weibull). The experiments are focused on fault tolerance mechanisms for the Compute Unit as explained in Sect. 3 Thus, we assume that the only component that may fail is the Compute Unit and that other components are fully reliable.

Our execution environment is the Polaris supercomputer hosted by Argonne Leadership Computing Facilities (ALCF) [1]. To evaluate our approach, we use the implementation of the matrix multiplication algorithm in SCM that was also used in [10]. Each codelet executes a tile that is of size 128 by 128 double elements. The program executes square matrix multiplication of size M=N=K=768 doubles (i.e., 6 by 6 tiles. For the Weibull fault model, we use a beta of 0.7 previously used by [22,31]. For Lambda, we precalculate a range that could demonstrate the benefits of the approach based on the codelet execution time. In Polaris, the `MatMul_2048L` codelet for a single tile runs in approximately 2.5 ms. Based on our calculation the ranges of $\lambda = [0.0002, 0.008]$ for the Poisson model, and $\lambda = [0.002, 0.08]$ for Weibull were considered appropriate values. We perform 30 repetitions per lambda, increasing lambda by 0.0002 and 0.002 for Poisson and Weibull respectively.

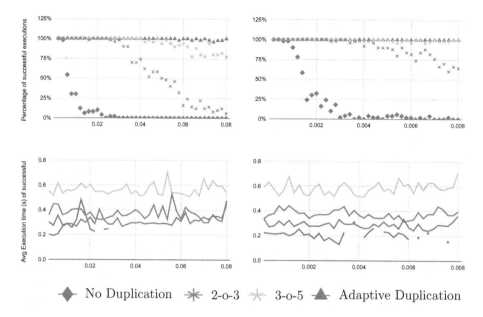

◆ No Duplication ✳ 2-o-3 ✲ 3-o-5 ▲ Adaptive Duplication

Fig. 15. Percentage of successful trials (Top Row) and execution time (Bottom Row) vs fault rate λ (horizontal axis) for two fault injection models: Weibull (left) and Poisson (Right). Weibull uses $\beta = 0.7$ in all the experiments. (Color figure online)

Our experiments are summarized in Fig. 15. The top row shows the results for the number of experiments that yield a successful run. The bottom row shows the average execution time of those results that were successful. If no results were successful, no data point for the time was considered, hence the breaking line in No Duplication (red).

Experiments show a considerable improvement in reliability across the different mechanisms. The average overhead of execution time for Weibull was 1.15, 1.37, and 2.07 times the baseline (no duplication). For Poisson on the other hand overheads were 1.39, 1.80, and 2.81 times the baseline (no duplication). In general, the adaptive solution presented a considerable advantage both in reliability and performance overhead, consequently demonstrating the advantage of scheduling-driven approaches.

5   Conclusion

This paper presents a possible implementation of resilience within the Sequential Codelet PXM. Our main contribution consists of identifying, categorizing, and adapting state-of-the-art resilience techniques for integration within the SCM. We demonstrated the real-world applicability of these adapted techniques within an emulated Codelet Model. We believe our work lays the foundation for enhancing resilience in similarly complex systems. Furthermore, our in-depth analysis of the performance implications of these techniques offers critical, data-driven insights. These insights will assist in understanding the trade-offs between resilience and performance, guiding decisions that balance system robustness with efficiency. We recognize that our work is only one step in the ongoing journey towards improving resilience in complex systems like the Codelet PXM.

References

1. Argonne leadership computing facility. https://www.alcf.anl.gov/, Accessed 22 July 2023
2. GitHub - josemonsalve2/SCM: Sequential Codelet Model of Program Execution – github.com. https://github.com/josemonsalve2/SCM/. Accessed 22 July 2023
3. Aguilera, M., Chen, W., Toueg, S.: Heartbeat: a timeout-free failure detector for quiescent reliable communication, vol. 1320, pp. 126–140 (1997). https://doi.org/10.1007/BFb0030680
4. Ahmad, I., Yu-Kwong Kwok, Y.K.K.: A new approach to scheduling parallel programs using task duplication. In: 1994 International Conference on Parallel Processing, vol. 2, pp. 47–51 (1994). https://doi.org/10.1109/ICPP.1994.37
5. Ansel, J., Arya, K., Cooperman, G.: DMTCP: transparent checkpointing for cluster computations and the desktop. In: 2009 IEEE International Symposium on Parallel & Distributed Processing, pp. 1–12 (2009). https://doi.org/10.1109/IPDPS.2009.5161063
6. Bolchini, C., Miele, A., Sciuto, D.: An adaptive approach for online fault management in many-core architectures (2012). https://doi.org/10.1109/DATE.2012.6176589
7. Bosilca, G., Delmas, R., Dongarra, J., Langou, J.: Algorithmic based fault tolerance applied to high performance computing (2008)
8. Dennis, J.: A parallel program execution model supporting modular software construction. In: Proceedings. Third Working Conference on Massively Parallel Programming Models (Cat. No. 97TB100228), pp. 50–60 (1997). https://doi.org/10.1109/MPPM.1997.715961
9. Diaz, J.M.M.: Sequential Codelet Model A SuperCodelet Program Execution Model and Architecture. Phd thesis, University of Delaware, Newark, DE (2021)
10. Diaz, J.M.M., Harms, K., Guaitero, R.A.H., Perdomo, D.A.R., Kumaran, K., Gao, G.R.: The supercodelet architecture. In: Proceedings of the 1st International Workshop on Extreme Heterogeneity Solutions. ExHET 2022. Association for Computing Machinery, New York (2022). https://doi.org/10.1145/3529336.3530823
11. DiTomaso, D., Kodi, A., Louri, A.: QORE: a fault tolerant network-on-chip architecture with power-efficient quad-function channel (qfc) buffers. In: 2014 IEEE 20th International Symposium on High Performance Computer Architecture (HPCA), pp. 320–331 (2014). https://doi.org/10.1109/HPCA.2014.6835942
12. Egwutuoha, I.P., Levy, D., Selic, B., Chen, S.: A survey of fault tolerance mechanisms and checkpoint/restart implementations for high performance computing systems. J. Supercomput. **65**(3), 1302–1326 (2013). https://doi.org/10.1007/s11227-013-0884-0
13. Fang, Y., Zou, C., Elmore, A.J., Chien, A.A.: UDP: a programmable accelerator for extract-transform-load workloads and more. In: Proceedings of the 50th Annual IEEE/ACM International Symposium on Microarchitecture, MICRO-50 2017, pp. 55–68. Association for Computing Machinery, New York (2017). https://doi.org/10.1145/3123939.3123983
14. Fox, D., Diaz, J.M.M., Li, X.: Chiplets and the codelet model (2022)

15. Fox, D., Diaz, J.M., Li, X.: On memory codelets: prefetching, recoding, moving and streaming data (2023)
16. Gao, G., Suetterlein, J., Zuckerman, S.: Toward an Execution Model for Extreme-Scale Systems - Runnemede and Beyond (2011). technical Memo
17. Gizopoulos, D., et al.: Architectures for online error detection and recovery in multicore processors. In: 2011 Design, Automation & Test in Europe (2011). https://doi.org/10.1109/date.2011.5763096
18. IEC: Functional safety of electrical/electronic/programmable electronic safety-related systems. Standard IEC 61508–1:2010. International Electrotechnical Commission, Geneva, CH (2010). https://webstore.iec.ch/publication/5515
19. Iyer, R., Nakka, N., Kalbarczyk, Z., Mitra, S.: Recent advances and new avenues in hardware-level reliability support. IEEE Micro **25**(6), 18–29 (2005). https://doi.org/10.1109/MM.2005.119
20. Kadri, N., Koudil, M.: A survey on fault-tolerant application mapping techniques for network-on-chip. J. Syst. Arch. **92**, 39–52 (2019). https://doi.org/10.1016/j.sysarc.2018.10.001. https://www.sciencedirect.com/science/article/pii/S1383762118301498
21. Kasap, S., Wächter, E.W., Zhai, X., Ehsan, S., McDonald-Maier, K.D.: Novel lockstep-based fault mitigation approach for socs with roll-back and roll-forward recovery. Microelectron. Reliabil. **124**, 114297 (2021). https://doi.org/10.1016/j.microrel.2021.114297. https://www.sciencedirect.com/science/article/pii/S0026271421002638
22. Koren, I., Krishna, C.M.: Fault-Tolerant Systems. Organ Kaufmann (2007)
23. Landwehr, A.: An experimental exploration of self-aware systems for exascale architectures (2016)
24. Linguaglossa, L., et al.: Survey of performance acceleration techniques for network function virtualization. Proc. IEEE **107**(4), 746–764 (2019). https://doi.org/10.1109/JPROC.2019.2896848
25. Monsalve, J., Harms, K., Kalyan, K., Gao, G.: Sequential codelet model of program execution - a super-codelet model based on the hierarchical turing machine. In: 2019 IEEE/ACM Third Annual Workshop on Emerging Parallel and Distributed Runtime Systems and Middleware (IPDRM), pp. 1–8 (2019). https://doi.org/10.1109/IPDRM49579.2019.00005
26. Nicolae, B., Moody, A., Gonsiorowski, E., Mohror, K., Cappello, F.: Veloc: towards high performance adaptive asynchronous checkpointing at large scale. In: 2019 IEEE International Parallel and Distributed Processing Symposium (IPDPS), pp. 911–920 (2019). https://doi.org/10.1109/IPDPS.2019.00099
27. Patterson, D.A., Hennessy, J.L.: Computer Architecture: A Quantitative Approach. Morgan Kaufmann Publishers Inc., San Francisco (1990)
28. Platunov, A., Sterkhov, A.: Whatchdog mechanisms in embedded systems. Sci. Tech. J. Inf. Technol. Mech. Opt. 301–311 (2017). https://doi.org/10.17586/2226-1494-2017-17-2-301-311
29. Poledna, S.: Fault-Tolerant Real-Time Systems: The Problem of Replica Determinism. Kluwer Academic Publishers, Boston (1996)
30. Qu, P., Yan, J., Zhang, Y., Gao, G.: Parallel turing machine, a proposal. J. Comput. Sci. Technol. **32**, 269–285 (2017). https://doi.org/10.1007/s11390-017-1721-3
31. Rozo Duque, L.A., Monsalve Diaz, J.M., Yang, C.: Improving mpsoc reliability through adapting runtime task schedule based on time-correlated fault behavior. In: 2015 Design, Automation & Test in Europe Conference & Exhibition (DATE), pp. 818–823 (2015)

32. Safari, S., et al.: A survey of fault-tolerance techniques for embedded systems from the perspective of power, energy, and thermal issues. IEEE Access **10**, 12229–12251 (2022). https://doi.org/10.1109/ACCESS.2022.3144217

33. Sahoo, S.S., Ranjbar, B., Kumar, A.: Reliability-aware resource management in multi-/many-core systems: a perspective paper. J. Low Power Electron. Appl. **11**(1) (2021). https://doi.org/10.3390/jlpea11010007. https://www.mdpi.com/2079-9268/11/1/7

34. Salehi, M., Khavari Tavana, M., Rehman, S., Shafique, M., Ejlali, A., Henkel, J.: Two-state checkpointing for energy-efficient fault tolerance in hard real-time systems. IEEE Trans. Very Large Scale Integr. (VLSI) Syst. **24**(7), 2426–2437 (2016). https://doi.org/10.1109/TVLSI.2015.2512839

35. Sastry Hari, S.K., Li, M.L., Ramachandran, P., Choi, B., Adve, S.V.: Mswat: low-cost hardware fault detection and diagnosis for multicore systems. In: Proceedings of the 42nd Annual IEEE/ACM International Symposium on Microarchitecture, MICRO 42, pp. 122–132. Association for Computing Machinery, New York (2009). https://doi.org/10.1145/1669112.1669129

36. Subasi, O., Unsal, O., Krishnamoorthy, S.: Automatic risk-based selective redundancy for fault-tolerant task-parallel hpc applications. In: Proceedings of the Third International Workshop on Extreme Scale Programming Models and Middleware, ESPM22017. Association for Computing Machinery, New York (2017). https://doi.org/10.1145/3152041.3152083

37. Suettlerlein, J., Zuckerman, S., Gao, G.R.: An implementation of the codelet model. In: Wolf, F., Mohr, B., an Mey, D. (eds.) Euro-Par 2013. LNCS, vol. 8097, pp. 633–644. Springer, Heidelberg (2013). https://doi.org/10.1007/978-3-642-40047-6_63

38. Tomasulo, R.M.: An efficient algorithm for exploiting multiple arithmetic units. IBM J. Res. Dev. **11**(1), 25–33 (1967). https://doi.org/10.1147/rd.111.0025

39. Weis, S., Garbade, A., Fechner, B., Mendelson, A., Giorgi, R., Ungerer, T.: Architectural support for fault tolerance in a teradevice dataflow system. Int. J. Parallel Program. (2014). https://doi.org/10.1007/s10766-014-0312-y

40. Weis, S., et al.: A fault detection and recovery architecture for a teradevice dataflow system. In: 2011 First Workshop on Data-Flow Execution Models for Extreme Scale Computing, pp. 38–44 (2011). https://doi.org/10.1109/DFM.2011.9

Artificial Intelligence using HPC Scale

Parallel-Distributed Implementation of the Lipizzaner Framework for Multiobjective Coevolutionary Training of Generative Adversarial Networks

Sergio Nesmachnow[1,2]([✉]) [ID], Jamal Toutouh[2] [ID], Guillermo Ripa[1],
Agustín Mautone[1], and Andrés Vidal[1]

[1] Universidad de la República, Montevideo, Uruguay
[2] Universidad de Málaga, Málaga, Spain
sergion@fing.edu.uy, jamal@uma.es

Abstract. This article presents a parallel-distributed implementation of the Lipizzaner framework for multiobjective coevolutionary Generative Adversarial Networks training. A specific design is proposed following the messagge passing paradigm to execute in high performance computing infrastructures. The implementation is validated for the generation of handwritten digits problems. Accurate efficiency and scalability results, and a proper load balancing are reported.

Keywords: Computational Intelligence · Generative Adversarial Networks · High Performance Computing

1 Introduction

Generative Adversarial Networks (GANs) are computational methods in the field of artificial intelligence that aim to learn generative models to estimate the distribution of a given training dataset to generate new, synthetic data.

GANs consist of two neural networks, the generator and the discriminator, which compete against each other during the learning process. The generator strives to produce synthetic data that is indistinguishable from real data, whereas the discriminator aims to differentiate between real and generated data. GANs have demonstrated their effectiveness in a variety of tasks, including image and video generation [6]. Despite their success, GANs training remains a challenging task due to unstable training dynamics and pathologies such as oscillation, mode collapse, discriminator collapse, and vanishing gradients [1,2].

Evolutionary computation has shown promising results for GANs training. Evolutionary Algorithms and Coevolutionary Algorithms have been used to optimize GAN parameters or design spatial systems to improve the learning process.

C. J. Barrios H. et al. (Eds.): CARLA 2023, CCIS 1887, pp. 97–112, 2024.
https://doi.org/10.1007/978-3-031-52186-7_7

Evolutionary computation-based GAN training methods have guided populations of neural networks towards convergence, resulting in comparable or better results than traditional GAN training methods.

This article focuses on the spatially-distributed competitive coevolutionary algorithm for GAN training proposed in the Lipizzaner framework [13]. The method specifies a spatial topology, such as a two-dimensional toroidal grid or a ring, to position pairs of generators and discriminators in each cell of the spatial topology. Additionally, neighborhood relationships between cells and migration policies allow for the definition of subpopulations and signal propagation across the topology. As a result, a cellular algorithm is used to optimize the parameters of the generators and the discriminators by applying gradient-based training.

The complex optimization strategy proposed by Lipizzaner is effective for GAN training, but has a specific major drawback: it is computationally expensive. To alleviate the computational cost of the GAN training process, parallel computing techniques can be applied to distribute the populations handled by Lipizzaner and evolve them in parallel. This article presents a parallel distributed implementation of Lipizzaner, designed to execute in cluster infrastructures. Furthermore, instead of the single objective optimization approach in Lipizzaner, focused on improving the quality of synthetic samples produced by the generator, a multiobjective optimization aproach is applied. By considering a second objective function that also optimizes the diversity of the synthetic samples, the multiobjective approach is more able to represent the distribution of the real data and it is more robust to specific patologies such as mode collapse. However, the multiobjective optimization training introduces a new source of complexity and computational cost. It is not uncommon that a single instance of the training process for a GAN demands more than a day of execution time [4,14].

The proposed implementation is validated for a benchmark problem in the field of artificial intelligence generation models, the generation of handwritten digits. The computed result demonstrate the correctness of the proposed approach. accurate results of both efficiency and scalability were computed, and the algorithm showed a proper load balancing.

The article is organized as follows. Section 2 introduces coevolutionary GANs training, the Lipizzaner framework, and reviews related works. Section 3 describes the proposed approach for developing the parallel-distributed multiobjective version of Lipizzaner. Section 4 reports the experimental evaluation. Finally, Sect. 5 presents the conclusions of the research.

2   Generative Adversarial Networks and Coevolutionary Training

This section describes the Lipizzaner framework and reviews related works. The coevolutionary GAN training approach involves modeling the GAN training process as a two-player game between the generator and discriminator. The game is solved by implementing gradient-based optimization on the GAN minmax objective [5]. In contrast, competitive coevolutionary GAN training involves two populations of generators and discriminators that co-evolve against each other, while addressing the minmax objective, as described in evolutionary game theory and the competitive coevolutionary neural population model [9].

2.1   The Lipizzaner Framework

The Lipizzaner framework employs a spatially-distributed competitive coevolutionary algorithm for GAN training [13]. This method coevolves populations of generators and discriminators, with individual members of each population located in the cells of a toroidal grid. Overlapping neighborhoods facilitate migration among cells to propagate models across the grid. Each cell contains two competitive subpopulations defined by individuals in the cell and those gathered from the neighborhood. Training occurs in pairs throughout the subpopulations by implementing stochastic gradient descent with a minmax objective. Gaussian mutation is applied to adjust the stochastic gradient descent training parameters during evolution. After each training epoch, the competing subpopulations are updated with copies of the best generator and discriminator from each neighborhood cell.

2.2   Related Work

Evolutionary computation methods using populations of generators and discriminators are a promising research line for GAN training. However, few articles have proposed explicit parallel-distributed approaches to improve the computational efficiency of the training process.

Liu et al. [8] presented the first implementatioin of a decentralized parallel gradient-based algorithm for GANs training. A master-worker design was proposed where workers performs several rounds of communications per iteration, updating both the discriminator and generator simultaneously. The proposed method was useful to deal with the main challenges of handling the nonconvex-nonconcave min-max optimization for GANs training. The method was evaluated for training WGAN-GP on the CIFAR10 dataset and Self-Attention GAN on the ImageNet dataset. The computed results showed the effectiveness of the proposal on a low latency cluster with four servers equipped with a 14-core IntelXeon E5-2680 (2.4GHz) processor and four Nvidia P100GPUs.

Hardy et al. [7] proposed a distributed training approach for GANs, using several datasets on multiple workers. A single generator is kept in a centralized server and a global learning iteration approach is applied, where each worker has its own discriminator an performs learning iterations over it to computes an error feedback to be sent to the central server. The server then computes the gradient of the generator and optimizes/updates its parameters using Adam. A swap of discriminators is applied to avoid especialization and overfiting when performing too many learning iterations over the same data subset. The workload of workers is kept as reduced as possible, i.e., avoiding moving data shares during training. The proposal was evaluated for the standard MNIST and CIFAR10 datasets and compared with a variant of federated learning over a GPU-based server with two Intel Xeon Gold 6132 processors and NVIDIA Tesla M60 or P100 GPUs. Acceptable efficiency values were obtained (reduction by a factor of two) improvinig over a variant of federated learning approach for both datasets.

Cardoso et al. [3] explored the parallelization of GANs training on cloud services. Parallel approaches were proposed to train on multiple GPUs over Google Tensor Processing Units (TPU). A synchronous parallel strategy was applied over multiple GPUs on a single node. A multiworker strategy to use multiple nodes and a TPU strategy for synchronous training on TPUs using all_reduce and collective operations. The proposal was evaluated on Google Cloud and Microsoft Azure. Linear speedup of the training process was achieved.

The original Lipizzaner implementation applies a task-based workload distribution implemented using the `Flask` library from Python and the `HTTP` protocol for communications. Master and slave processes are executed on predefined nodes and ports, available for communications. The processes open an API on the assigned port and wait for the `start execution` message. The master recognizes the network ports exposed to the clients. Once all clients are identified, a thread is created for each one that is responsible for checking that they are still running (a heartbeat mechanism). The threads send a message to each client at a fixed interval and wait for a response; if no response is received, the client is restarted or the entire algorithm is terminated. Afterwards, the master sends the execution start message to each client and blocks until the clients finish executing the algorithm. Once the clients receive the message to start executing, they create a new thread that is responsible for executing the algorithm, while the main process handles arriving requests. At the beginning of each generation, each client sends a request to its neighbors, to be responded with the network that was most recently selected in their cells. This method avoids synchronization, since the last selection is always responded regardless of whether the nodes are in different generations. A class is used to control read/write access to the local networks, avoiding race conditions between the thread that executes the algorithm and the control thread. When all clients have finished their generations, they send a completion message to the master as a response to the heartbeat. Once all clients have notified their completion, the master makes an `HTTP` request to all clients for them to send the generators and discriminators. With the obtained networks, the master generates an ensemble of models, whose weights are optimized via the evolutionary algorithm, based on a given performance metric.

The proposed approach for distributed execution has several drawbacks:

- Requires nodes to have visibility of the IP and port of other nodes. This functionality is not allowed in many clusters as it could be a security vulnerability. This restricts the environments in which the model can be executed.
- Manual load balancing of processes is necessary. There is no system to determine an optimal distribution of processes on nodes, and the distribution must be done manually, adding work when running the algorithm.
- Introduces a high level of complexity, since the implementation uses control threads to handle the API while the experiment is running. Due to the use of threads, there is a need for resource access control to avoid race conditions.

- To obtain the networks of neighbors, it is necessary to make a request for sending, increasing the number of necessary messages and the delay in being able to continue the training.

Our previous article [11] presented a parallel implementation of a cellular competitive coevolutionary method to train two populations of GANs. A distributed memory parallel implementation was proposed for execution in high performance/supercomputing centers. Accurate efficiency results were reported, showing that the proposed implementation was able to reduce the training times and scale properly when considering different grid sizes for training.

The analysis of related works allows concluding that few explicit parallel-distributed approaches have been proposed for GAN training. Most proposals rely on implicit parallelization provided by built-in functions in GPUs.

3   Parallel Distributed Multiobjective Lippizaner

This section describes the design and implementation of the parallel distributed multiobjective Lippizzaner version.

3.1   Methodology and Design

The applied methodology consisted in reimplementing the original distribution scheme in Lipizzaner (developed under the client-server model, based on *sockets* and the HTTP protocol), to work under the message passing paradigm.

The reimplementation is needed since the distributed computing paradigm works on specific middleware and not using low-level implementations. For the distribution of the algorithm, the message passage paradigm was applied. It communicates information by the explicit passage of messages between the populations in Lipizzaner. The design is conceived to be used in high-performance computing platforms, via the standardization provided by the MPI library.

The methodology applied to carry out the adaptation consisted of the analysis of the existing structures in Lipizzaner, with emphasis on the structures related to the main training cycle and the distribution of individuals. The adaptation procedure was useful to evaluate the coupling of the structures in the original communication protocol, identifying the structures that should be discarded and those that should be reused.

The main design decisions when reimplementing Lipizzaner with MPI consisted of: 1) basing the interactions between processes on the Cartesian grid intracommunicator; 2) not using a separate master process from the processes that handle the evolutionary cycle; 3) have a single thread of execution in each process, and 4) minimize synchronization points between processes.

3.2   Implementation Details

The new architecture was designed and implemented, using the mpi4py library for Python. It allows an easy integration with the source code of Lipizzaner and also allows integrating other machine learning modules and libraries developed in Pyton and PyTorch.

mpi4py is responsible of initializing and terminating the MPI context via the MPI_INIT and MPI_FINALIZE functions. In turn, provides an object-oriented interface for defining communicators and accessing MPI functions, and handles serialization and deserialization of Python objects to make it possible to send them as MPI messages using the Pickle library.

Regarding the serialization of GANs, the coding for discriminators and generators defined by the original algorithm was maintained. Both networks are packaged in a map where the discriminator is indexed by the letter "D" and the generator is indexed by the letter "G", to be sent in a single message to neighboring processes. Each process uses lists to represent separate populations of discriminators and generators. Two neighborhood dictionaries (one for discriminators and one for generators) are maintained. Both are indexed by the rank of neighboring processes. The neighborhoods are used during the communication routines to keep track of the MPI ranks (origin neighborhoods) associated with each Lipizzaner process, to know the origin of the individuals. Populations are used to execute the evolutionary cycle.

The Cartesian grid topology provided by MPI makes it easy to identify neighboring processes. In addition, it allows taking advantage of the physical location in the computing nodes to improve the performance of sending messages, since communications between neighboring nodes are the most frequent in the Lipizzaner algorithm. In the Lipizzaner reimplementation, as many processes are launched as many cells are required in the grid and the process with rank zero is determined as master. The master process is responsible for the initial loading of the data into shared memory and the assembly of the final model. However, unlike the original Lipizzaner algorithm, the master process also participates in the execution of the evolutionary algorithm as another grid process., following an active master-slave pattern.

Figure 1 shows a diagram with the execution flow of the process of the redesigned Lipizzaner algorithm. Labels are included for the steps in which an MPI function is used. When a process starts its execution and mpi4py implicitly initializes the MPI context, the process checks if its rank is 0 (corresponding to the master process). If the process has a different rank, it waits at the first synchronization barrier until the training data is loaded into memory and can be used. If the process has rank 0, it is the master process. Thus, it is in charge of reading the configuration of the algorithm, loading the training data into memory and waiting at the synchronization barrier for the other processes. Once all the processes are in the synchronization barrier, the barrier is opened to continue.

After passing the barrier that controls the availability of data, each process initializes its population, distributes it using the MPI_ALLGATHER function over a communicator that contains only its neighbors, and begins the first generation of the evolutionary algorithm. From the second generation, the usual migration flow begins: the process obtains immigrant individuals from its neighbors and updates its population, executes the evolutionary cycle to select and mutate its best individual, and begins the emigration process sending the best individual to its four neighbors.

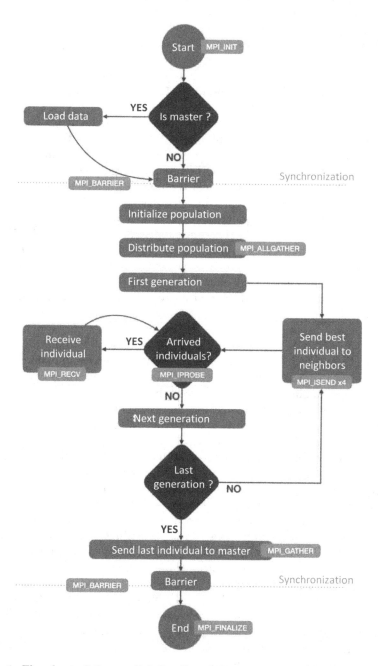

Fig. 1. Flowchart of the parallel distributed Lipizzaner redesigned with MPI

According to the original specification of Lipizzaner, the evolutionary cycles of the different subpopulations are not synchronized at any time. The specification implies that the number of immigrants at the beginning of a generation is not deterministic. Therefore, each process updates its population with the available information and proceeds to execute the evolutionary cycle. The immigration is executed iteratively: the existence of individuals in the message queue is checked with the non-blocking function MPI_IPROBE and if the function returns true, the function MPI_RECV is executed to consume the message. The process is repeated until the MPI_IPROBE function indicates that there are no new messages about immigrant individuals available. Since MPI guarantees the order of arrival of the messages, if several individuals come from the same neighbor, the local population would be updated only with the most recent one.

At the end of an intermediate generation, each process sends its best individual to its four neighbors with four independent non-blocking MPI_ISEND functions. At the end of the last generation the best individual is sent only to the master process through the collective communication function MPI_GATHER. After that, the process is blocked in a final barrier to wait for the completion of any ongoing message Once all the processes are synchronized on the final barrier, all but the master finish their execution. Then, the master process assembles the final model using the final generators sent by the processes and ends its execution.

Figure 2 presents a diagram with the relevant classes of the new architecture. The main class is LipizzanerWorker, responsible for executing the main algorithm. The class cell is responsible for handling communications via MPI and LipizzanerTrainer executes the evolutionary cycle. Neighbourhood and Population are auxiliary classes that model the notion of neighborhood between processes and the concept of population, respectively.

At the entry point, each process loads the configuration file and waits for the data to be loaded by the master according to the diagram in Fig. 1. Then, the LipizzanerWorker class is instantiated, which allows the training algorithm to be started using the run method. The LipizzanerWorker class performs the main loop of each Lipizzaner process, maintaining the current iteration and coordinating messaging operations with the evolution loop.

The messaging functionality is encapsulated in the Cell class, which maintains local individuals, provides methods for encoding and decoding messages, and implements the immigration from (in the collect method) and migration to (in distribute method) neighboring subpopulations.

The Population and Neighbourhood classes are collections of individuals that represent the local population in different contexts of the algorithm. On the one hand, Population extends the concept of a list of individuals by adding functionalities to determine if a multidimensional fitness is used (is_multidimensional), to obtain the best individual of the population (best); and to calculate the Pareto front (pareto_front). The Population class models the simplest and most ubiquitous notion of population in Lipizzaner, so it is used in all stages of the algorithm. On the other hand, the Neighbourhood

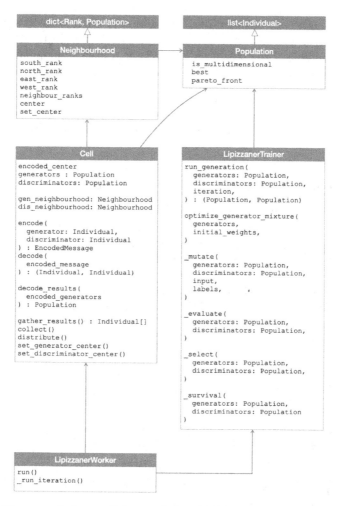

Fig. 2. Diagram of classes of the parallel multiobjective version of Lipizzaner

is a dictionary that models the neighborhood between subpopulations, keeping the ranks of the adjacent processes in the grid (South, North, East and West) and storing the local individuals according to the rank of the source process. Unlike `Population`, the `Neighbourhood` class represents a notion of population coupled to algorithm distribution and messaging operations, so it is only used as an auxiliary to the `Cell` class.

Finally, the `LipizzanerTrainer` class is responsible for executing generations (`run_generation`) on the current population and returning the descendant population. This class has access to the evolutionary operators and encapsulates their call through the `_evaluate` method to calculate the fitness of each individual; `_select` to select the individuals to be mutated; `_mutate` to generate new individuals through mutation, and `_survival` to determine which individuals will be in the new population. `LipizzanerTrainer` also implements the `optimize_generator_mixture` method, responsible for adjusting the parameters of the ensemble of the optimized generators in each subpopulation.

4   Experimental Evaluation

This section describes the experimental evalauation of the developed parallel distributed multiobjective version of Lipizzaner.

4.1   Methodology for Performance Evaluation

GAN Architecture, Dataset, and Parameters. The performance evaluation is performed using a Deep Convolutional GAN architecture over the MNIST dataset. MNIST gathers images of handwritten digits, including 70,000 images of handwritten digits (60,000 for training and 10,000 for validation) of size 28×28 pixels on a single color channel. The parametric configuration, the chosen dataset, the network architecture, and the hyperparameters are based on the Lipizzaner original article. This choice allows the standard implementation of Lipizzaner to be used as a baseline for comparing results. Table 1 reports the parameter values used in the performance evaluation (Fig. 3).

Fig. 3. Sample images in MNIST

Table 1. Parameter values used in the performance evaluation

parameter	value
batch size	64
# iterations	50
learning rate	5×10^{-5}
population size	2
replacement size	1
tournament size	2

Efficiency Metrics. The execution time is used as the main metric for performance evaluation. The traditional approach for algorithmic speedup evaluation is applied to evaluate efficiency, computing the ratio of the the execution time of the algorithm on a single compute resource (TP_1) and the execution time of the algorithm on N compute resources (TP_N) (Eq. 1).

An adapted formulation of the parallelizability is used to evaluate the scalability of the developed implementation. The approach is based on increasing the number of computing resources while keeping the amount of work constant. However, in the case of Lipizzaner, there is a one-to-one relationship between grid cells (work performed) and the processing cores (available computing resources), so the work to be done does not remain constant, but increases proportionally to computing resources. Given this proportional increase, the adapted formulation for evaluating scalability (SL_N) is defined by Eq. 2, where TP_M is the Lipizzaner execution time using M processes and M processing cores and TP_N the Lipizzaner execution time using N processes and N processing cores.

$$S_N = \frac{TP_1}{TP_N} \quad (1) \qquad SL_N = \frac{TP_M - TP_N}{M - N}, \text{ for } N < M \quad (2)$$

For a perfectly parallelizable algorithm, the execution time is constant when increasing both variables proportionally, therefore $SL_L = 0$. If there are steps that cannot be parallelized, $SL_L > 0$. The analysis is performed for 4, 9, and 16 resources, corresponding to Lipizzaner grids of dimensions 2×2, 3×3, and 4×4.

Finally, the load balance of the algorithm is also evaluated. The start and end times of iteration are studied for each process in the grid. The evaluation was meant to detect situations with load not evenly distributed between the processes or when some process is benefited by the resource manager.

The experimental analysis was performed on the high performance computing platform of National Supercomputing Center (Cluster-UY), Uruguay [10]. Experiments were performed on Intel Xeon-Gold 6138 2.00GHz with GPUs NVIDIA Tesla P100 (12GB RAM) and NVIDIA Ampere A100 (40GB RAM, 6912 CUDA cores FP32, 3456 CUDA cores FP64 and 422 núcleos Tensor cores) and trying to run the algorithm in the same conditions. All metrics were computed as averages in ten independent executions for each experiment.

4.2   Results Quality

Figure 4 presents a summary of the analysis of results quality. The Q-Q plots for quality metrics (coverage, density, and Frechet Inception Distance (FID) [12]) are reported. Results obtained in the plane of the theoretical quantiles of a reference normal distribution and the observed quantiles are shown in green. The identity line, in orange, is a graphic reference of the approximation of the results to the reference distribution. Results are correctly aligned, so they are distributed similar to a normal distribution, i.e., the reference distribution has mean and standard deviation equal to the empirical generated by the GAN.

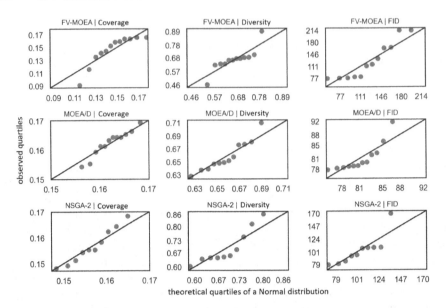

Fig. 4. Q-Q plots for result quality metrics

4.3   Performance Results

Analysis of Diversity and Replacement Strategies. Two diversity functions were implemented in the proposed multiobjective evolutionary algorithm (EGAN and GDPP). In turn, three replacement algorithms werer implemented and evaluated (FV-MOEA, MOEA/D, an NSGA-2) [12].

Figure 5(a) presents the scalabilty evaluation of execution times for the two diversity measures studied. Results show a proper almost-linear speedup when using the GDPP function and a poor sub-linear behaviour for EGAN. Overall, GDPP is more efficient since it is strictly higher in total execution time for all grid sizes. Figure 5(b) presents the scalabilty evaluation for the three replacement algorithms. The three distributions coincide in median and variance, indicating that the replacement algorithm has a low incidence in the total execution time.

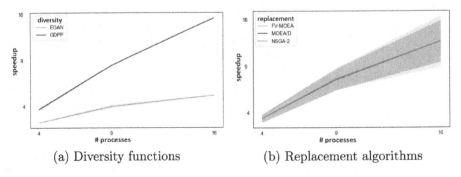

(a) Diversity functions   (b) Replacement algorithms

Fig. 5. Scalability analysis for diversity and replacement algorithms

Scalability Analysis. The scalability analysis studied the relation between the execution time and the size of the grid/number of computing resources. Figure 6 summarizes the dependency relationship between execution time and grid size using a linear regression model. When considering all Lipizzaner executions (Fig. 6(a)), the linear regression model did not fit the data precisely (the coefficient of determination $R^2 = 0.860$). For GDPP executions (Fig. 6(b)), the linear regression model had a coefficient of determination $R^2 = 0.996$, so it achieved a better fit to the data. Scalability values (SL_N) are reported in Table 2.

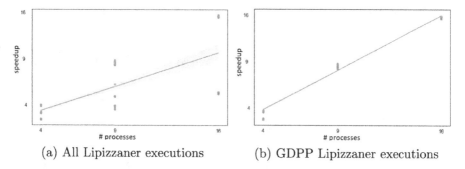

(a) All Lipizzaner executions   (b) GDPP Lipizzaner executions

Fig. 6. Scalability analysis for parallel distributed Lipizzaner

Load Balancing and Resource Utilization. The workload in Lipizzaner is distributed by assigning the same number of network training iterations to all processes in a grid. Furthermore, each process works on a portion of the used dataset, which is the same size for each process. When the algorithm to execute, the number of iterations, are the same between processes, and and the datasets have the same size, it can be guaranteed that the load between processes is fair.

Table 2 reports the mean and variance in iteration times for each process. The variance in the duration of the iterations was low, less than 15% of the average in all cases, which indicates an equitable allocation of resources among the processes.

Table 2. Scalability results and iteration times

grid size	diversity function	replacement strategy	scalability			iteration time	
			SL_4	SL_9	SL_{16}	mean (s)	stdev (s)
2×2	E–GAN	FV–MOEA	0.71	0.66	0.58	10.39	0.23
		MOEA/D	0.70	0.64	0.59	10.38	0.17
		NSGA–II	0.71	0.68	0.60	10.37	0.18
	GDPP	FV–MOEA	0.41	0.36	0.32	16.10	1.46
		MOEA/D	0.41	0.36	0.32	16.00	1.50
		NSGA–II	0.41	0.36	0.32	16.07	1.46
3×3	E–GAN	FV–MOEA	0.62	0.60	0.59	17.25	2.85
		MOEA/D	0.60	0.58	0.58	16.84	1.95
		NSGA–II	0.60	0.57	0.56	16.86	1.90
	GDPP	FV–MOEA	0.36	0.34	0.31	32.34	3.76
		MOEA/D	0.33	0.33	0.32	32.16	3.63
		NSGA–II	0.32	0.31	0.31	32.38	3.63
4×4	E–GAN	FV–MOEA	0.52	0.49	0.47	21.48	0.86
		MOEA/D	0.50	0.47	0.45	21.37	0.80
		NSGA–II	0.48	0.46	0.43	21.46	0.83
	GDPP	FV–MOEA	0.32	0.29	0.27	54.92	4.00
		MOEA/D	0.31	0.31	0.28	54.81	3.89
		NSGA–II	0.30	0.28	0.26	54.83	3.88

Figure 7 presents the execution time needed for each iteration of processes belonging to a Lipizzaner grid. Figures 7(a) and 7(b) indicate that the processes remained at the same or one iteration distance throughout training. However, in Fig. 7(c) it is shown that process 10 ended its execution while process 9 still had two iterations to process. The difference between the end of the iterations increases as time progresses for the case of the 4×4 grid.

Summarizing, no pathologies were detected in the load distribution or in the allocation of resources. An interesting line of future work is to explore how the difference between the final iteration times behaves for larger grid sizes, since if the difference were to increase, it could result in training problems.

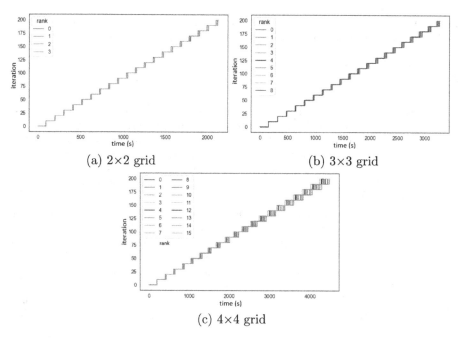

(a) 2×2 grid   (b) 3×3 grid

(c) 4×4 grid

Fig. 7. Execution time of iterations for each process

5   Conclusions and Future Work

This article presented a parallel distributed implementation of the multiobjec-tive optimization strategy for coevolutionary training of Generative Adversarial Networks implemented in Lipizzaner.

A redesign of the execution and load distribution methods of Lipizzaner was proposed and implemented, for execution in high performance computing plat-forms. Specific synchronization and communications were included using the Cartesian grid topology provided by MPI, to improve the overall efficiency of message passing. Asynchronous and collective communications were used for a correct implementation of the coevolutionary training approach. Several combi-nations of diversity functions and replacemnt algorithms were included in the implementation.

The different variants of the proposed approach were validated for the hand-written digits generation problem, evaluating the efficiency, scalability, and load balancing of the parallel distributed training algorithm. The main results demon-strated that the developed implementation scales properly for different grid sizes, taking advantage of additional computing resources. A correct load balancing pattern was also corroborated.

The main lines for future work are related to extend the experimental vali-dation of the proposed parallel approach, and conceive and implement different multiobjective strategies. The approach should be validated over other standard datasets to analyze the efficiency and scalability of the proposed parallel distributed training strategy for larger and more complex problems.

References

1. Arjovsky, M., Bottou, L.: Towards principled methods for training generative adversarial networks. arXiv preprint arXiv:1701.04862 (2017)
2. Arora, S., Risteski, A., Zhang, Y.: Do GANs learn the distribution? some theory and empirics. In: International Conference on Learning Representations (2018)
3. Cardoso, R., Golubovic, D., Lozada, I.P., Rocha, R., Fernandes, J., Vallecorsa, S.: Accelerating GAN training using highly parallel hardware on public cloud. EPJ Web Conf. **251**, 02073 (2021)
4. Esteban, M., Toutouh, J., Nesmachnow, S.: Parallel/distributed intelligent hyperparameters search for generative artificial neural networks. In: Jagode, H., Anzt, H., Ltaief, H., Luszczek, P. (eds.) ISC High Performance 2021. LNCS, vol. 12761, pp. 297–313. Springer, Cham (2021). https://doi.org/10.1007/978-3-030-90539-2_20
5. Goodfellow, I., et al.: Generative adversarial nets. In: Advances in Neural Information Processing Systems, pp. 2672–2680 (2014)
6. Gui, J., Sun, Z., Wen, Y., Tao, D., Ye, J.: A review on generative adversarial networks: algorithms, theory, and applications. IEEE Trans. Knowl. Data Eng. **35**(4), 3313–3332 (2021)
7. Hardy, C., Merrer, E.L., Sericola, B.: MD-GAN: multi-discriminator generative adversarial networks for distributed datasets. In: IEEE International Parallel and Distributed Processing Symposium (2019)
8. Liu, M., et al.: A decentralized parallel algorithm for training generative adversarial nets (2019). https://arxiv.org/abs/1910.12999
9. Moran, N., Pollack, J.: Coevolutionary neural population models. In: Artificial Life Conference Proceedings, pp. 39–46. MIT Press One Rogers Street, Cambridge, MA 02142–1209, USA (2018)
10. Nesmachnow, S., Iturriaga, S.: Cluster-UY: collaborative scientific high performance computing in Uruguay. In: Torres, M., Klapp, J. (eds.) ISUM 2019. CCIS, vol. 1151, pp. 188–202. Springer, Cham (2019). https://doi.org/10.1007/978-3-030-38043-4_16
11. Perez, E., Nesmachnow, S., Toutouh, J., Hemberg, E., O'Reily, U.M.: Parallel/distributed implementation of cellular training for generative adversarial neural networks. In: IEEE International Parallel and Distributed Processing Symposium Workshops (2020)
12. Ripa, G., Mautone, A., Vidal, A., Nesmachnow, S., Toutouh, J.: Multiobjective coevolutionary training of generative adversarial networks. In: Genetic and Evolutionary Computation Conference (2023)
13. Schmiedlechner, T., Yong, N., Al-Dujaili, A., Hemberg, E., O'Reilly, U.: Lipizzaner: a system that scales robust generative adversarial network training (2018). https://arxiv.org/abs/1811.12843
14. Toutouh, J., Esteban, M., Nesmachnow, S.: Parallel/distributed generative adversarial neural networks for data augmentation of COVID-19 training images. In: Nesmachnow, S., Castro, H., Tchernykh, A. (eds.) CARLA 2020. CCIS, vol. 1327, pp. 162–177. Springer, Cham (2021). https://doi.org/10.1007/978-3-030-68035-0_12

Provenance-Based Dynamic Fine-Tuning of Cross-Silo Federated Learning

Camila Lopes[iD], Alan L. Nunes[iD], Cristina Boeres[iD],
Lúcia M. A. Drummond[iD], and Daniel de Oliveira[✉][iD]

Universidade Federal Fluminense, Niterói, Brazil
{camila_ol,alan_lira}@id.uff.br, {boeres,lucia,danielcmo}@ic.uff.br

Abstract. Federated Learning (FL) is a distributed technique that allows multiple users to train models collaboratively without accessing private and sensitive data. Iteratively, each user trains a "local" model in a specific machine consuming private data and then sends the model updates to a server for their fusion into a centralized one. Although FL represents a step forward, the training duration in each iteration directly depends on the several configurations set, *e.g.*, hyperparameters. Analyzing hyperparameters during the FL workflow allows for dynamic fine-tuning that can improve the performance of FL regarding training time and quality of results. However, due to its exploratory nature, the user may lose track of which configurations have been used to train the model with the best accuracy if the choices are not correctly registered. Provenance is the natural choice to represent data derivation traces to help hyperparameters fine-tuning by providing a global data-oriented picture of the FL workflow. Yet, the existing FL frameworks do not provide dynamic fine-tuning nor support provenance capturing. Therefore, this paper introduces an FL framework named `Flower-PROV` that uses provenance data for tracking configurations and evaluation metrics during the FL execution to allow for dynamic fine-tuning of hyperparameters, thus saving training time. We show a use case with Cross-Silo FL where `Flower-PROV` dynamic fine-tuning reduced the FL training time up to 94.24% when compared with the fine-tuning using grid-search.

Keywords: Federated learning · Provenance data · Dynamic fine-tuning

1 Introduction

Over the last few years, Machine Learning (ML) has gained much attention from both academia and industry [3,8,17]. Although several ML techniques were proposed decades ago, many factors explain the cause of ML usage becoming grandly boosted more recently. The first one is data availability. Massive datasets are available and can be used to train a myriad of ML models. The second factor is that many computing resource types are available for any user, especially in

C. J. Barrios H. et al. (Eds.): CARLA 2023, CCIS 1887, pp. 113–127, 2024.
https://doi.org/10.1007/978-3-031-52186-7_8

public clouds. Finally, ML has been fostered by the emergence of Deep Learning (DL) [6], an essential technique for pattern matching at scale.

Although ML and DL represent a step forward, their learning workflow requires that all available data are fully accessible to train a model, becoming a problem for two primary reasons: *Privacy* and *Volume*. Regarding privacy, many datasets contain sensitive data of individuals that cannot be publicized, according to regulations such as GDPR in Europe (https://gdpr-info.eu/). Even though anonymization techniques can be applied, due to reverse engineering, anonymized datasets usage is often ineffective. Regarding data volume, datasets often have hundreds of gigabytes. Despite various initiatives aimed at providing advanced network infrastructure to facilitate research collaborations among different organizations and, consequently, handle large volumes of data transfers (*e.g.*, RedCLARA within Latin America), not all organizations or institutions have access to these resources. As a result, data transfers can still pose challenges.

To bridge this gap between ML and privacy, Federated Learning (FL) [13] has been proposed. FL is a distributed technique that allows multiple users to train models collaboratively while maintaining their training data private, thus not exposing sensitive data. The final trained model is obtained iteratively, and in each iteration, the users (*i.e.*, workers) train their model locally and send an updated version of the model (not sensitive data) back to the server that aggregates the received locally trained models and sends the updated parameters to the workers, so that they can continue their local training in the following iteration. Besides the clear advantage of keeping data private, FL also reduces costly data transfers since it removes the need to pool data into a single server.

Despite the evolution of FL in the last few years [11], there are some open, yet crucial, problems to be addressed. One problem is that each iteration of the FL workflow may last from a few minutes to several hours, depending on the model type, the volume of input data, and the worker's computing power, which can limit the local training of large models. The training time and the quality of the trained model in each iteration are directly associated with the input dataset and the choice of a set of hyperparameters. Although the user can explore several configurations of hyperparameter values by executing multiple FL workflows, this can be time-consuming. One attractive option is to analyze the evaluation metrics values (*e.g.*, accuracy) after each iteration and then perform Dynamic Fine-tuning of hyperparameters, *i.e.*, depending on the metric values, hyperparameters are adjusted at runtime. According to da Silva *et al.* [24], there is a lack of capabilities for enabling ML (and consequently FL) steering and dynamic execution. One of the challenges is how to properly register which hyperparameter configurations have been used to train a specific model. If this information is not recorded, the user may lose track of it, mainly due to the exploratory nature of the FL workflow and its distributed execution.

Provenance data [4] can help the dynamic fine-tuning of hyperparameters by providing a global data picture with exact dependencies. It supplies a series of metadata that describes how data are produced in each iteration of the FL workflow by registering hyperparameter and parameter values, evaluation metrics, *etc.* Although recently proposed approaches use a provenance database to integrate data from ML applications to improve data analyses and decisions [19–21], it has not been applied in the context of FL, especially to foster dynamic fine-tuning of hyperparameters.

In this paper, we use provenance data to monitor and dynamically fine-tune hyperparameters in the FL workflow, especially in the Cross-Silo scenario where workers represent clients and companies, and their number is usually small (see Subsect. 2.1 for more details). In particular, we propose an extension of the well-known *Flower* framework [2], named `Flower-PROV`. By using `Flower-PROV`, workers perform multiple epochs of training, send the locally trained model to the server that updates its global model, evaluates it, and adjusts the hyperparameters at runtime for the next iteration, depending on the results returned by a query on provenance database, which contains metadata collected throughout the whole execution of the FL workflow. `Flower-PROV` was evaluated by training a classification model based on CIFAR-10 [9] benchmark. Results show that the `Flower-PROV` dynamic fine-tuning reduces the overall training time up to 94.24% when compared to static fine-tuning and finds hyperparameter values configurations not commonly explored by users.

The remainder of this paper is organized as follows. Section 2 discusses essential concepts such as FL and Provenance. Section 3 brings related work. Section 4 presents the `Flower-PROV` approach while Sect. 5 shows the experimental results. Finally, Sect. 6 concludes this paper and proposes future directions.

2   Background

This section discusses two important concepts tackled by this paper: (i) Federated Learning and (ii) Provenance data.

2.1   Federated Machine Learning in a Nutshell

Federated Machine Learning [13], henceforth named Federated Learning (FL), allows users to train models using multiple workers (commonly managed by a central server) of a distributed environment without the requirement to access the whole dataset. This technique is gaining much attention mainly due to privacy issues since the raw datasets in worker nodes are not required to be shared with all users involved in the training process. Moreover, FL can be applied to train models using different algorithms [14], and it is also receiving attention due to its applicability to training Deep Neural Networks (DNN).

FL has a well-known workflow, where, in each iteration, the server defines the model type for training (*e.g.*, a DNN) and forwards this information to the workers alongside with the necessary hyperparameters. Then, each worker executes the training phase in the light of its local data, consuming a subset of the dataset (accessible by the worker). Finally, each worker sends information regarding the trained model (*e.g.*, weights of a DNN) to the server. The server combines the parameters of locally trained models and generates an aggregated global model, which can be achieved using different aggregation strategies. One common strategy is Federated Averaging (*FedAvg*), which involves several local stochastic gradient descent updates and one aggregation by the server in each round. Once the aggregated global model is obtained, the server starts a new iteration by sending it back to them.

Although the trained model has its hyperparameters (*e.g.*, dropout and activation function for DNNs), the FL workflow itself has specific parameters that must be set. These include the number T of rounds (one round is associated with one iteration of the learning phase), the number of workers nodes K, the fraction of workers C used in each round, and the batch size B (the number of examples used for training) consumed in each iteration. Such parameters commonly have to be fine-tuned together with the model's hyperparameters to optimize the execution both in terms of the accuracy of the result (or any other evaluation metric) or training time consumption. This fine-tuning is a complex yet essential task. For example, depending on the heterogeneity of the computing power in worker nodes, one can define a small value for parameter C, which reduces the necessary computing power per round.

This server client architecture of FL, also called Model-Centric FL [27], is classified into Cross-Device, where the clients are mobile devices typically and can reach up to a scale of millions of workers, or Cross-Silo (which is the focus of this paper), where workers are usually associated with organizations and their number is commonly reduced. In this second type of FL, the central server can assume that all clients are available during the whole execution, as they are robust machines or even clusters. There are some frameworks capable of executing FL workflows. One of the most prominent is *Flower* [2], open-source, which enables train models using FL on large numbers of workers. Besides, it has compatibility with most existing ML frameworks like *Keras, TensorFlow,* and *PyTorch*, allowing research across different servers and devices, including *Cloud, Mobile,* and *Edge* Computing. *Flower* is interoperable with many operating systems and hardware platforms, works well in heterogeneous edge device environments, and is used as the basis for the approach proposed in this paper.

2.2 A Brief Tour Through Provenance

Provenance may be defined as the "lineage and processing history of data" [4]. It refers to the metadata that describes the process of generating a piece of data and is used to register, in a structured and queryable form, the data derivation path of a specific context. Here, provenance data describes how data are produced during the FL workflow, although it was initially used to assess the quality and reliability and foster reproducibility. Yet, it contains rich information (*e.g.*, consumed parameter values and datasets, execution times) that can be used in other tasks such as scheduling, fault-tolerance, and parameter tuning [16].

Although provenance data can be represented and stored in many ways, the W3C standard, named PROV [7], defines a data model for representing provenance. This model represents provenance in terms of *Entities, Agents, Activities*, and multiple types of relationships as presented in Fig. 1. An *Entity* represents a *thing.* In the context of this paper, an entity can be a trained model, the aggregated model, a set of hyperparameter values, *etc. Activities* are actions executed within the FL workflow and act upon entities, *e.g.*, the local training in a worker node or the model aggregation in the server. Finally, an *Agent* is a user responsible for starting/stopping activities, providing datasets, *etc.* Although PROV is an agnostic model, *i.e.*, not tied to a specific knowledge domain, it can be extended to distinct fields, such as FL.

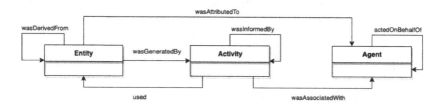

Fig. 1. PROV data model, adapted from Groth *et al.* [7].

The FL workflow is composed of multiple steps (*e.g.*, local training, aggregation, *etc.*), as discussed in Subsect. 2.1, where a dataset will undergo when subjected to the FL workflow execution. The specification of this workflow can be seen as *Prospective Provenance* (*p-prov*), a type of provenance data that registers the steps performed during data processing. Another type of provenance is *Retrospective Provenance* (*r-prov*), which in turn records information regarding the execution, *i.e.* when an activity of the workflow is executed, the parameters consumed in an execution, errors, *etc.* Provenance data can be available at runtime or after the execution of a workflow. When both *p-prov* and *r-prov* are available for querying during the FL workflow execution, they can be used jointly to foster the analysis and fine-tune hyperparameters. For instance, if the value defined for a parameter is not producing results with expected accuracy after the aggregation in a specific round, its value can be updated at runtime.

3   Related Work

This section discusses existing approaches that use provenance data for analyzing and fine-tuning hyperparameters in general ML and FL-specific approaches. Many use provenance data to foster data analytics of ML workflow [5,12,20,21, 23,26]. ModelDB [26] and ModelKB [5] are model management systems that collect provenance data and other metadata related to the ML workflow. ModelDB provides specific interfaces to well-known tools, such as SparkML and scikit-learn, and ModelKB is based on callbacks in native ML frameworks, *e.g.*, TensorFlow), to collect metadata about the workflow. Similarly, Schelter *et al.* [23] propose a system to track the metadata and provenance for SparkML pipelines and scikit-learn. The previous three approaches provide ways to submit analyses to the provenance database allowing users to trace back results, but they do not supply dynamic fine-tuning of hyperparameters.

BugDoc [12] is an approach that captures provenance data from ML workflows to help users to understand the reason for failed executions. Once it is identified, BugDoc suggests parameter values for future executions to improve efficiency and reduce the number of iterations in the learning workflow. Although BugDoc represents a step forward, it does not support dynamic fine-tuning or FL. Similarly, Pina *et al.* [20,21] propose an approach to capture provenance data from Deep Learning applications to foster analytics and interpretability of the trained model. Although Pina *et al.* use a provenance database to store and query provenance data at runtime, it does not provide dynamic fine-tuning and is not designed for the FL workflow.

Some provenance-based approaches are specific to FL [1,18]. The framework Bassa-ML proposed [1] is a blockchain-based FL platform that is built on top of the TensorFlow model card toolkit (a model card is an ML document that encapsulates metadata and some level of provenance) and implements a blockchain-based coordinator-less FL scheme to manage provenance data in a decentralized way. The authors claim that using the generated ML documents permits the addition of trust to blockchain applications while preventing attacks. Nonetheless, it was not reported how the shared information in the Model Card was used for analysis, and the proposed approach does not allow for dynamic fine-tuning.

Peregrina *et al.* [18] propose a framework for data governance in the FL workflows. The data governance framework has a metadata model and management system for tracing the participants' operations and collecting all information regarding the definition of the goals and configuration of the FL workflow. Their model, however, lacks some relevant information, such as the activities executed in the FL workflow. Besides, the proposal does not consider the dynamic tuning of the FL hyperparameters.

4   Dynamic Fine-Tuning with `Flower-PROV`

Fine-tuning hyperparameters in FL is far from trivial. Besides the hyperparameters of the chosen model (*e.g.*, DNN), the FL framework has its parameters (*e.g.*, number of rounds, and number of epochs in each worker). One challenge when fine-tuning FL workflows is that popular AutoML techniques are not directly applied due to the distributed nature of the execution [10]. To support the fine-tuning of hyperparameters at runtime, we propose `Flower-PROV` framework. By using provenance data captured throughout the FL workflow, `Flower-PROV` can identify the relationship between the hyperparameter values and the evaluation metrics (*e.g.* accuracy), thus allowing the system to change the hyperparameter values at runtime according to a pre-defined dynamic fine-tuning policy (*dfp*).

`Flower-PROV` extends the *Flower* framework [2] by adding provenance capabilities and dynamic-tuning, where a server is responsible for model aggregation and each client trains local models. Particularly, `Flower-PROV` is focused on Cross-Silo FL workflow. Figure 2 presents the architecture of `Flower-PROV`,

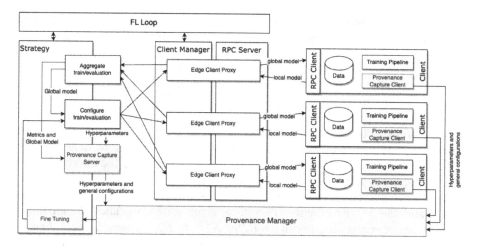

Fig. 2. Flower-PROV architecture.

where the light gray rectangles are the contributions of this paper and the white ones are present at the *Flower* core framework. The architecture is composed of six main components: (i) Strategy, (ii) Client Manager, (iii) FL Loop, (iv) RPC Server, (v) Client, and (vi) Provenance Manager. The *Client Manager* is responsible for sampling *Clients* that will train multiple local models. In coordination with the RPC Server, it manages numerous *ClientProxy* objects, which are objects associated with a client connected to the server. A *ClientProxy* is responsible for sending and receiving messages to each of the *Clients*, which performs local model training. The entire FL workflow orchestration is performed by *FL Loop*. It invokes the *Strategy*, an abstraction of how the FL algorithm works in the server, to prepare the next round of FL and sends the configurations to the clients involved in the training process. After each *Client* generates a new local model, the *FL Loop* receives the updates, *e.g.*, weights of a DNN, and invokes the *Strategy* for aggregating results (*Aggregate Train/Evaluation* in Fig. 2). After aggregation, the *Strategy* evaluates the aggregated model (*Configure Train/Evaluation* in Fig. 2) according to the chosen evaluation metrics (*e.g.*, accuracy).

In each of the forenamed steps, provenance data are captured. The *Provenance Manager* is the component responsible for receiving provenance data from the *Server* and *Clients* and structuring it in a queryable form. In the current version of Flower-PROV, the *Provenance Manager* is built on top of the DfAnalyzer provenance library [25] that provides generic methods for capturing and querying provenance. On the server side, the *Provenance Capture Server* component captures metadata regarding the aggregation and evaluation steps, such as the evaluation metrics and the model sent to the clients. Client-side activities and metadata are collected from each *Client* using the *Provenance Capture Client* component. All data are stored in a W3C PROV-compliant provenance database and are available at runtime, *i.e.*, as soon as they are captured, they can be queried, which allows for using such data for dynamic fine-tuning.

When the provenance data are available, the *Fine Tuning* component can be invoked, triggered by a series of events identified in the provenance database. Such events can be identified according to user-defined criteria that we call *Dynamic Fine-tuning Policy* (*dfp*). In this work, the FL workflow can be viewed as a directed graph $F = (S, Dep)$, where S are the vertices representing the workflow steps to be executed in *Server* or *Client* (*e.g.*, local training or model aggregation) and Dep is a set of arcs that represents the data dependencies amongst steps in S (*i.e.*, the local training in *Clients* can only be executed after receiving updates from the *Server*). Let us also represent the execution environment as $R = \{r_1, \ldots, r_k\}$, which is the set of computing resources where the *Clients* and the *Server* execute. Therefore, given an FL workflow F, an input D, and a set of computing resources R, let $X(F, D, R) = \{hpv_1, hpv_2, ..., hpv_m\}$ be the set of hyperparameter values defined for executing the FL workflow F. Each hyperparameter value hpv_i represents one of the configuration parameters of the FL framework and model, *e.g.*, number of rounds (as detailed in Subsect. 2.1). Thus, the goal of the *Fine Tuning* component is to use provenance data to adjust hyperparameter values at runtime seeking the set of hyperparameter values $X^*(F, D, R)$ that satisfy a set of user-defined criteria C.

To find X^*, the hyperparameter values need runtime adjustment following a procedure. In addition, the moment it is performed has to be identified by querying the provenance database. The *dfp* is the abstraction used to define how parameters are changed and how to identify them. A *dfp* can be formalized as $dfp = \{e, C, A\}$, where e is a type of the *dfp* (*i.e.*, user-defined or automatic, although in this paper only user-defined *dfps* are applied), C is the set of constraints that have to be satisfied to change hyperparameters, and A are fine-tuning actions that can be performed. Such constraints are translated to a database function in the provenance database (named `update_hyperparameters`), which is triggered every time new metadata is collected. This function returns 1 if changes are required and 0, otherwise. Figure 3 shows an example of some defined constraints using SQL.

Finally, when it is defined that a change will be performed, the actions in A are executed. One example of action is the *increment* on the number of epochs in the *Clients*, which will be increased by 1 when a change is required in the hyperparameters. These changes repeat until the *dfp* does not trigger any hyperparameter changes after some θ rounds.

In the next section, we present the evaluation of the dynamic fine-tuning mechanism in `Flower-PROV`. `Flower-PROV` is being open-sourced and will be available at https://github.com/UFFeScience/Flower-PROV.

5   Experimental Evaluation

To evaluate dynamic fine-tuning of hyperparameters in `Flower-PROV` we have chosen as a case study the MobileNetV2 architecture [22], a general-purpose

```
[...]
SELECT
    CASE WHEN (
        LAST_VALUE(accuracy_training) OVER () < accuracy_goal
        AND LAST_VALUE(training_time) OVER () < limit_training_time * 60
        AND (LAST_VALUE(accuracy_training) OVER () > FIRST_VALUE(accuracy_training) OVER ()
            AND LAST_VALUE(val_accuracy) OVER () > FIRST_VALUE(val_accuracy) OVER ()
        )
        AND LAST_VALUE(accuracy_training) OVER () - FIRST_VALUE(accuracy_training) OVER ()
            < limit_accuracy_change
    )
        THEN 1
        ELSE 0
    END
[...]
```

Fig. 3. Example of constraints of the dynamic fine-tuning policy

computer vision convolution DNN. The dataset used was CIFAR-10 [9], a popular multi-class balanced dataset of colored 32 $\times$ 32 pixels images formed by ten classes, each having 6,000 images. In total, 50,000 ($\approx$ 83.33%) images were used for training and 10,000 ($\approx$ 16.66%) for testing. To emulate the data privacy attribute in `Flower-PROV`, each *Client* received a balanced and distinct partition of the original CIFAR-10 generated with the dataset-splitter[1] tool. We fixed 10% of the local training datasets for the validation split in all experiments presented in this section.

A set of virtual machines in Amazon AWS were deployed to compose the Cross-Silo FL system comprised of one server and five clients, where all clients are available during the entire FL workflow execution, *i.e.*, no churn is considered. All clients in `Flower-PROV` execute the training and evaluation of the local ML model in *g4dn.xlarge* virtual machines, which feature 4 vCPUs, 16 GiB memory, and 1 GPU NVIDIA T4 Tensor Core with 2560 CUDA cores and 16 GB memory, costing USD 0.5260 per hour in the On-Demand market. The server, responsible for aggregating local models, executes in a *t2.2xlarge* virtual machine, which features 8 vCPUs and 32.0 GiB memory and costs USD 0.3712 per hour in the On-Demand market.

5.1 Provenance Capture Overhead Evaluation

The first experiment evaluates the overhead imposed by provenance capture in `Flower-PROV`. Although the provenance data provide a rich source of information for dynamic fine-tuning, capturing provenance imposes an overhead. We have executed the FL workflow for training MobileNetV2 multiple times by varying the values of hyperparameters batch size ($bs = \{32, 64, 128, 256, 512\}$) and client epochs ($e = \{1, 2, 3, 4, 5\}$) in each execution, which results in 25 workflow executions. In these executions, the *Fine Tuning* component was disabled, *i.e.*, there are no runtime changes in hyperparameters, and the number of rounds was fixed to 100. Figure 4 presents the execution time (in seconds) with and without capturing provenance data. One can note that except by the execution with $bs = 32$ and $e = 1$, the provenance capture imposes an overhead in the order of single-digit, which is acceptable considering the benefits of provenance for

[1] dataset-splitter - https://github.com/alan-lira/dataset-splitter.

dynamic fine-tuning. Concerning all the 25 executions, the provenance capture overhead was 7.54% on average, having a standard deviation of 0.06.

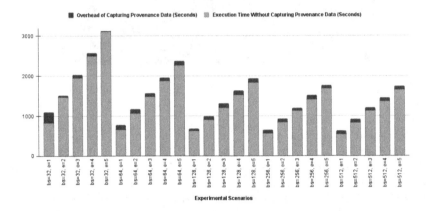

Fig. 4. Provenance data capturing overhead.

5.2   Evaluation of Hyperparameter Fine-Tuning Using Grid-Search

The second experiment evaluates the fine-tuning of hyperparameters using grid-search [15] and querying captured provenance data. In this scenario, the fine-tuning involves defining a n-dimensional search space, where each hyperparameter represents a different dimension, and the dimension scale is the possible value of that hyperparameter. In grid-search, the search space is represented as a grid, and each position in the grid has to be evaluated, *i.e.*, the FL workflow has to be executed multiple times, varying the combination of hyperparameters values, to define the best possible combinations. Although provenance data can help with this analysis, this type of tuning is time-consuming due to the considerable number of executions to evaluate.

In this experiment, we executed the FL workflow for training MobileNetV2 25 times, varying the values of hyperparameters batch size $bs = \{32, 64, 128, 256, 512\}$ and client epochs $e = \{1, 2, 3, 4, 5\}$. Figure 5 and Fig. 6 summarize the training accuracy and time obtained after executing `Flower-PROV` for each configuration during 100 rounds, respectively. All data presented were queried at the provenance database.

As expected, Fig. 5 and Fig. 6 show that, as the number of epochs increases for a given batch size, the training accuracy and the execution time also rise. Nevertheless, it is not simple nor intuitive to set the best combination of hyperparameters *a priori*. For example, the best accuracies were achieved for $bs = \{32, 64\}$, thus showing that incrementing the batch size higher than 64 may not be beneficial.

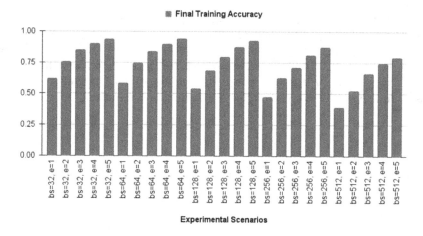

Fig. 5. Accuracy in Grid-search results after 100 rounds.

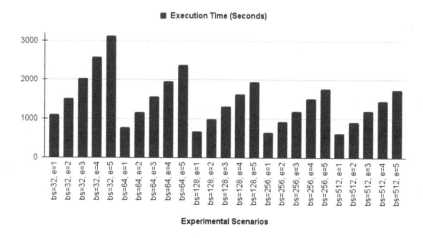

Fig. 6. Execution time of Grid-search after 100 rounds.

In addition, in each execution of the workflow, all 100 rounds were executed. However, if the user defines a target accuracy, this value can be achieved with less than 100 rounds, and the workflow execution could be stopped, sparing execution time and computing resources. If the user also defines a deadline for the execution, the FL workflow may not finish executing all rounds in time. Figure 7 presents the accuracy evolution over the 100 rounds of each of the 25 executions of the workflow. Let the user set the target accuracy as 0.8. Analyzing Fig. 7, one can note that after 100 rounds, only 10 out of the 25 hyperparameter configurations achieve the target accuracy value. On the other hand, if the target accuracy is 0.5 and a deadline of 700 s, only one hyperparameter configuration is successful. Therefore, executing all the configurations would be a time and computing resource waste, even considering the limited search space used.

Although the analysis provided by Fig. 7 represents a step forward, it may not deliver the best hyperparameter configuration. Grid-search is an interesting fine-tuning strategy if the well-performing hyperparameter combinations are known *a priori*. For example, in the experiments, we consider batch size values as the power of two. However, the best parameter combinations sometimes cannot be guessed intuitively. Thereby, dynamic fine-tuning is a promising approach.

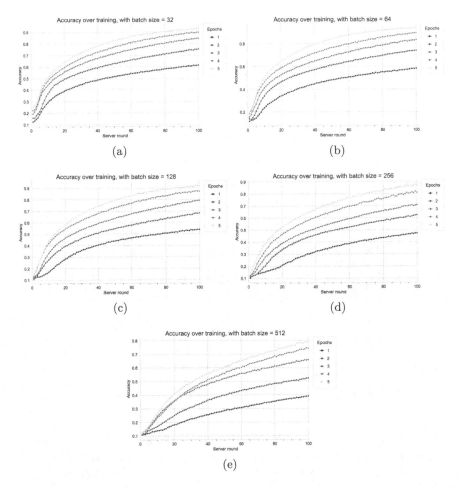

Fig. 7. Accuracy evolution over 100 rounds for fine-tuning using grid-search with batch size (a) $bs = 32$, (b) $bs = 64$, (c) $bs = 128$, (d) $bs = 256$, and (e) $bs = 512$.

5.3   Evaluation of the Dynamic Fine-Tuning

For this evaluation, we first define the *dfp*, as detailed in Sect. 4. The set constraints that trigger the tuning are: (i) the accuracy of the last round has to be smaller than the target accuracy defined by the user, (ii) if the hyperparameters were not changed in the last two rounds (this allows for the latest hyperparameter change to take effect), (iii) if the accuracy varies less than 0.01 after two rounds. We have also to define the set of actions to be performed: (i) batch size is increased by 10% and (ii) the number of epochs is increased by 2. It is worth noticing that although provenance data are captured since the first round, the changes in hyperparameter values start on the third round since the constraints require analyzing a 2-round window.

Four different scenarios are set by varying the target accuracy: (i) 0.5 (DS_1), (ii) 0.6 (DS_2), (iii) 0.7 (DS_3), and (iv) 0.8 (DS_4) and the execution deadline as 10 min. Table 1 presents the number of changes in hyperparameter values, the chosen batch size, the chosen number of epochs, the required rounds to obtain the best configuration, the accuracy, and the execution time. It is worth noticing that fine-tuning hyperparameters using grid search required 25 workflow executions to obtain the best hyperparameters configuration for a given accuracy goal, demanding a total of 36,570.32 s ($\approx$ 10 h). Moreover, using the grid-search approach, the user only explores intuitive values for the hyperparameters. However, Table 1 shows that the hyperparameter values selected cannot be guessed intuitively, $e.g.$, $bs = 41$ and $e = 7$. In addition, the target accuracy was achieved for DS_1, DS_2, DS_3 and DS_4, respectively, in less than 20 rounds (as presented in Fig. 8), taking no more than 2,104.95 s ($\approx$ 0.5 h), depicting a 94.24% reduction in execution time.

Table 1. The chosen values for batch size and number of epochs for each scenario.

Experimental Scenario	Number of Updates	Batch Size	Epochs	Round	Training Accuracy	Time (s)
DS_1	3	41	7	11	0.5261	420.01
DS_2	4	45	9	13	0.6094	388.53
DS_3	5	49	11	17	0.7165	586.76
DS_4	6	53	13	19	0.8020	709.65

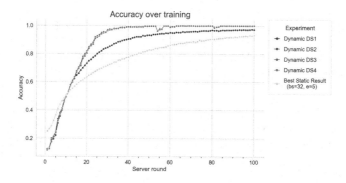

Fig. 8. Training accuracy over rounds.

6   Concluding Remarks

The collaborative nature of a Federated Learning system allows multiple users to evaluate their private and sensitive data without sharing it. The user seeks the desired quality metric of the training results, which can be time-consuming and may require a great effort from the user's side to set the proper configuration values. This work proposes `Flower-PROV`, an FL framework for dynamically fine-tuning the hyperparameters based on provenance data captured in a queryable form to achieve an evaluation target. An experimental analysis demonstrates that the `Flower-PROV` dynamic fine-tuning shortens the training time up to 94.24% when compared with an exploratory grid-search to reach the desired target evaluation metrics, under an overhead of no more than 8%. Concerning future perspectives, `Flower-PROV` will be expanded to Cross-Device FL, where clients may not participate in all rounds. Also, it will regard non-IID datasets since clients can have different data sample sizes and probability distributions. Furthermore, we plan to apply the framework in real-data scenarios.

References

1. Bandara, E., Shetty, S., Rahman, A., Mukkamala, R., Zhao, J., Liang, X.: Bassa-ML – a blockchain and model card integrated federated learning provenance platform. In: IEEE 19th Annual Consumer Communications and Networking Conference (CCNC), pp. 753–759 (2022)
2. Beutel, D.J., et al.: Flower: a friendly federated learning research framework. arXiv (2020)
3. Fernandes, E., Moro, S., Cortez, P.: Data science, machine learning and big data in digital journalism: a survey of state-of-the-art, challenges and opportunities. Expert Syst. Appl. **221**, 119795 (2023)
4. Freire, J., Koop, D., Santos, E., Silva, C.T.: Provenance for computational tasks: a survey. Comput. Sci. Eng. **10**(3), 11–21 (2008)
5. Gharibi, G., Walunj, V., Nekadi, R., Marri, R., Lee, Y.: Automated end-to-end management of the modeling lifecycle in deep learning. Empir. Softw. Eng. **26**, 1–33 (2021)
6. Goodfellow, I., Bengio, Y., Courville, A.: Deep Learning. MIT Press, Cambridge (2016)
7. Groth, P., Moreau, L.: W3C PROV - an overview of the prov family of documents (2013). https://www.w3.org/TR/prov-overview/
8. Kamm, S., Veekati, S.S., Müller, T., Jazdi, N., Weyrich, M.: A survey on machine learning based analysis of heterogeneous data in industrial automation. Comput. Ind. **149**, 103930 (2023)
9. Krizhevsky, A.: Learning multiple layers of features from tiny images. Technical report. University of Toronto (2009)
10. Li, T., Sahu, A.K., Talwalkar, A., Smith, V.: Federated learning: challenges, methods, and future directions. IEEE Sig. Process. Mag. **37**(3), 50–60 (2020)
11. Li, T., Sahu, A.K., Zaheer, M., Sanjabi, M., Talwalkar, A., Smith, V.: Federated optimization in heterogeneous networks. In: Proceedings of Machine Learning and Systems (MLSys). mlsys.org (2020)

12. Lourenço, R., Freire, J., Simon, E., Weber, G., Shasha, D.E.: BugDoc. VLDB J. **32**(1), 75–101 (2023)
13. McMahan, B., Moore, E., Ramage, D., Hampson, S., Arcas, B.A.: Communication-efficient learning of deep networks from decentralized data. In: Proceedings of the 20th (AISTATS), vol. 54, pp. 1273–1282. PMLR (2017)
14. Nair, D.G., Aswartha Narayana, C.V., Jaideep Reddy, K., Nair, J.J.: Exploring SVM for federated machine learning applications. In: Rout, R.R., Ghosh, S.K., Jana, P.K., Tripathy, A.K., Sahoo, J.P., Li, K.C. (eds.) Advances in Distributed Computing and Machine Learning. LNNS, vol. 427, pp. 295–305. Springer, Singapore (2022). https://doi.org/10.1007/978-981-19-1018-0_25
15. Nogay, H.S., Adeli, H.: Diagnostic of autism spectrum disorder based on structural brain MRI images using, grid search optimization, and convolutional neural networks. Biomed. Sig. Process. Control. **79**(Part), 104234 (2023)
16. de Oliveira, D.C.M., Liu, J., Pacitti, E.: Data-Intensive Workflow Management: For Clouds and Data-Intensive and Scalable Computing Environments. Synthesis Lectures on Data Management. Morgan & Claypool Publishers, San Rafael (2019)
17. Parmar, J., Chouhan, S.S., Raychoudhury, V., Rathore, S.S.: Open-world machine learning: applications, challenges, and opportunities. ACM Comput. Surv. **55**(10), 205:1–205:37 (2023)
18. Peregrina, J.A., Ortiz, G., Zirpins, C.: Towards a metadata management system for provenance, reproducibility and accountability in federated machine learning. In: Zirpins, C., et al. (eds.) ESOCC 2022. CCIS, vol. 1617, pp. 5–18. Springer, Cham (2022). https://doi.org/10.1007/978-3-031-23298-5_1
19. Pina, D.B., Chapman, A., de Oliveira, D., Mattoso, M.: Deep learning provenance data integration: a practical approach. In: Ding, Y., Tang, J., Sequeda, J.F., Aroyo, L., Castillo, C., Houben, G. (eds.) Companion Proceedings of the ACM Web Conference 2023. WWW 2023, Austin, TX, USA, 30 April 2023–4 May 2023, pp. 1542–1550. ACM (2023)
20. Pina, D., Kunstmann, L., de Oliveira, D., Valduriez, P., Mattoso, M.: Provenance supporting hyperparameter analysis in deep neural networks. In: Glavic, B., Braganholo, V., Koop, D. (eds.) IPAW 2020-2021. LNCS, vol. 12839, pp. 20–38. Springer, Cham (2021). https://doi.org/10.1007/978-3-030-80960-7_2
21. Pina, D., et al.: Capturing provenance from deep learning applications using Keras-Prov and Colab: a practical approach. J. Inf. Data Manag. **13**(5) (2022)
22. Sandler, M., Howard, A., Zhu, M., Zhmoginov, A., Chen, L.C.: MobileNetV2: inverted residuals and linear bottlenecks. In: Proceedings of the IEEE Conference on Computer Vision and Pattern Recognition, pp. 4510–4520 (2018)
23. Schelter, S., Boese, J.H., Kirschnick, J., Klein, T., Seufert, S.: Automatically tracking metadata and provenance of machine learning experiments. In: Machine Learning Systems Workshop at NIPS (2017)
24. da Silva, F., Casanova, R., et al.: Workflows community summit: bringing the scientific workflows research community together (2021)
25. Silva, V., et al.: Dfanalyzer: runtime dataflow analysis tool for computational science and engineering applications. SoftwareX **12**, 100592 (2020)
26. Vartak, M., Madden, S.: MODELDB: opportunities and challenges in managing machine learning models. IEEE Data Eng. Bull. **41**(4), 16–25 (2018)
27. Yang, Q., Liu, Y., Chen, T., Tong, Y.: Federated machine learning: concept and applications. ACM Trans. Intell. Syst. Technol. **10**(2) (2019)

High Performance Computing Applications

A GPU Numerical Implementation of a 2D Simplified Wildfire Spreading Model

Daniel San Martin[1]([✉])(iD) and Claudio E. Torres[1,2](iD)

[1] Departamento de Informática, Universidad Técnica Federico Santa María,
Valparaíso, Chile
daniel.sanmartinr@usm.cl, ctorres@inf.utfsm.cl
[2] Centro Científico Tecnológico de Valparaíso, Universidad Técnica Federico Santa
María, Valparaíso, Chile

Abstract. Wildfires are a latent problem worldwide that every year burns thousands of hectares, negatively impacting the environment. To mitigate the damage, there is software to support wildfire analysis. Many of these computational tools are based on different mathematical models, each with its own advantages and disadvantages. Unfortunately, only a few of the software are open source. This work aims to develop an open-source *GPU* implementation of a mathematical model for the spread of wildfires using *CUDA*. The algorithm is based on the Method of Lines, allowing it to work with a system of partial differential equations as a dynamical system. We present the advantages of a *GPU* versus *C* and an *OpenMP* multi-threaded *CPU* implementation for computing the outcome of several scenarios.

Keywords: Wildfires · Numerical Methods · GPU · CUDA · Scientific Computing

1 Introduction

Wildfires are a worldwide problem that each year consumes large extensions of area, generating environmental, and socioeconomic, among other damages. Most fires, for example in Chile [8], are caused by human negligence, being natural causes, such as extreme weather conditions, thunderstorms or volcanic eruptions, less frequent compared to the former. The season of greatest occurrence of this phenomenon is in summer and generally in areas with a Mediterranean climate, conditions that favor the uncontrolled spread of fire.

The devastating effects and behavior of this type of disaster have led to the importance of developing technology for the study of the phenomenon, especially, to mitigate the damage they generate. For this purpose, several types of models have been developed which, according to [28], can be grouped into risk, propagation, and effect assessment models, which are closely related to each other. These models have a variety of approaches and may involve different mathematical techniques, mainly based on cellular automata or partial differential equations.

C. J. Barrios H. et al. (Eds.): CARLA 2023, CCIS 1887, pp. 131–145, 2024.
https://doi.org/10.1007/978-3-031-52186-7_9

For the development of this work, we focus on fire propagation models that use a mathematical representation to describe its behavior. Specifically, this work uses a physical model based on partial differential equations as described by [4,12], and [30]. For a comparison between the modeling approaches and the details of the models on which this work is based, see [30,33]. The main objective of this work is to extend a numerical implementation of the selected mathematical model, which is capable of processing multiple simulations efficiently, allowing a contribution to the study of wildfires. This allows for a more in-depth analysis of the phenomenon by knowing the behavior of the fire and fuel for different scenarios, for instance: varying ignition sources, wind direction, fuel characteristics, etc. The use of Graphics Processing Units (*GPU*) is introduced as a High-performance Computing (*HPC*) tool for processing this large number of case studies.

For an overview of the main approaches used in modeling the phenomenon, related work is presented in Sect. 2. Subsequently, in Sect. 3, the insight behind the model studying the dynamics of wildfires is briefly described. In Sect. 4 we present the numerical method which approximates the solution of the model used, in addition to the proposed *GPU* implementation. The numerical experiments and analysis of the implementation are presented in Sect. 5. Finally, the conclusions and future work are presented in Sects. 6 and 7 respectively.

2   Related Work

Currently, there is a wide range of tools for the analysis of forest fires, including numerical simulation software. Most of this technology is based on mathematical models that, very generally, can be grouped into discrete and continuous approaches. Within the discrete approach are Cellular Automata (*CA*), which are widely used for their simplicity of implementation, however, it is a challenge to relate the state update rules with the physical phenomenon to be modeled, see [1,2,7,14,18,19,21]. In the continuous approach, there are models based on Partial Differential Equations (*PDE*), which build the model from the underlying physical process; however, these usually derive in computationally intensive implementations; see [4,13,15–17,22,24,30]. In many cases, these models are used to complement information systems for wildfire analysis (see [3,38]).

In terms of implementation, many of the software uses *HPC* tools such as *OpenMP* or *MPI*. Recently, due to the capabilities of *GPU*s, and through General-Purpose Computing on Graphics Processing Units (*GPGPU*) approach, some of the new software provides implementations using frameworks such as *CUDA* or *OpenCL*. See [5,6,9–11,25,34,35,37]. Since most of the references using *GPU* are *CA*-based models, this work explores the development of an open-source *PDE*-based model implementation, that includes an efficient numerical method compatible with the use of the *CUDA* framework for *GPU*s.

3   Mathematical Model

The mathematical model used in this work is based on the model originally proposed by Asensio & Ferragut [4], also derived by Mandel et al. [22] and Eberle et al. [13], and recently studied by San Martin & Torres in [29, 30, 33].

Conceptually, the model describes the temperature behavior through a process of diffusion, convection, and reaction, in addition to fuel consumption by the chemical reaction of the process. Diffusion represents the propagation of temperature from a zone of higher temperature to a zone of lower temperature. Convection is the heat transfer induced by the effect of a fluid, such as wind in this case. The reaction process is an exothermic chemical process between temperature and vegetable fuel.

Let $u(\mathbf{x}, t)$ the temperature value and $\beta(\mathbf{x}, t)$ the fuel fraction, both defined in the spatial coordinates $\mathbf{x} = (x, y)$ at time t, where $\mathbf{x} \in \Omega =]x_{\min}, x_{\max}[\times]y_{\min}, y_{\max}[\subset \mathbb{R}^2$ y $t \in [t_{\min}, t_{\max}]$. Let $\mathbf{v}(\mathbf{x}, t) = \mathbf{w}(t) + \nabla T(\mathbf{x})$ the vector field which models the effect of wind and topography, and $f(u, \beta)$ a non-linear heat source. Then, the mathematical model is defined as,

$$
\begin{aligned}
u_t &= \kappa \nabla^2 u - \mathbf{v} \cdot \nabla u + f(u, \beta), && \text{in } \Omega \times]0, t_{\max}], \\
\beta_t &= g(u, \beta), && \text{in } \Omega \times]0, t_{\max}], \\
u(\mathbf{x}, t) &= h_1(\mathbf{x}, t), && \text{on } \Gamma \times]0, t_{\max}], \\
\beta(\mathbf{x}, t) &= h_2(\mathbf{x}, t), && \text{on } \Gamma \times]0, t_{\max}], \\
u(\mathbf{x}, 0) &= u_0(\mathbf{x}), && \text{in } \Omega, \\
\beta(\mathbf{x}, 0) &= \beta_0(\mathbf{x}), && \text{in } \Omega,
\end{aligned}
\tag{1}
$$

where Γ represents the boundary of Ω and,

$$
f(u, \beta) = s(u)^+ \beta \exp\left(\frac{u}{1 + \varepsilon u}\right) - \alpha u,
$$

$$
g(u, \beta) = -s(u)^+ \frac{\varepsilon}{q} \beta \exp\left(\frac{u}{1 + \varepsilon u}\right),
$$

with

$$
s(u)^+ = \begin{cases} 1, & \text{if } u \geq u_{pc}, \\ 0, & \text{otherwise.} \end{cases}
$$

The gradient is defined as $\nabla = \left(\frac{\partial}{\partial x}, \frac{\partial}{\partial y}\right)$ and $\nabla^2 = \frac{\partial^2}{\partial x^2} + \frac{\partial^2}{\partial y^2}$ is the Laplace operator. The mathematical model is presented in its non-dimensional form. More details of the model and the parameters can be found in Asensio [4] and Eberle [13].

4   Algorithm

The algorithm used in this work is derived from a numerical approximation using the *Method of Lines* representing the *PDEs* system (1) as the following *Initial Value Problem (IVP)*

$$
\dot{\mathbf{y}}(t) = \Phi(t, \mathbf{y}(t)),
\tag{2}
$$

where,

$$\dot{\mathbf{y}}(t) = \left(\text{vec}\left(\dot{U}(t) \right), \text{vec}\left(\dot{B}(t) \right) \right)^{\top}$$

and

$$\Phi(t, \mathbf{y}(t)) = \begin{pmatrix} \text{vec}\left(\kappa \left(U(t) D_{N_x}^{(2)} + D_{N_y}^{(2)} U(t) \right) - \left(V_1(t) \odot (U(t) D_{N_x}) + V_2(t) \odot (D_{N_y} U(t)) \right) + F(t) \right) \\ \text{vec}\left(G(U(t), B(t)) \right) \end{pmatrix}$$

with $\mathbf{y}(0) = (\text{vec}\,(U(0)), \text{vec}\,(B(0)))^{\top}$ the initial condition. vec $(\cdot)$ denotes the vectorization operator applied in column-major order. Boundary conditions are imposed in each time step according to the values of $h_1(\mathbf{x}, t)$ and $h_2(\mathbf{x}, t)$ from (1).

The problem (2) is solved numerically using Second-Order Finite Difference (*FDM*) and Fourth-Order Runge-Kutta Method (*RK4*) over a discrete spatial and time domain

$$\begin{aligned} x_i &= x_{\min} + i\,\Delta x, \quad i = 0, ..., N_x, \quad \Delta x = (x_{\max} - x_{\min})/N_x, \\ y_j &= y_{\min} + j\,\Delta y, \quad j = 0, ..., N_y, \quad \Delta y = (y_{\max} - y_{\min})/N_y, \\ t_n &= t_{\min} + n\,\Delta t, \quad n = 0, ..., N_t, \quad \Delta t = (t_{\max} - t_{\min})/N_t. \end{aligned}$$

N_x, N_y, and N_t correspond to the number of intervals for the spatial and temporal domains. U stores the temperature discretization, B stored the discretization of fuel, V_1, V_2 are the matrices corresponding to the approximation of the components of the vector field $\mathbf{v}$, F y G are the numerical representation of the functions f and g defined in (1). D_N y $D_N^{(2)}$ are the differentiation matrices that allow us to approximate the first and second spatial partial derivatives; see [30, 36]. $\odot$ represents the Hadamard product or element-wise multiplication.

The derivation, analysis of the convergence, and theoretical and numerically observed computational complexity of the algorithm can be found in [30, 33].

4.1   Applications

This algorithm allows us to study, for example, the vulnerability of fuel zones or risk maps (see examples in [30]), calculating the damage that fires can cause at different initial ignition points. This analysis requires a large number of numerical simulations since there is uncertainty in the initial conditions of the problem. For example, the location of the initial fire sources, and the meteorological conditions, among others. See Fig. 1. Therefore, it is crucial to develop an implementation that keeps computation times in the order of minutes or seconds, since the shorter the execution time, the higher the number of fire scenarios that can be simulated.

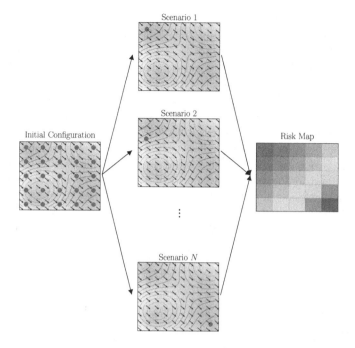

Fig. 1. Risk maps generation scheme. (source: [30])

4.2   CPU Implementation

The basic implementation of the algorithm was carried out in *Python*, using the libraries *NumPy* for the vector handling of the structures and *SciPy* for the handling of sparse matrices. It is important to point out that these libraries have an optimized implementation of linear algebra algorithms and are mostly developed in *C/C++* [27]. This version can be accessed in [31].

To compare the performance of our implementation, we also include a sequential version in *C* and another with a *CPU* multi-thread management using *OpenMP*.

4.3   GPU Implementation

Graphics processing units (*GPU*s), included on graphics cards, have been widely used over the past few years because of the amount of computation that can be processed, including numerical simulations of *PDE*s. While the video cards were developed primarily for graphics work, the concept *General-Purpose GPU* (*GPGPU*) has been widely used in scientific applications because of the computational advantages they present over *CPU*s [20]. The parallel programming model for *GPU*s allows an instruction to be performed on multiple threads and is known as *Single Instruction, Multiple Threads* (*SIMT*). *CUDA* is a platform for *GPU* software development, providing a set of directives for working with the $C/C{+}{+}$ language, but extending its use to other languages. The execution of code on GPU is performed in functions called *kernels*, which are executed in parallel on the available threads according to the characteristics of the graphics card. More details about $CUDA$ programming can be accessed in the official development documentation [26].

The general parameters for the execution of a *kernel* are the number of blocks per grid and the number of threads per block. The performance of the code on GPU often depends on the correct selection of these parameters.

Due to the need to perform multiple numerical simulations, a GPU implementation is proposed where each thread processes the $\mathbf{Y}_l^{[m]}$ element of the scheme described in Fig. 2. Each scenario m is associated with an independent numerical simulation with $m \in [0, N_s-1]$, $l \in [0, 2\,(N_x+1)\,(N_y+1)\,N_s-1]$, and N_s the number of scenarios/simulations. The idea is to process $2\,(N_x+1)\,(N_y+1)\,N_s$ elements in parallel for each *timestep* of the time integration method.

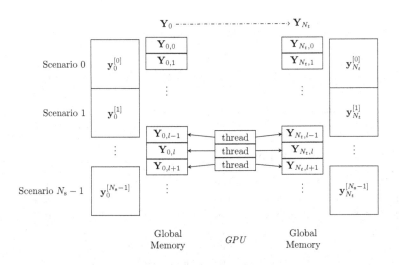

Fig. 2. GPU implementation description.

In summary, the approach we propose solves an *Initial Value Problem(IVP)*

$$\dot{\mathbf{Y}}(t) = \boldsymbol{\Phi}(t, \mathbf{Y}(t)) \tag{3}$$

where

$$\mathbf{Y}(t) = \left(\mathbf{y}(t)^{[0]}, \ldots, \mathbf{y}(t)^{[N_s-1]}\right)^{\top},$$

represents the vector with all the numerical simulations, and

$$\boldsymbol{\Phi}(t, \mathbf{Y}(t)) = \left(\boldsymbol{\Phi}(t, \mathbf{y}(t))^{[0]}, \ldots, \boldsymbol{\Phi}(t, \mathbf{y}(t))^{[N_s-1]}\right)^{\top}$$

is the evaluation of the right-hand side of (2) for each fire scenario.

The computational effort is performed in the evaluation of $\boldsymbol{\Phi}(t, \mathbf{Y}(t))$, and this is the reason because it is processed by the *GPU*.

The algorithm 1 shows the calculation of the right-hand side of equation (3) using *GPU* threads. Algorithm 2 presents the computation of the next time step using *RK4* method. The operation "vector plus scalar times another vector" is described in Algorithm 3. This is used for *RK4* method for *GPU* threads. Finally, Algorithm 4 shows the *RK4* loop performed by the *CPU*, calling the *GPU CUDA* kernels.

Algorithm 1. Computation of right-hand-side of equation (2) $\boldsymbol{\Phi}$.

1: **procedure** RHSVEC(Parameters, $\mathbf{Y}$, $\mathbf{Y}_{\mathrm{tmp}}$)
2:     $t_{\mathrm{id}} \leftarrow$ `threadIdx.x` $+$ `blockIdx.x` $\cdot$ `blockDim.x`
3:     **while** $t_{\mathrm{id}} < N_{\mathrm{s}}\,(N_x + 1)(N_y + 1)$ **do**
4:         $m \leftarrow t_{\mathrm{id}}/((N_x + 1)(N_y + 1))$
5:         row $\leftarrow (t_{\mathrm{id}} - m\,(N_x + 1)(N_y + 1))\%(N_y + 1)$
6:         col $\leftarrow (t_{\mathrm{id}} - m\,(N_x + 1)(N_y + 1))/(N_y + 1)$
7:         offset $\leftarrow 2\,m\,(N_x + 1)(N_y + 1)$
8:         $l \leftarrow$ offset $+$ col $(N_y + 1)$ + row
9:         $u_{\mathrm{idx}} \leftarrow l$
10:         $b_{\mathrm{idx}} \leftarrow l + (N_x + 1)(N_y + 1)$
11:         $u_{\mathrm{k}} \leftarrow h_1(x, y, t)$
12:         $b_{\mathrm{k}} \leftarrow h_2(x, y, t)$
13:         **if** $\neg(\mathrm{row} = 0 \vee \mathrm{row} = N_y \vee \mathrm{col} = 0 \vee \mathrm{col} = N_x)$ **then**
14:             $u \leftarrow \mathbf{Y}_{\mathrm{tmp}_{u_{\mathrm{idx}}}}$
15:             $b \leftarrow \mathbf{Y}_{\mathrm{tmp}_{b_{\mathrm{idx}}}}$
16:             $v_1, v_2 \leftarrow \mathbf{v}(x, y, t)$
17:             $u_{\mathrm{r}} \leftarrow \mathbf{Y}_{\mathrm{tmp}_{\mathrm{offset}+(\mathrm{col}+1)\cdot(N_y+1)+\mathrm{row}}}$
18:             $u_{\mathrm{l}} \leftarrow \mathbf{Y}_{\mathrm{tmp}_{\mathrm{offset}+(\mathrm{col}-1)\cdot(N_y+1)+\mathrm{row}}}$
19:             $u_{\mathrm{u}} \leftarrow \mathbf{Y}_{\mathrm{tmp}_{\mathrm{offset}+\mathrm{col}\cdot(N_y+1)+\mathrm{row}+1}}$
20:             $u_{\mathrm{d}} \leftarrow \mathbf{Y}_{\mathrm{tmp}_{\mathrm{offset}+\mathrm{col}\cdot(N_y+1)+\mathrm{row}-1}}$
21:             $u_{\mathrm{x}} \leftarrow (u_{\mathrm{r}} - u_{\mathrm{l}})/(2\Delta x)$
22:             $u_{\mathrm{y}} \leftarrow (u_{\mathrm{u}} - u_{\mathrm{d}})/(2\Delta y)$
23:             $u_{\mathrm{xx}} \leftarrow (u_{\mathrm{r}} - 2u + u_{\mathrm{l}})/\Delta x^2$
24:             $u_{\mathrm{yy}} \leftarrow (u_{\mathrm{u}} - 2u + u_{\mathrm{d}})/\Delta y^2$
25:             $u_{\mathrm{k}} \leftarrow \kappa\,(u_{\mathrm{xx}} + u_{\mathrm{yy}}) - (v_1\,u_{\mathrm{x}} + v_2\,u_{\mathrm{y}})$
26:             $u_{\mathrm{k}} \leftarrow u_{\mathrm{k}} + H_{pc}(u)b\exp(u/(1 + \varepsilon\,u)) - \alpha u$
27:             $b_{\mathrm{k}} \leftarrow -H_{pc}(u)\varepsilon\,b\exp(u/(1 + \varepsilon\,u))/q$
28:         **end if**
29:         $\mathbf{Y}_{u_{\mathrm{idx}}} \leftarrow u_{\mathrm{k}}$
30:         $\mathbf{Y}_{b_{\mathrm{idx}}} \leftarrow b_{\mathrm{k}}$
31:         $t_{\mathrm{id}} \leftarrow t_{\mathrm{id}} +$ `gridDim.x` $\cdot$ `blockDim.x`
32:     **end while**
33: **end procedure**

Algorithm 2. *RK4* scheme using *GPU* approach.

```
1: procedure RK4SCHEME(Parameters, Y_new, Y_old, k_1, k_2, k_3, k_4, Δt, size)
2:     t_id ← threadIdx.x + blockIdx.x · blockDim.x
3:     while t_id < size do
```
$$4: \qquad \mathbf{Y}_{\mathrm{new}\,t_{\mathrm{id}}} \leftarrow \mathbf{Y}_{\mathrm{old}\,t_{\mathrm{id}}} + \frac{\Delta t}{6}\left(\mathbf{k}_{1\,t_{\mathrm{id}}} + 2\mathbf{k}_{2\,t_{\mathrm{id}}} + 2\mathbf{k}_{3\,t_{\mathrm{id}}} + \mathbf{k}_{4\,t_{\mathrm{id}}}\right)$$
```
5:         t_id ← t_id + gridDim.x · blockDim.x
6:     end while
7: end procedure
```

Algorithm 3. Vector sum implementation using *GPU* approach.

```
1: procedure SUMVECTOR(Parameters, c, a, b, size, scalar)
2:     t_id ← threadIdx.x + blockIdx.x · blockDim.x
3:     while t_id < size do
4:         c_{t_id} ← a_{t_id} + scalar · b_{t_id}
5:         t_id ← t_id + gridDim.x · blockDim.x
6:     end while
7: end procedure
```

Algorithm 4. Code extract implementing the *RK4* loop.

```
1: ...
2: for n = 1 to N_t do
3:     Copy Y into Y_tmp
4:     RHSVec<<<N_BLOCKS, N_THREADS>>>(Parameters, k_1, Y_tmp)
5:     sumVector<<<N_BLOCKS, N_THREADS>>> (Parameters, k_tmp, Y_tmp, k_1, 0.5Δt, size)
6:     RHSVec<<<N_BLOCKS, N_THREADS>>>(Parameters, k_2, Y_tmp)
7:     sumVector<<<N_BLOCKS, N_THREADS>>> (Parameters, k_tmp, Y_tmp, k_2, 0.5Δt, size)
8:     RHSVec<<<N_BLOCKS, N_THREADS>>>(Parameters, k_3, Y_tmp)
9:     sumVector<<<N_BLOCKS, N_THREADS>>> (Parameters, k_tmp, Y_tmp, k_3, Δt, size)
10:     RHSVec<<<N_BLOCKS, N_THREADS>>>(Parameters, k_4, Y_tmp)
11:     RK4Scheme<<<N_BLOCKS, N_THREADS>>>(Parameters, Y, Y_tmp, k_1, k_2, k_3, k_4, Δt, size)
12: end for
13: ...
```

The parameters of the functions are detailed in equation (1) and *N_BLOCKS*, *N_THREADS* are the parameters of *CUDA kernels*. In particular, the RHSVec *kernel* consumes approximately the 90% of the execution time.

5   Numerical Experiments

5.1   Numerical Simulations

Some numerical examples are presented below.

The first experiment presented in Fig. 3 is defined in the domain $\Omega =]0, 90[^2$, $t \in]0, 50]$. Initial conditions are $u_0(x, y) = 6 \exp(-((x - 20)^2 + (y - 70)^2)/20)$ for temperature and for fuel is $\beta_0 \sim \mathcal{U}(0, 1)$. The boundary conditions are $h_1 = h_2 = 0$. The vector field is defined as $\mathbf{v}(x, y, t) = (\cos(-\pi/4 + 0.01\,t), \sin(-\pi/4 + 0.01\,t))$. The model parameters are $\kappa = 0.1$, $\varepsilon = 0.3$, $u_{pc} = 3$, $q = 1$ y $\alpha = 0.001$, and the number of intervals is $N_x = N_y = 127$ and $N_t = 1000$.

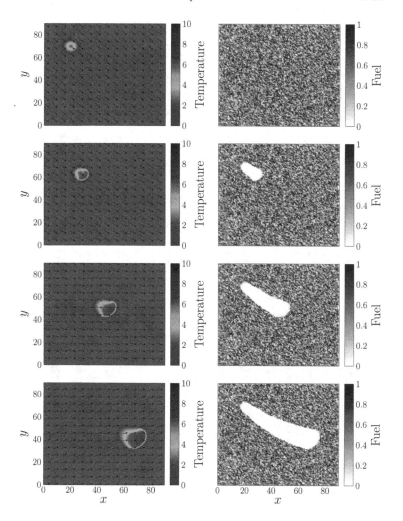

Fig. 3. First experiment using a dynamic vector field.

The second experiment, Fig. 4, has the spatial domain $\Omega =]-100, 100[^2$ and temporal $t \in]0, 30]$. The initial condition for temperature is

$$u_0(x,y) = \begin{cases} 6 & \text{if } (x,y) \in \Omega_0, \\ 0 & \text{otherwise,} \end{cases}$$

with $\Omega_0 = [-100, -93.7] \times [-21.3, 21.3]$ and for $\beta_0 \sim \mathcal{U}(0,1)$. The vector field used is $\mathbf{v}(x,y,t) = (1,0)$. The boundary conditions are $h_1 = h_2 = 0$. The model parameters are $\kappa = 10$, $\varepsilon = 0.3$, $u_{pc} = 3$, $q = 1$ y $\alpha = 0.01$, and the number of intervals is $N_x = N_y = 127$ and $N_t = 900$.

Figs. 3 and 4 show how the fire front, the highest temperature zone, and fuel consumption follow the dynamics of the wind, as expected.

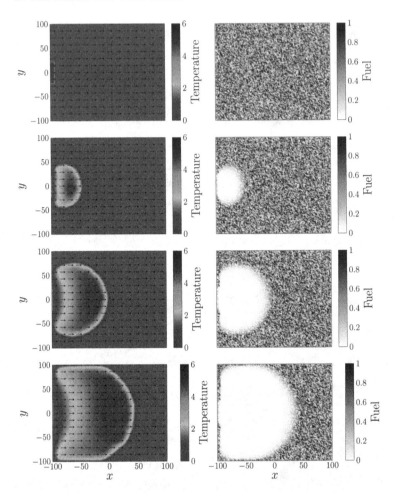

Fig. 4. Second experiment with a rectangular initial fire source. This experiment aims to replicate the output presented by Mell et al. [23].

5.2   Comparison

To compare the performance of each implementation, an equispaced ignition points grid is defined as described in Fig. 1. Using this definition, N_s simulations are executed with $N_s \in \{1, 10, 100, 1000, 8100\}$. The aim is to process a high number of simulations, to compare the execution times for both *CPU* and *GPU* implementations. It is important to point out that this comparison does not include the implementation developed in [33], because the idea presented in this article highlights the difference between the multithreaded *CPU* and *GPU* paradigms, being *CuPy* an intermediate *GPU* implementation between *NumPy* and *CUDA*, thus, *CuPy* will be bounded by their behavior.

The code was executed in the computer cluster of the *Centro Científico Tecnológico de Valparaíso* from *Universidad Técnica Federico Santa María* (*CCT-Val*). Computer nodes have an Intel(R) Xeon(R) E5-2643 v2 *CPU* with 3.9 GHz frequency, 6 physical nodes and 12 logical cores. These nodes include a Tesla K20m graphic card with 2496 cores, 706 MHz frequency, and 5 GB of *vRAM*. Additionally, they have 64 GB of *RAM*.

For the *OpenMP* implementation, 12 threads were selected due to the shorter average execution time. To select the *CUDA kernel* parameters, we performed 10 experiments for 8100 simulations. The results are presented in Table 1.

Table 1. Average execution times (s) of the algorithm for different numbers of threads and blocks.

		# Blocks				
		32	64	128	256	512
# Threads	128	116.7	74.2	60.5	62.1	61.1
	256	74.0	59.1	59.7	58.8	**57.7**
	512	73.4	65.8	60.7	60.9	59.0

Using the previous results, the configuration of 512 blocks and 256 threads obtains the shorter average execution time, being 49.42% smaller than the worst cases with 32 blocks and 128 threads. Figure 5a presents the average times of experiments performed with the configuration described before. In addition, we define the *speedup* as the quotient between the execution time of the *CPU* implementations included in the article versus the *GPU* version using *CUDA*. Figure 5b shows these values.

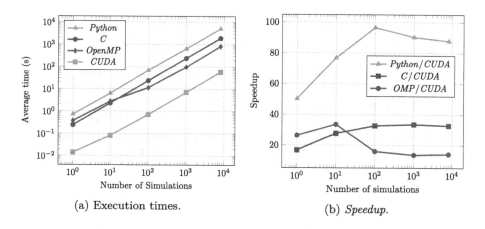

(a) **Execution times.**

(b) *Speedup.*

Fig. 5. Implementation results.

When analyzing the curves in the execution times plot, we can see how the *GPU* implementation considerably reduces the computation time required for processing the different scenarios. Notice that over 1000 execution scenarios, the *GPU* implementation is approximately 88 times faster than the first version in *Python*. As well, the *CUDA* version is 14 times faster than the *CPU* multi-threaded *OpenMP* implementation.

Regarding degradation of *speedup*, it is mainly because the number of threads available is lower than the number of tasks that need to be computed under this approach, thus, the computation has to be performed in batches.

6   Conclusions

This work has presented an open-source *GPU* implementation of the wildfire spread model proposed by [4] with the simplification introduced by [13]. A description of the mathematical model, the algorithm, and a *GPU* implementation strategy is provided. To validate the implementation, an extensive comparison has been made with *CPU* versions, including an implementation on *C* and *OpenMP*, both in the numerical results obtained and in their execution times.

The algorithm has been successfully adapted to take advantage of the power of graphics cards. The results show that the proposal is 88 times faster than the version in [30], 32 times faster than a sequential version in *C* and approximately 14 times faster than a version in a multi-threaded *CPU* implementation using *OpenMP*.

In addition, the described implementation is publicly available on *GitHub* [32], therefore the results can be reproduced and the code can be used as an active tool in the study of wildfires.

7   Future Work

Due to the limitations associated with the parallelization approach used in this work, specifically, using one thread to process each element of the vector of simulations, it is open to explore other strategies to improve the performance of the implementation. For example, using each thread to process more than one element of the vector considering the local relationship when approximating the spatial partial derivatives.

Further extensions of the current work are the utilization of different types of available memory to further reduce *GPU* computation times, the use of code profiling in order to optimize and avoid possible bottlenecks, and the extension of the presented framework to the use of multi-*GPU* or hybrid *CPU-GPU* architecture to solve even more scenarios in parallel.

Acknowledgment. This work was partially supported by ANID-Subdirección de Capital Humano/Doctorado Nacional/2019-21191017, ANID PIA/APOYO AFB220004 Centro Científico Tecnológico de Valparaíso - CCTVal, and Programa de Iniciación a la

Investigación Científica (*PIIC*) from Dirección de Postgrado y Programas, Universidad Técnica Federico Santa María, Chile.

Powered@NLHPC: This research was partially supported by the supercomputing infrastructure of the NLHPC (ECM-02).

References

1. Alexandridis, A., Vakalis, D., Siettos, C., Bafas, G.: A cellular automata model for forest fire spread prediction: the case of the wildfire that swept through Spetses Island in 1990. Appl. Math. Comput. **204**(1), 191–201 (2008). https://doi.org/10.1016/j.amc.2008.06.046
2. Almeida, R.M., Macau, E.E.N.: Stochastic cellular automata model for wildland fire spread dynamics. J. Phys: Conf. Ser. **285**(1), 12038 (2011). https://doi.org/10.1088/1742-6596/285/1/012038
3. Arganaraz, J., Lighezzolo, A., Clemoveki, K., Bridera, D., Scavuzzo, J., Bellis, L.: Operational meteo fire risk system based on space information for Chaco Serrano. IEEE Lat. Am. Trans. **16**(3), 975–980 (2018). https://doi.org/10.1109/TLA.2018.8358681
4. Asensio, M.I., Ferragut, L.: On a wildland fire model with radiation. Int. J. Numer. Meth. Eng. **54**(1), 137–157 (2002). https://doi.org/10.1002/nme.420
5. Carrillo, C., Margalef, T., Espinosa, A., Cortés, A.: Accelerating wild fire simulator using GPU. In: Rodrigues, J.M.F., et al. (eds.) ICCS 2019. LNCS, vol. 11540, pp. 521–527. Springer, Cham (2019). https://doi.org/10.1007/978-3-030-22750-0_46
6. Carrillo, C., Cortés, A., Margalef, T., Espinosa, A., Cencerrado, A.: Applying GPU parallel technology to accelerate FARSITE forest fire simulator. In: Advances in Forest Fire Research, pp. 913–921 (2018). https://doi.org/10.14195/978-989-26-16-506_100
7. Chopard, B., Droz, M.: Cellular automata model for the diffusion equation. J. Stat. Phys. **64**(3), 859–892 (1991). https://doi.org/10.1007/BF01048321
8. CONAF: Incendios Forestales en Chile (2021). http://www.conaf.cl/incendios-forestales/incendios-forestales-en-chile/
9. Denham, M., Laneri, K.: Using efficient parallelization in graphic processing units to parameterize stochastic fire propagation models. J. Comput. Sci. **25**, 76–88 (2018). https://doi.org/10.1016/J.JOCS.2018.02.007
10. Denham, M.M., Waidelich, S., Laneri, K.: Visualization and modeling of forest fire propagation in Patagonia. Environ. Model. Softw. **158**, 105526 (2022). https://doi.org/10.1016/J.ENVSOFT.2022.105526
11. D'Ambrosio, D., Gregorio, S.D., Filippone, G., Rongo, R., Spataro, W., Trunfio, G.A.: A Multi-GPU approach to fast wildfire hazard mapping. Adv. Intell. Syst. Comput. **256**, 183–195 (2014). https://doi.org/10.1007/978-3-319-03581-9_13
12. Eberle, S.: Modeling and simulation of forest fire spreading. In: Eulogio, P.I., Guardiola-Albert, Carolina, Javier, H., Luis, M.M., José, D.J., Antonio, V.G.J. (eds.) Mathematics of Planet Earth, pp. 811–814. Springer, Berlin Heidelberg, Berlin, Heidelberg (2014). https://doi.org/10.1007/978-3-642-32408-6_175
13. Eberle, S., Freeden, W., Matthes, U.: Forest fire spreading. In: Freeden, W., Nashed, M.Z., Sonar, T. (eds.) Handbook of Geomathematics, pp. 1349–1385. Springer, Berlin Heidelberg, Berlin, Heidelberg (2015). https://doi.org/10.1007/978-3-642-54551-1_70

14. Fernandez-Anez, N., Christensen, K., Rein, G.: Two-dimensional model of smoul-
dering combustion using multi-layer cellular automaton: the role of ignition location and direction of airflow. Fire Saf. J. **91**, 243–251 (2017). https://doi.org/10.
1016/J.FIRESAF.2017.03.009

15. Ferragut, L., Asensio, M.I., Cascón, J.M., Prieto, D.: A wildland fire physical model
well suited to data assimilation. Pure Appl. Geophys. **172**(1), 121–139 (2015).
https://doi.org/10.1007/s00024-014-0893-9

16. Ferragut, L., Asensio, M.I., Monedero, S.: Modelling radiation and moisture content in fire spread. Commun. Numer. Meth. Eng. **23**, 819–833 (2006). https://doi.
org/10.1002/cnm.927

17. Ferragut, L., Asensio, M.I., Monedero, S.: A numerical method for solving
convection-reaction-diffusion multivalued equations in fire spread modelling. Adv.
Eng. Softw. **38**(6), 366–371 (2007). https://doi.org/10.1016/J.ADVENGSOFT.
2006.09.007

18. Ghisu, T., Arca, B., Pellizzaro, G., Duce, P.: An improved cellular automata for
wildfire spread. Procedia Comput. Sci. **51**, 2287–2296 (2015). https://doi.org/10.
1016/J.PROCS.2015.05.388

19. Hansen, P.B.: Parallel cellular automata: a model program for computational science. Concurrency Pract. Experience **5**(5), 425–448 (1993). https://doi.org/10.
1002/cpe.4330050504

20. Harris, M.: Introducing parallel forall. https://developer.nvidia.com/blog/?p=8.
Accessed 3 Oct 2023

21. Karafyllidis, I., Thanailakis, A.: A model for predicting forest fire spreading using
cellular automata. Ecol. Model. **99**(1), 87–97 (1997). https://doi.org/10.1016/
S0304-3800(96)01942-4

22. Mandel, J., et al.: A wildland fire model with data assimilation. Math. Comput.
Simul. **79**(3), 584–606 (2008). https://doi.org/10.1016/j.matcom.2008.03.015

23. Mell, W., Jenkins, M.A., Gould, J., Cheney, P.: A physics-based approach to modelling grassland fires. Int. J. Wildland Fire **16**(1), 1–22 (2007). https://doi.org/10.
1071/WF06002

24. Montenegro, R., Plaza, A., Ferragut, L., Asensio, M.I.: Application of a nonlinear
evolution model to fire propagation. Nonlinear Anal. Theory Methods Appl. **30**(5),
2873–2882 (1997). https://doi.org/10.1016/S0362-546X(97)00341-6

25. Ntinas, V.G., Moutafis, B.E., Trunfio, G.A., Sirakoulis, G.C.: GPU and FPGA
parallelization of fuzzy cellular automata for the simulation of wildfire spreading. In: Wyrzykowski, R., Deelman, E., Dongarra, J., Karczewski, K., Kitowski,
J., Wiatr, K. (eds.) PPAM 2015. LNCS, vol. 9574, pp. 560–569. Springer, Cham
(2016). https://doi.org/10.1007/978-3-319-32152-3_52

26. NVIDIA: CUDA C++ Programming Guide. https://docs.nvidia.com/cuda/cuda-
c-programming-guide/. Accessed 3 Oct 2023

27. Oliphant, T.E.: Python for scientific computing. Comput. Sci. Eng. **9**(3), 10–20
(2007). https://doi.org/10.1109/MCSE.2007.58

28. Preisler, H.K., Ager, A.A.: Forest-Fire Models. Encycl. Environmetrics (2013).
https://doi.org/10.1002/9780470057339.vaf010.pub2

29. San Martín, D., Torres, C.E.: Exploring a spectral numerical algorithm for solving a wildfire mathematical model. In: 2019 38th International Conference of the
Chilean Computer Science Society (SCCC), pp. 1–7 (2019). https://doi.org/10.
1109/SCCC49216.2019.8966412

30. San Martín, D., Torres, C.E.: Ngen-Kütral: Toward an open source framework
for chilean wildfire spreading. In: 2018 37th International Conference of the

Chilean Computer Science Society (SCCC), pp. 1–8 (2018). https://doi.org/10.1109/SCCC.2018.8705159

31. San Martin, D., Torres, C.: Open source framework for chilean wildfire spreading (2019). https://github.com/dsanmartin/ngen-kutral. Accessed 1 Mar 2019

32. San Martin, D., Torres, C.: Open source framework for Chilean wildfire spreading: GPU implementation (2019). https://github.com/dsanmartin/ngen-kutral-gpu. Accessed 1 Mar 2019

33. San Martin, D., Torres, C.E.: 2D simplified wildfire spreading model in Python: from NumPy to CuPy. CLEI Electron. J. **26**, 5:1-5:18 (2023). https://doi.org/10.19153/CLEIEJ.26.1.5

34. Smith, J., Barfed, L., Dasclu, S.M., Harris, F.C.: Highly parallel implementation of forest fire propagation models on the GPU. In: 2016 International Conference on High Performance Computing and Simulation, HPCS 2016, pp. 917–924 (2016). https://doi.org/10.1109/HPCSIM.2016.7568432

35. Sousa, F.A., dos Reis, R.J., Pereira, J.C.: Simulation of surface fire fronts using fireLib and GPUs. Environ. Model. Softw. **38**, 167–177 (2012). https://doi.org/10.1016/J.ENVSOFT.2012.06.006

36. Trefethen, L.N.: Spectral Methods in MATLAB. Society for Industrial and Applied Mathematics, Philadelphia, PA, USA (2000). https://doi.org/10.1137/1.9780898719598

37. Wu, R., et al.: vFirelib: a GPU-based fire simulation and visualization tool. SoftwareX **23**, 101411 (2023). https://doi.org/10.1016/J.SOFTX.2023.101411

38. Zambrano, M., Pérez, I., Carvajal, F., Esteve, M., Palau, C.: Command and control information systems applied to large forest fires response. IEEE Lat. Am. Trans. **15**(9), 1735–1741 (2017). https://doi.org/10.1109/TLA.2017.8015080

Towards a Multi-GPU Implementation of a Seismic Application

Pedro H. C. Rigon[1,2](✉) ⓘ, Brenda S. Schussler[1,2]ⓘ, Edson L. Padoin[1,2]ⓘ,
Arthur F. Lorenzon[1,2]ⓘ, Alexandre Carissimi[1,2]ⓘ,
and Philippe O. A. Navaux[1,2]ⓘ

[1] Institute of Informatics, Federal University of Rio Grande do Sul, Porto Alegre,
Brazil
{phcrigon,bsschussler,aflorenzon,asc,navaux}@inf.ufrgs.br,
padoin@unijui.edu.br
[2] Regional University of Northwestern Rio Grande do Sul, Porto Alegre, Brazil

Abstract. This study explores the implementation and analysis of a
Multi-GPU system for the application of the Fletcher Method in geophysical exploration, essential in the discovery and extraction of energy
sources such as oil and gas. The scalability of the software for the use of
multiple GPUs (Graphics Processing Units) allows for improved performance of these applications due to their parallel processing capacity. The
proposed strategy emphasizes a judicious approach to workload division,
considering the data location and the GPU's processing capacity. This
implementation stands out as the first in the seismic application field
to utilize multiple V100 GPUs and assess the impact on performance.
The experiments results demonstrated that the proposed Multi-GPU
implementation provides significant performance improvements over the
Single-GPU version (e.g., 2.77 times using 4 GPUs). Furthermore, the
Multi-GPU implementation exhibits linear growth in performance and
efficiency as the input grid size increases.

Keywords: Multi-GPU · Fletcher · Performance · GPU · CUDA

1 Introduction

Geophysical exploration methods play a vital role in our society as they enable
the discovery of fundamental resources (e.g., oil and gas) that drive the economic
development of nations. However, pursuing new oil reservoirs usually involves
destructive practices like drilling in environmentally sensitive areas and improper
waste disposal. Hence, researchers have developed applications that simulate
seismic imaging for oil detection to mitigate these adverse effects and enhance
drilling precision. On top of that, given that these applications involve a huge
amount of data and naturally lend themselves to parallel processing, graphics
processing units (GPUs) have become extensively employed to accelerate such
tasks [Lukawski et al., 2014].

GPUs are architectures designed with a single instruction, multiple data
(SIMD) approach and incorporate thousands of processing cores. This design

C. J. Barrios H. et al. (Eds.): CARLA 2023, CCIS 1887, pp. 146–159, 2024.
https://doi.org/10.1007/978-3-031-52186-7_10

makes them well-suited as accelerator devices for executing applications that efficiently handle array and matrix data structures. However, despite their impressive computing capabilities, GPUs demand significant power during their operation. Consequently, optimizing the utilization of the available hardware resources on GPUs, such as cores and memory, becomes imperative when executing parallel applications [Lorenzon and Beck Filho, 2019]. By doing this, we can effectively reduce energy consumption while mitigating the associated environmental and economic impacts [Navaux et al., 2023].

With the increasing availability of multiple GPUs in high-performance servers, one can further explore the processing potential through Multi-GPU systems [Papadrakakis et al., 2011]. In this scenario, by distributing the workload among all the GPUs available in the system, one can take advantage of the parallel processing power of each one, achieving significant performance improvements [Liu et al., 2019]. Furthermore, the improvement in scalability provided by multiple GPUs allows the handling of increasingly larger datasets, improving the analysis capacity and quality of the generated seismic images through the greater density of data incorporated in the final result.

However, effectively implementing seismic applications that can fully leverage the processing power of Multi-GPU systems poses a significant challenge. A key obstacle lies in achieving efficient utilization of GPUs. Therefore, striking a balance in workload distribution across the GPUs becomes crucial to optimize the available processing power. Additionally, employing efficient strategies for workload partitioning and thread coordination is vital to prevent resource underutilization or overload on the GPUs. By addressing these challenges, one can maximize the efficiency and performance of parallel applications on Multi-GPU systems.

Considering the aforementioned scenario, we propose a Multi-GPU implementation for the Fletcher Method. Our main objective is to provide a workload division strategy that considers fundamental aspects such as data locality and maximizes GPU processing capacity. To validate the proposed implementation, we performed extensive experiments using twenty-nine different grid input sets on a system with eight GPUs. With that, we can verify the performance gains and energy consumption reductions a Multi-GPU implementation provides as the grid input set changes.

Through the experiments, we demonstrate that the proposed Multi-GPU implementation can provide significant performance improvements over the Single-GPU version (e.g., 2.77 times using 4 GPUs). Moreover, the results indicate that more GPUs are associated with greater throughput, highlighting scalability as a critical aspect of optimizing performance in this application. We also show that the performance and efficiency of multi-GPU implementations are directly proportional to the size of the input grid. However, it is essential to highlight that for smaller input grids, the multi-GPU performance is degraded due to the cost of inter-GPU synchronization and data communication, characteristics inherent to these implementations.

The remainder of this paper is organized as follows. In Sect. 2 we describe the Fletcher model and list the Related Work. In Sect. 3, the proposed Multi-GPU implementation is discussed. The methodology followed during the experiments is described in Sect. 4. Performance and power demand results are discussed in Sect. 5 while the final considerations are drawn in Sect. 6.

2   Background and Related Work

2.1   Fletcher Modeling

Fletcher modeling works as a technique for simulating wave propagation over time. This propagation is expressed through the acoustic Eq. (1), where the velocity varies according to the specific geological layers (Eq. 2). Referring to the equations, $p(x, y, z, t)$ indicates the pressure at each location in the domain with respect to time, $V(x, y, z)$ is a representation of the propagation velocity, and $\rho(x, y, z)$ reflects the density [Fletcher et al., 2009].

$$\frac{1}{V^2}\frac{\partial^2 p}{\partial t^2} = \nabla^2 p \tag{1}$$

$$\frac{1}{V^2}\frac{\partial^2 p}{\partial t^2} = \nabla^2 p - \frac{\nabla \rho}{\rho} \cdot \nabla p \tag{2}$$

Seismic modeling initializes by collecting data in a seismic survey, as illustrated in (Fig. 1). The procedure begins with equipment attached to a ship, which at regular intervals emits seismic waves that reflect and refract in interactions with different environmental undergrounds, working as a sonar to map geological structures. When these waves return to the ocean's surface, specific sensors installed on cables towed by the ship capture and record seismic variations. These variations, a.k.a. seismic traces, correspond to the set of signals obtained by each sensor during the wave emission. Therefore, with each emission of waves, the seismic traces of all the microphones on the cable are recorded, providing an understandable overview of the subsoil. During this operation, the ship continues to move and emit signals periodically, thus producing a detailed image of the seabed and underground [Chu et al., 2011].

The Fletcher method models the acoustic wave propagation in a Tilted Transversely Isotropic (TTI) environment through a three-dimensional grid, in which the size of each dimension (x, y, and z) is defined by the variables sx, sy, and sz, respectively. Each point on this grid represents a point in the physical environment being modeled, and this point is associated with physical characteristics such as pressure, density, and wave velocity. In the case of TTI media, the wave velocity varies depending on the direction. That is, each point has an associated slope direction.

We illustrate the single-GPU implementation of the Fletcher method in the Algorithm 1. It requires as input the following parameters: the number of iterations the wave will propagate (*endTime*), a value that defines the period in which the state of the wave will be stored in the disk (*threshToWriteWave*), and the

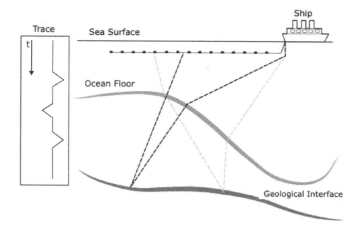

Fig. 1. Data collection in a marine seismic survey

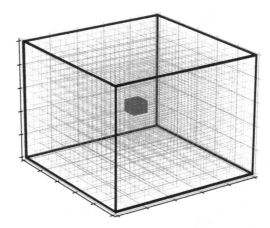

Fig. 2. The pressure point inserted (in red) at the center of the three-dimensional pressure vector. (Color figure online)

dimensions of the grid (*sx*, *sy*, and *sz*). The procedure starts by initializing the grid with the physical characteristics of the environment through the *initialize-Grid()* function. Initially, a pressure point that represents the amplitude of the seismic wave for a given instant is inserted at the central position of the three-dimensional pressure vector (Fig. 2). Then, before the kernel starts the execution on the GPU, this three-dimensional array is mapped to a one-dimensional array, following the traditional (*x*, *y and z*) order. This means that the points *x* of the same line are mapped contiguously in the one-dimensional vector resulting from the mapping.

Algorithm 1. Fletcher: Single-GPU Implementation

Input: *endTime*: number of iterations the wave will propagate.

      threshToWriteWave: number of iterations where the wave will be stored in disk.

      sx: size of dimension x.

      sy: size of dimension y.

      sz: size of dimension z.

 1: *initializeGrid(grid, sx, sy, sz)*

 2: *initPropagatePointers(grid, initPoint)*

 3: *allocateDataDevice()*

 4: *copyDataToDevice()*

 5: *calculateExecutionConfiguration(blocks, threadsPerBlock, sx, sy, sz).*

 6: **for** each *dt* in *endTime* **do**

 7:     *insertSourcePointToDevice()*

 8:     *kernelPropagate <<< blocks, threadsPerBlock >>> (...)*

 9:     *updatePointers()*

10:     **if** *dt == threshToWriteWave* **then**

11:       *writeWave()*

12:     **end if**

13: **end for**

The loop from line *6* to *13* is responsible for iterating until the simulation is performed. Then, for each iteration, a modulated Gaussian pulse representing the amplitude of the seismic wave at a given time instant is inserted in the center of the three-dimensional grid (*insertSourcePointToDevice()*). Then, the CUDA Kernel is launched for execution, which will propagate this pressure point in time. The propagation of the seismic wave is based on the computation of a 5-point stencil during the Kernel execution. Stencil computation is a technique that involves computing a center point based on reading neighboring points that are the results of previous kernel computation. This approach is widely used in parallel processing algorithms and [Pearson et al., 2020] image processing. During computation using the Stencil (Fig. 3) technique, there is no dependency between the calculations of individual points, which means that they can be computed independently and in parallel. This property makes processing highly parallelizable, allowing multiple points to be calculated simultaneously, speeding up execution [Pavan et al., 2019].

Once the point associated with the acoustic wave is computed, the wave state is propagated to the previous state to proceed with the next iteration. In this scenario, two buffers are used: *pp* (previous state) and *pc* (current state). The current state of the wave is moved to the *pp* buffer, which now becomes the previous state. At the same time, the newly calculated next state is stored in the *pc* buffer, which now becomes the current state. Furthermore, when the number of iterations reaches a defined threshold, the wave is written to the disk (*writeWave()*).

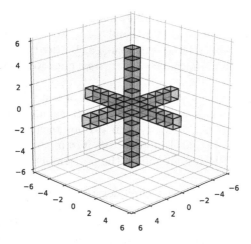

Fig. 3. 5-points 3D Stencil representation

In summary, for each time step, the pressure values at each grid point are updated based on the wave equation and the previous pressure, density, and wave velocity values of the point and its neighbors. To avoid artificial reflections from the border of the grid, which can interfere with the wave propagation characteristic, an absorption zone of 16 points is applied. The seismic waves are artificially damped in this region according to the distance from the inner grid. In this way, the closer to the border of the grid, within the absorption region, the greater the smoothing velocity at these points, so the velocity set at the border is zero.

2.2 Related Work

In this section, we list the works that exploit the parallelism of seismic applications. They are organized in chronological order.

[Liu et al.,2019] explore using GPUs to accelerate the Reverse Time Migration (RTM) algorithm. The parallelization scheme focuses on using two GPUs by employing a workload division strategy. The authors also consider a version that relies on the unified memory scheme available in CUDA. The results suggest that the workload division strategy presents better results than unified memory in a multi-GPU environment. Furthermore, the authors argue that computational efficiency grows linearly with the increase in GPUs. In contrast, our paper extends the scope to use Multi-GPU systems with up to eight GPUs, with a balanced workload distribution approach across all these components.

[Serpa and Mishra, 2022] address optimizing the Fletcher method on multi-core and single-GPU architectures focusing on portability. The paper analyzes the performance, energy consumption, and energy efficiency of two versions of the code, an original version and an optimized version for OpenMP, OpenACC, and CUDA. The results indicate that the CUDA version has the best performance and energy efficiency among all evaluated versions. While it focuses on multicore architectures and single-GPU only, our work focuses on Multi-GPU architectures and addresses related topics such as border exchange between algorithm iterations and the performance and energy improvements as the grid size increases.

[Liu et al., 2012] discuss the implementation of the GPU-accelerated RTM algorithm. It also addresses specific issues such as uneven topography and anisotropic environment, i.e., it focuses on various technical aspects of implementing GPU-accelerated RTM. Different from it, our work focuses on the implementation of a Multi-GPU system and on the performance and energy efficiency results.

[Pearson et al., 2020] explore techniques to improve 3D stencil communication on heterogeneous supercomputers using strategies such as hierarchical partitioning and optimization of data exchange between GPUs. Through tests on up to 256 nodes, the authors demonstrate the efficiency of these techniques in improving communication and reducing data exchange time. On the other hand, our work uses concepts of stencil communication to implement Fletcher's method of propagating seismic waves in a Multi-GPU environment in CUDA, exploring aspects such as performance and energy efficiency.

[Okamoto et al., 2010] describe how the use of multiple GPUs can significantly speed up simulations of seismic wave propagation. A particular challenge faced when using multiple GPUs is non-contiguous memory alignment in the overlapping regions between subdomains processed by different GPUs. This can lead to delays in data transfer between the device and the host node. Differently, in our work, we address this scenario and show that with the increase in the grid input size, there is a proportional increase in the synchronization time between the subdomains processed by different GPUs.

3   Multi-GPU Implementation of Fletcher

Given the Single-GPU implementation of the Fletcher method described in Sect. 2, we discuss next the modifications we have done for the Multi-GPU version. Because proper workload distribution and memory management across many GPUs are key performance aspects in Multi-GPU environments, we consider a workload division that can take advantage of (i) the intrinsic parallelism available in the calculation of each grid point; (ii) the memory management between the GPUs; and (iii) the data locality aspect [Padoin et al., 2013].

For the workload distribution, we consider the division of the z-axis among all GPUs, as illustrated in Fig. 4 for the distribution across 4 GPUs. This partitioning divides the three-dimensional grid into subdomains in the z-axis direction, and each of these subdomains is assigned to a specific GPU for processing. The outcome of this strategy is an even distribution of the workload across the available GPUs. This strategy aims to optimize the data locality since the execution of the CUDA kernel is based on the computation of a 5-point Stencil (Fig. 3). Hence, when mapping the three-dimensional grid to a one-dimensional grid in

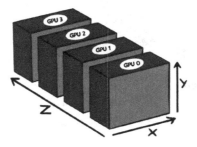

Fig. 4. Workload distribution strategy along z-axis across 4 GPUs

the traditional way (x, y, z), it is essential to note that the neighboring addresses along the x and y axes will be closer in memory than the neighboring points along the z-axis. In this scenario, assigning a continuous block in the z-axis direction to each GPU can increase memory locality on L1 and L2 GPU caches, reducing the need for slower global memory accesses.

Moreover, we explore memory coalescence because GPUs are designed to be more efficient when threads of the same warp access data stored in contiguous memory addresses. Hence, decreasing the distance between the points ensures that memory data access will happen more cohesively. This allows GPU memory reads and writes to be combined into fewer memory transactions, resulting in a more efficient use of memory bandwidth. However, although there is immediate parallelism during kernel execution, it is worth mentioning that each call to the CUDA kernel advances the solution by a single dt time step. Hence, to propagate the wave by several time steps, the kernel needs to be iterated, and between these iterations, we must ensure the exchange of information between the different GPUs. This communication occurs through synchronizing and updating variables in the border regions of the computing domain.

For the 5-point Stencil computation, the edges represent intersection zones of the three-dimensional grid data mapped to the GPUs used for processing. These borders are needed to synchronize data across all GPUs, ensuring the correct reading of data throughout the execution of the CUDA kernel. Hence, computing the Stencil requires that each subdomain, present on each GPU, have a 5-point border in the z dimension for each intersection point with the subdomain of other GPUs. Therefore, after the kernel execution, it is necessary to exchange the upper and lower borders across the neighbors' GPUs to propagate the updated data to the next iteration of wave propagation. During this exchange operation, $cudaMemCpyDeviceToDevice$ was used to assess the impact of the border exchange considering an indirect communication. When using this function, the communication always passes through the Host.

Moreover, the workload distribution along the z-axis also provides benefits in reducing the number of operations performed only to exchange borders through GPUs. Although it is not possible to eliminate all communications, this strategy minimizes the need for inter-GPU communication because threads on each GPU

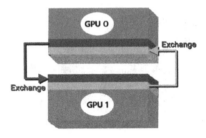

Fig. 5. Border exchange across GPUs along the z-axis.

can process their grid points independently without synchronizing and updating data from other GPUs. In addition, the cost associated with border synchronization reduces since this overhead increases with the growth of the grid size (Fig. 5).

4   Methodology

The experiments were performed on a *p3.16xlarge* AWS instance (Table 1), which is equipped with 64 Intel Xeon E5-2686 v4 (Broadwell) VCPUs, each supporting two threads per core, resulting in a total of 128 available execution threads. In addition, the instance has 8 NVIDIA Tesla V100-SXM2 16Gb GPUs and offers 488 GiB of RAM. Also, the following versions were used: CUDA v.12.0, NVIDIA driver 525.85.12, and gcc 9.4.0 with the −O3 optimization flag.

Table 1. Specifications of the Architecture

Processor Specification	
Processor	Intel Xeon E5-2686 v4
Architecture	Broadwell
Processor/GPU	Intel(R) Xeon(R) CPU E5-2686 v4 @ 2.30 GHz, 64 VCPUs
Memory	1 MiB L1d, 1 MiB L1i, 8 MiB L2, 90 MiB L3
GPU Specifications	
GPU	NVIDIA Tesla V100-SXM2
Architecture	Volta
Processor/GPU	GV100
Registers	256 KB/SM, 20480 KB/GPU
Memory	4096-bit HBM2, 16 GB, 6144 KB L2 Cache

We have considered twenty-nine different input grid sizes for the Fletcher method: ranging from 88 to 984 (the maximum size we could allocate in the architecture), in intervals of 32. We have chosen to use 3D input vectors with a dimension multiple of 32 to match the size of the CUDA warps. In this scenario, the following versions were implemented and tested: Single-GPU, 2-GPUs, 4-GPUs, and 8-GPUs, indicating the number of used GPUs.

We compare the Single and Multi-GPU versions regarding performance and energy consumption. The performance is represented by the number of samples computed per second (MSamples/s). We collected the energy consumption via the NVIDIA-SMI command line tool provided by NVIDIA. The results presented in the next section are the average of 10 runs with a 95% confidence interval based on the *Student's t* distribution. In addition, each graph identifies the confidence intervals of the results for each problem size and GPU version.

5   Results

In this section, we present, analyze, and discuss the results obtained from the experiments. First, we discuss the performance of the Multi-GPU implementation of the Fletcher method for 1, 2, 4, and 8 GPUs. The energy efficiency is analyzed, comparing the average power demand (in Watts) of the GPU during the iteration of the CUDA kernel with the performance (in MSamples/s) to assess the energy efficiency of the application.

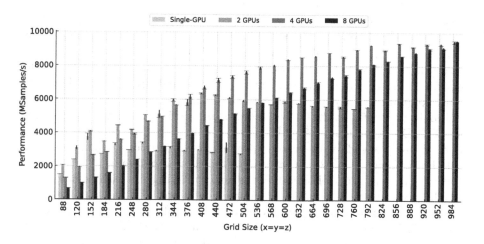

Fig. 6. Performance results for each grid size and implementation. The higher the bar, the better the performance.

Figure 6 shows the performance results for the entire experiment set. It is worth mentioning that the grid set computed on the Single-GPU and 2-GPUs versions is limited by the GPU VRAM, which in this case is 16Gb per Device (NVIDIA Tesla V100-SXM2). Therefore, the first observation is that the Multi-GPU implementation of Fletcher allows the execution of larger grid sizes, improving the capability and quality of seismic images generated through higher data density incorporated into the final result.

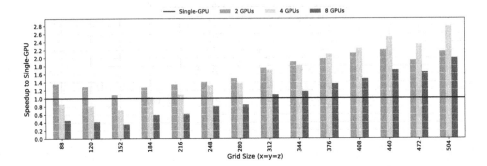

Fig. 7. Performance Speedup over Single-GPU implementation.

By analyzing the behavior of Fig. 7, one can highlight that the performance grows along with the increase in the grid size, allowing the user to increase application throughput. As an example, for a grid size equal to 504, the maximum speedup of 2.77 is achieved over the Single-GPU with 4 GPUs. Moreover, by using 2 GPUs, we observed a speedup over the Single-GPU greater than 2 for grid sizes 376 and larger, indicating efficient scalability for this configuration. However, when increasing the number of GPUs to eight, we could not obtain proportional gains to this increase in computational capacity because of the cost of inter-GPU communication. That is, with a small grid size, parallelism in Kernel computation is not exploited to the maximum, and the cost of border synchronization between the GPU is more significant in relation to the execution time of CUDA kernel computing. Therefore, we argue that the effectiveness of an 8-GPU strategy would require a larger problem, where the cost of communication would have a smaller impact in relation to the throughput gain.

This statement is corroborated by the analysis of Fig. 6, which demonstrates that the performance of multi-GPU implementations exhibits a positive linear trend with increasing input grid size. This implies that the effectiveness of Multi-GPU computing amplifies proportionally to the scale of the problem. Thus, its performance becomes especially notable for large-scale computational tasks, where the ratio between the cost of inter-GPU communication and Kernel CUDA computation is optimized. Additionally, the use of 2 GPUs reaches its Performance peak for input grid sizes close to 408. Afterward, a slight decrease in performance is observed as the grid size increases, until GPU memory capacity (VRAM) limits computation, which it does for input sizes greater than 792.

Figure 8 illustrates the maximum power achieved while running the CUDA kernel for different versions and grid input sizes. The maximum power increases as the number of GPUs also increase. The Single-GPU approach consistently

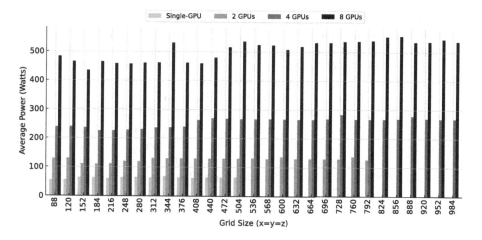

Fig. 8. Maximum Power dissipation for each version and grid input set.

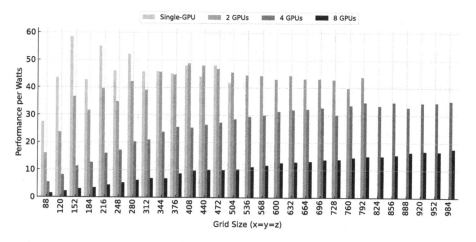

Fig. 9. Performance per Watts comparison

presents the lowest power across all problem sizes. This increase in maximum power with the use of more GPUs is expected, as more processing units mean more power dissipated. However, it is important to highlight that an increase in power does not always translate into a proportional increase in performance, highlighting the importance of considering energy efficiency when analyzing and optimizing applications for multi-GPU systems, aiming to achieve the best balance between performance and power consumption.

Extending the analysis through the data of the average power consumed during the execution of the CUDA kernel. Figure 9 shows that the single-GPU implementation has high efficiency for small input grid sizes. This is due to the fact that there is no cost of inter-GPU edge synchronization and also the fact that computing power does not become a performance limiting factor for these input sizes, due to the reduced scale of the grid Furthermore, we confirmed the low power efficiency of multi-GPU implementations for lower problem sizes. This is because the cost of inter-GPU synchronization and data communication inherent in such implementations results in unnecessarily high power consumption for issues that could be efficiently managed by a single GPU.

Furthermore, the energy efficiency of multi-GPU grows linearly with the size of the input grid. This indicates that to achieve high efficiency with multi-GPU, a large input set is needed, in order to ensure that throughput inherent to the multi-GPU implementation significantly outweighs the cost associated with data synchronization. This reinforces the idea that the best performance between single-GPU and multi-GPU implementations depends on factors such as the input grid and the complexity of modeling wave and medium characteristics.

6   Conclusions and Future Work

In this work, we have explored the implementation of Fletcher's multi-GPU method and compared it with the single-GPU approach. This implementation provided an innovative technical analysis for seismic applications using Multi-GPU systems with NVIDIA Tesla V100. Therefore, we studied the variations in performance and energy efficiency according to the variation in the size of the input grid. The presented results reinforce the importance of choosing the appropriate implementation method, given the size of the grid and the complexity of the modeled problem to be treated.

The results indicate that the multi-GPU implementation offers greater scalability, allowing the handling of larger input sets. However, it should be noted that for smaller input grids, multi-GPU performance is degraded due to the cost associated with inter-GPU edge synchronization. We have found that the performance of multi-GPU implementations is directly proportional to the input grid size, reaching peak efficiency and performance, with a Speedup of 2.77 when employing 2 GPUs for grid sizes around 408. However, within the dataset analyzed, the configuration with 8 GPUs did not generate gains proportional to the increase in the available computational load, being more suitable for problems with a larger grid dimension, where the cost of inter-GPU communication is small concerning the throughput provided. In future work, we intend to reduce the cost of inter-GPU communication by implementing a direct approach, which incorporates peer-to-peer (P2P) communication and the use of NVIDIA's NVLINK technology.

Acknowledgment. This work has been partially supported by Petrobras under number 2020/00182-5, by the call CNPq/MCTI/FNDCT - Universal 18/2021 under grants 406182/2021-3, and by the Coordenação de Aperfeioamento de Pessoal de Nível Superior - Brazil (CAPES) - Finance Code 001.

References

Chu, C., Macy, B.K., Anno, P.D.: Approximation of pure acoustic seismic wave propagation in TTI media. Geophysics **76**(5), WB97–WB107 (2011)

Fletcher, R.P., Du, X., Fowler, P.J.: Reverse time migration in tilted transversely isotropic (TTI) media. Geophysics **74**(6), WCA179–WCA187 (2009)

Liu, G.-F., Meng, X.-H., Yu, Z.-J., Liu, D.-J.: An efficient scheme for multi-GPU TTI reverse time migration. Appl. Geophys. **16**(1), 56–63 (2019)

Liu, H., Li, B., Liu, H., Tong, X., Liu, Q., Wang, X., Liu, W.: The issues of prestack reverse time migration and solutions with graphic processing unit implementation. Geophys. Prospect. **60**(5), 906–918 (2012)

Lorenzon, A.F., Beck Filho, A.C.S.: Parallel computing hits the power wall: principles, challenges, and a survey of solutions. Springer Nature (2019)

Lukawski, M.Z., et al.: Cost analysis of oil, gas, and geothermal well drilling. J. Petrol. Sci. Eng. **118**, 1–14 (2014)

Navaux, P.O.A., Lorenzon, A.F., da Silva Serpa, M.: Challenges in high-performance computing. J. Braz. Comput. Soc. **29**(1), 51–62 (2023)

Okamoto, T., Takenaka, H., Nakamura, T., Aoki, T.: Accelerating large-scale simulation of seismic wave propagation by multi-GPUS and three-dimensional domain decomposition. Earth Planets Space **62**(12), 939–942 (2010)

Padoin, E.L., Pilla, L.L., Boito, F.Z., Kassick, R.V., Velho, P., Navaux, P.O.: Evaluating application performance and energy consumption on hybrid CPU+ GPU architecture. Clust. Comput. **16**, 511–525 (2013)

Papadrakakis, M., Stavroulakis, G., Karatarakis, A.: A new era in scientific computing: Domain decomposition methods in hybrid cpu-gpu architectures. Comput. Methods Appl. Mech. Eng. **200**(13), 1490–1508 (2011)

Pavan, Pablo J.., Serpa, Matheus S.., Carreño, Emmanuell Diaz, Martínez, Víctor., Padoin, Edson Luiz, Navaux, Philippe O. A.., Panetta, Jairo, Mehaut, Jean-François.: Improving Performance and Energy Efficiency of Geophysics Applications on GPU Architectures. In: Meneses, Esteban, Castro, Harold, Barrios Hernández, Carlos Jaime, Ramos-Pollan, Raul (eds.) High Performance Computing: 5th Latin American Conference, CARLA 2018, Bucaramanga, Colombia, September 26–28, 2018, Revised Selected Papers, pp. 112–122. Springer International Publishing, Cham (2019). https://doi.org/10.1007/978-3-030-16205-4_9

Pearson, C., Hidayetoğlu, M., Almasri, M., Anjum, O., Chung, I.-H., Xiong, J., Hwu, W.-M.W.: Node-aware stencil communication for heterogeneous supercomputers. In: 2020 IEEE International Parallel and Distributed Processing Symposium Workshops (IPDPSW), pp. 796–805. IEEE (2020)

Serpa, M., Mishra, P.: Performance evaluation and enhancement of the fletcher method on multicore architectures (2022)

What Does a Nation-Wide Digital Nervous System Use for an Operating System?

Nicolás Erdödy[1]([✉]), Richard O'Keefe[2], and Ian Yule[3]

[1] Open Parallel Ltd., Oamaru, New Zealand
nicolas.erdody@openparallel.com
[2] Open Parallel Ltd., Dunedin, New Zealand
[3] Stoneleigh Consulting, Tauranga, New Zealand

Abstract. Concerns over climate change and sustainable agriculture have made nation-wide high resolution environment monitoring and modelling desirable. Recent developments in technology have made it affordable. An environment modelling network is a supercomputer, but not of a familiar kind. Conventional supercomputing approaches are appropriate for the modelling aspect, but not the monitoring aspect. While sensor networks are familiar in the Internet of Things (IoT), geographically remote sensors without access to mains power have harsher resource constraints than, say, internet-ready light bulbs. A "two-realm" approach to system software is needed.

Keywords: Operating System · Sensor Network · Messaging · AI · Edge Computing · km-scale Simulations

1 Introduction

Like most nations worldwide, New Zealand is highly dependent on its primary sector. Land is a diminishing resource, and we must make better use of it and take better care of it. The dual needs of sustainability and economic exploitation are not symbiotic, at least in the short term, so we need to develop much more informed methods of management which will ensure that we can preserve and improve our environment while improving our economic exploitation of the land. But biology is complicated, variable, riddled with uncertainty, and highly integrated. It is difficult to be cognisant of all of the moving parts and it is very difficult to predict beyond the most immediate time period.

Operational response lies mostly with individual producers, while governments have responsibility for creating the right conditions for sustainable economic exploitation. The complexity draws comparison to a nervous system which responds to continuous and varied inputs to maintain health. One of the key components of a nervous system is continuous sensory input. One of the problems the primary sector has even in a nation-wide context is that often the sensory mechanisms become compromised, communication can become discontinuous and input to decision making numbed.

Many of the crops and production systems used around the world are similar therefore there is further utility in linking up with international partners. We have a truly global

C. J. Barrios H. et al. (Eds.): CARLA 2023, CCIS 1887, pp. 160–169, 2024.
https://doi.org/10.1007/978-3-031-52186-7_11

food supply industry. If we look at crops like apples or avocados we can see that they are distributed around the world, but we can also see the importance of countries like Mexico to global supply (Mexico exported 50x more avocados than New Zealand[1] in 2021) [21]. One example would be the fight against pests and diseases, newer Deep Learning and AI models are being used to detect defects and diagnose pest and disease problems, these models need to be trained with comprehensive and reliable data sets. These data sets could be created overseas before the problem occurs in a specific country. This type of wider diagnosis and cooperation would only work if the nervous system within each body (country) was functional and data interoperable. Thus, this multilevel or layering of decision making makes the need for integration of information flow to support decision making even more critical.

2   Background

There is an acknowledged yield gap in pretty much every growing system, that is the difference between what is biologically possible and what is actually achieved. It is suggested by the authors that it is because of non decisions, incomplete, or late decisions rather than wrong decisions. Which would point to the fact that the necessary information is not getting to the correct place to make decisions at the right time. It may be that preventative measures to yield limiting conditions were not taken or were taken too late and the damage was done. Having better information in the field to rapidly inform the grower is vital, this can be achieved by having adequate and continuous sensing of the crop and a nervous system capable of transmitting the information to the neural hub of the system.

We will discuss in this position paper that the amount of data and information required to make decisions in a complex environment involving e.g. weather forecast, climate variation, environment modification, and biology integrations requires a significant amount of processing capabilities -both distributed and centralised, fitting the definition of a supercomputer [22] -albeit not in the traditional way.

How much sensing is needed for weather/climate sensing?

Simulations and forecasts are too often based on incomplete data and assumptions and extrapolations are common, even if satellites are covering more and more areas. A sub-kilometre scale is presented in the Concept Paper for the Berlin Summit for EVE (Earth Visualization Engines) held in July 2023. [23] It says: "The demand for km-scale simulations is rooted in the global need for local information, at greater fidelity, both to advance scientific understanding as well as to link to impacts and better integrate local knowledge, including observations" [24].

The same paper gives some context for our approach: "The need to integrate local knowledge, sample uncertainty through complementary efforts, maintain access to a truly global talent pool, and establish global legitimacy, can likely only be met through regional or super-regional facilities [25] for instance, a lack of open observations throughout the Global South is crucial to fill" [26].

---

[1] Perú exported 22x more than New Zealand in 2021, and Chile and Colombia ~ 4x more each. But models tested and used in one country could be replicated in another if they are scalable and modular.

3   The Supercomputer

The supercomputer we are concerned with has not been built yet. It has not been funded yet. But some day soon we shall build it, because we'll have to.

There are about 250,000 nodes[2]. Each node contains 4 cores. The cores are 32-bit processors, running at 120 to 260 MHz depending on the model. At peak, a node draws about 0.45 A (two CPU packages + radio or camera) at 3.7 V, so the peak power demand is 0.42 MW. This is unambiguously a supercomputer.

Given the term "supercomputer", you have imagined a room, possibly a very large room, filled with racks and cables. There are no racks, no cables, and no room. What you must now imagine is the nodes moving apart, until they average about 1 km apart. That 0.42 MW peak power? It has to be supplied by batteries, which means that all these nodes have to spend most of their time powered almost completely down.

4   What is Such a Weird Machine for?

This is part of a long-term project called "Listen to the Land" (L2L), which envisages New Zealand (or a country with similar land area e.g. Ecuador) covered by a network of environmental sensors for climate monitoring and agriculture and forestry support. What's described here is just the weather/climate-sensing part. Given the scale of the task we want to start by describing a system that can be designed and built modularly[3].

Weather is patchy. Climate change is expected to be non-uniform. If you want to know how to react to climate change, you have an ethical duty to find out how the weather really is changing, not how your models tell you it ought to be changing. The traditional approach of "operating over a hundred [WMO quality] Electronic Weather Stations in [the] National Climate network" [1] cannot provide the fine-grained "ground truth" that a digital nervous system can. Nor can weather satellites provide the continuous coverage L2L can.

Think of a nervous system with sensory data flowing from skin to brain, integration in the brain, and responses floating from brain to muscles.

5   The Six-Layer Architecture

The diagram (Fig. 1) shows a distributed system with six layers. The ground layer is the physical ground. The land area of New Zealand is 264 537 km^2 [2], making it comparable to the United Kingdom at 241 930 km^2 [3] or Ecuador at 256,370 km^2 [4]. A recent article (2022) in Nature Climate Change [5] argues that climate models need 1 km resolution, so our current design calls for a similar resolution in ground truth data from sensor nodes.

The six layers involve:

---

[2] Based on New Zealand's land area.

[3] We are establishing a collaboration with the Sage project (Northwestern University, US), a novel cyberinfrastructure created also to exploit dramatic improvements in AI to build a continent-spanning network of smart sensors [26].

1) The sensor nodes have four 32-bit microcontroller cores performing specialised tasks: one to manage a camera or cameras (for cloud cover, global illuminance, frost and dew, and precipitation), one to manage encryption and the radio, one to collect temperature, pressure, humidity, and wind data and to do overall system management, and one to do compression, modelling, and forecasting. There will be on the order of 250,000

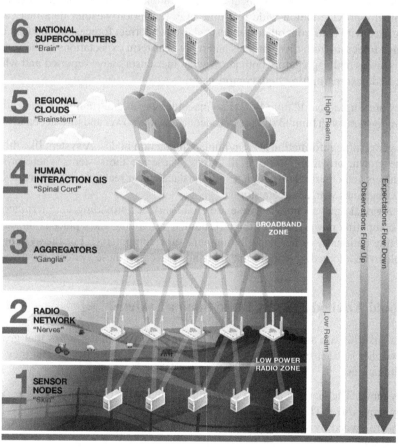

Fig. 1. A distributed system with six layers.

of these. Each node has about 1MB of ROM, about 1MB of RAM, and 2–8 MB of flash. Except for lacking MMUs and FPUs, these machines are much more powerful than those UNIX was designed for, and could run a fair approximation of Unix V7. There are no mass stores for virtual memory, and memory protection will be done by static analysis. Integer arithmetic is adequate for what the sensor nodes do. FPUs and MMUs would just increase price and current drain. "Operating system" services will be device drivers, scheduling, and communication stack.

2) The sensor nodes communicate with aggregators through a mesh network. That network is mostly the sensor nodes, filled out with communication nodes which have two 32-bit microcontroller cores: one to manage the radio and one for system management. How many are needed depends on the range of the radios in the sensor nodes, which will change over time. They are very similar to the sensor nodes but trade cameras for better radios.

3) The aggregators are unattended computers which receive observations from the sensor nodes, communicate with local data integration and modelling centres, which eventually provide nation-wide real-time high-resolution weather data that can be integrated with data from other sources and used to correct forecasting models. They receive forecasts from those models and relay near-term expectations to the sensors. The sensors and aggregators both know what the sensors have reported and what is expected next, permitting high compression.

They are single-board/"mini PC" class machines capable of running a conventional operating system, with limited storage but adequate mains power and internet bandwidth.

4) The geographic information system/human interaction nodes. A system like this has to be grown, providing value at all stages. These are the systems where primary producers and others can see high resolution data in near real time. These are desktop class machines with adequate storage.

5) The regional analysis nodes. These are cloud services providing long term storage and computing power. Most of the L2L number crunching takes place at this level.

6) Existing national weather and environment supercomputer(s). For the system as a whole to be adopted, the additional demands placed on these systems must be kept low.

6   Would Anybody Really Build Such a System?

Weather satellites are amazing, wonderful machines. They can do things that ground-based weather stations cannot do. And we need them to do those things. But they have some limitations.

- They move. The viewing angle is constantly changing.
- They move *away*. There isn't always a satellite overhead.
- They are owned by someone else. They show us whatever the owners decide they should show us.
- They are extremely expensive.
- If anything goes wrong, you can't send someone around with a van and a couple of spares.

Satellite estimates of things like precipitation are qualitatively good, but their quantitative agreement with ground truth has room for improvement. The same is true of rain radars, which trade wide coverage for reduced accuracy [6].

A review in 2017 found that access to weather data in New Zealand is more expensive than in many other countries. Indeed, many New Zealand farmers get their weather data from Norway (e.g., https://www.yr.no/nb/v) which is one of the most open countries. We estimate that the sensor and communicator nodes can be built for about USD 65 each. USD 18 million sounds like a lot of money for a network of tiny autonomous weather stations, but it is 38 times cheaper than launching our own weather satellite would be[4]. Each node will be available, providing data around the clock, easy to reach and cheap to replace.

It's not just New Zealand that has a use for such a network. Any nation or region that is seriously concerned about whether and how the climate is changing and what to do about it needs a good grasp on what is actually happening, and there is no substitute for actual measurement.

With hindsight, this nation-wide digital nervous system is an obvious answer to the needs of climate monitoring, precision agriculture and potentially earthquake prediction[5]. It is only within the last few years that it has become feasible to build sensor nodes cheap enough yet capable enough to be useful. This needed advances in microcontrollers, low power radio communication, and sensor technology. If we don't build such a system, someone else will. The issues for operating systems will remain.

7 Two Realms

Many people are working on Internet of Things/Edge Computing, and one would expect that this would be a solved problem. For example, one might turn to the Linux Foundation Edge consortium [7]. There [8] we read that "eKuiper is an edge lightweight IoT data analytics / streaming software implemented by Golang, and it can be run on all kinds of resource-constrained edge devices." Promising, very promising. "Features: Lightweight, Core service package is only about 4.5 M, initial memory footprint is 10 MB". 10 MB? That's not lightweight, that's huge! What happened to "can be run on resource-constrained devices"?

The six layer architecture divides into two realms, with one of the layers on the border between them. The "low realm" (layers 1 and 2 and in some ways 3) is very different from the "high realm" (layers 4–6 and in some ways 3). A lot of "edge" computing is actually pretty far from the edge. A device in a building with access to mains power, is living in the high realm, a very different world from the low realm where a device that's outside, nailed to a fencepost in a remote area, desperately trying to save battery power lives. The analogue of "edge" computing in L2L is the aggregators.

---

[4] USD 290 million for the satellite, USD 400 million for the launch, according to https://science.howstuffworks.com/satellite10.htm.

[5] "Movement along the Alpine Fault (in New Zealand), with its powerful uplift along the Southern Alps over millions of years, forms the geological foundations for our beautiful South Island and the stunning landscape we call home. The more we understand our natural environment and the forces that shape it, the better prepared we can be".[27].

A. Electrical power

High realm: mains power or own generator. Reducing energy use helps to keep prices down. Low realm: batteries + small solar panels. Keep energy use way down or it doesn't work at all.

B. Flexibility and maintainability

High realm: the computer should be able to do many things and be able to switch between them. Software changes fast. Patches are installed often. Low realm: the node has a fixed set of tasks, which changes very seldom. It makes economic sense to use formal methods such as SPARK/Ada [9] [10] and FRAMA-C [11] [12] to ensure that arithmetic errors, pointer errors, stack overflows, and scheduling errors will not occur.

Over-the-Air updates should be rare, but bugs happen. The software that runs in the sensor nodes must be structured so that updates are more like hot-loading a replacement module in an Erlang [13] program (which keeps right on running) than stopping a process and starting a new one in Unix. Updates must, in short, be small so that they can be transmitted and acted on without interruption to normal service.

C. Heterogeneity

Within a sensor node, each core has a different task. There is no particular benefit in all the cores having the same hardware architecture. Limited memory means that each core should store only the drivers for the devices attached to it and only the software (such as network stack, image processing, modelling, compression or whatever) relevant to its task. It also means that memory should be managed no later than system build time. This leaves mainly scheduling and core-to-core communication for a "common OS" to do.

The aggregators will be just sufficiently powerful single board computers, and it is here that we might expect to see synergy with Linux Foundation Edge. Fledge [14] in particular, with its focus on integrating and processing sensor data and forwarding the results to various destinations, looks attractive. EVE [15] on the other hand, with its support for "Docker containers, Kubernetes clusters and virtual machines", is over-engineered for the needs of this layer. In this layer there will be tens of thousands of nodes, so keeping price and power consumption down are still issues. This means just enough computer, and just enough operating system, to do the aggregation and forwarding job. As a nation-wide system will not be built all at once, and as it will need incremental maintenance/replacement, we must expect a mix of different hardware architectures and different capabilities.

The human interface layer takes us from grass [16] to GRASS [17]. For these systems unmodified Linux, macOS, and Windows are perfectly adequate. These devices will typically be owned by the people who use them.

Layers 5 and 6 are already familiar to the audience.

If there is no one kernel running at all levels that can be pointed to as "the OS", what can we mean when we talk about "an OS for a nation-wide supercomputer"?

The answer is that the systems are unified by their common task so that the collection of modules and services that enable the nodes to collaborate in their shared task is "the OS". A large part of this is communication support.

D. Communication is costly

Operating the radio is a major power drain for a sensor node. In a mesh where some of the nodes act as intermediaries between aggregators and other sensor nodes that are out of range, those intermediaries cannot afford to keep their receivers on at all times in case some neighbour has something to say. Most communication needs to be on a schedule where the radios are on at known times just enough to communicate. This means that keeping the sensor nodes associated with an aggregator tolerably well synchronised with it and each other is important for power economy. It is also useful because clock drift can be a sign of other problems.

Communication between aggregators and the geographical information layer is also difficult. Not depending on mobile phone networks or high-speed broadband is important -not even fully developed countries have homogeneous broadband coverage within their boundaries, and then you have to consider all the geographic variables (mountains, lakes, jungle, etc.). Once again, communicating on a regular schedule, using compression to keep data volumes down, and keeping software updates small and rare are important.

As we climb to higher layers, more, and more affordable, communication bandwidth is available, but greater volumes of data need to be transmitted. The two-way flow of information, with expectations flowing down and observations flowing up, means that only the surprise in the observations (the differences between what is observed and what is expected) need to be forwarded, not the raw observations.

Even messaging is heterogeneous however. AMQP [18] is well suited for the aggregators on up, using an implementation such as RabbitMQ. Communication is so costly and the sensor nodes so constrained that specialised, special-purpose lightweight protocols are needed at that level.

E. Failure

Suppose the sensor nodes are so well built that the probability that a specific one fails on any given day is $1/3653^6$. Then on any given day, out of 250,000 nodes, 68 ± 8 will fail. These failures will be scattered all over the nation, and it will be impractical to fix them all on the same day. This is going to happen to any large scale sensor network. The data that a failed node would have reported is irretrievably lost. However, for an isolated failure, an aggregator may be able to "fill in" estimated data using geostatistical [19] techniques such as kriging. (You would be astonished at how much on- the-ground weather data is estimated.) The good news is that with multiple sensors (such as temperature at worm height, at sheep height, at cow height, and at head height) failure will often be partial, so some data may be available from a "failed" node.

Data reported up-level from an aggregator needs to be tagged according to its reliability: actual measurements, corrected measurements (allowing for drift), or estimates.

Planning the process of repairing or replacing failed nodes is a well understood operations management task.

F. Ownership and authentication

---

[6] 1 in 10 years.

A typical supercomputer is owned by a single organisation. We expect the layer 1–4 devices to be owned by the individuals or organisations whose land they report on.

For a pure weather system, privacy is not much of an issue. We intend the system to be extended with sensors to "taste" the soil and watercourses for things like biologically available nitrogen and phosphorus (in New Zealand we should add selenium [20]). This could have legal and commercial consequences. It is always important to know that the data being built into our models is the real data. Even sensor nodes must do good encryption.

A sensor node needs to know its orientation (which way is down = 3-axis accelerometer, which way is North = 3-axis magnetometer) in order to calculate sunrise, sunset, moonrise, moonset, moon phase in order to predict illumination.

Fortunately, changes in orientation suggest either failure in electronics or someone moving the device, both of which are signs of unreliable data: a sensor which is no longer where it was supposed to be is no longer an authentic source of information about that place.

8 Summary

The operating system for a nation-wide supercomputer is a set of modules (such as conventional operating systems) and services communicating through messaging protocols that authenticate identity and location of sensors, respect rights to data, and ensure that quality-tagged reliable data are passed around while staying within resource limits. This requires machine learning and AI at the edge to cope with failure as well as to exploit success. A "two-realm" approach to system software is presented to start with the sensing capabilities and move up to the processing capabilities establishing the proposed architecture.

References

1. National Institute of Water and Air Instruments. https://niwa.co.nz/our-services/instruments/instrumentsystems/products/climate-stations, (Accessed 08 2022)
2. CIA World Factbook, 2022, entry New Zealand. https://www.cia.gov/the-world-factbook/countries/new-zealand/#geography, (Accessed 08 2022)
3. CIA World Factbook, 2022, entry United Kingdom. https://www.cia.gov/the-world-factbook/countries/united-kingdom/#geography, (Accessed 08 2022)
4. Cancillería de Ecuador (2023). https://www.cancilleria.gob.ec/bolivia/wp-content/uploads/sites/22/2021/07/ECUADOR.pdf, (Accessed 07 2022)
5. Slingo, J., et al.: Ambitious partnership needed for reliable climate prediction. Nat. Climate Change **12** (2022)
6. Schleiss, M., et al.: The accuracy of weather radar in heavy rain: a comparative study for Denmark. Hydrol. Earth Syst. Sci. **24**(6) (2020). https://hess.copernicus.org/articles/24/3157/2020/
7. Linux Foundation Edge home page. https://www.lfedge.org, (Accessed 08 2022)
8. Linux Foundation Edge "eKuiper project". https://www.lfedge.org/projects/ekuiper, (Accessed 08 2022)
9. Barnes, J.: SPARK: The Proven Approach to High Integrity Software. Altran Praxis (2012)

10. McCormick, J.W., Chapin, P.C.: Building High Integrity Applications with SPARK 2014. Cambridge University Press (2015)
11. Baudin, P., et al.: The dogged pursuit of bug-free C programs: the Frama-C software analysis platform. Commun. ACM **64**(8) (2021)
12. Kirchner, F., Kosmatov, N., Prevosto, V., Signoles, J., Yakobowski, B.: Frama-C, A software analysis. Perspect. Formal Aspects Comput. **27**(3) (2015)
13. Armstrong, J.: Programming Erlang: Software for a Concurrent World. 2nd edn. Pragmatic Programmers (2013)
14. Linux Foundation Edge Fledge project. https://www.lfedge.org/projects/fledge/, (Accessed 08 2022)
15. Linux Foundation Edge EVE project. https://www.lfedge.org/projects/eve, (Accessed 08 2022)
16. Champion, P.D., James, T., Popay, I., Ford, K.: An Illustrated Guide to Common Grasses. The New Zealand Plant Protection Society, Sedges and Rushes of New Zealand (2012)
17. Neteler, M., Mitasova, H. (eds.): Open Source GIS. Springer US, Boston, MA (2008). https://doi.org/10.1007/978-0-387-68574-8
18. OASIS, Advanced Message Queuing Protocol (AMQP) Version 1.0 (2012). http://docs.oasis-open.org/amqp/core/v1.0/amqp-core-complete-v1.0.pdf
19. Kitanidis, P.K.: Introduction to Geostatistics: Applications in Hydro-geology. Cambridge University Press (1997)
20. Gupta, U.C., Gupta, S.C.: Selenium in soils and crops, its deficiencies in livestock and humans: Implications for management. Commun. Soil Sci. Plant Anal. **31**(11–14), 1791–1807 (2008)
21. World Bank - World Integrated Trade Solution: Avocados, fresh or dried exports by country in 2021. http://wits.worldbank.org/trade/comtrade/en/country/ALL/year/2021/tradeflow/Exports/partner/WLD/product/080440, (Accessed 07 2023)
22. Supercomputing. https://www.ibm.com/topics/supercomputing, (Accessed 07 2023)
23. Conveners of the Berlin Summit for EVE (Earth Visualization Engines) (June 5 2023). https://owncloud.gwdg.de/index.php/s/rNWYNJSdJ19iwbJ, (Accessed 07 2023)
24. Ibid. Pg.8
25. Ibid. Pg.9
26. Ibid. Pg.15
27. Sage. https://sagecontinuum.org/, (Accessed 07 2023)
28. Alpine Fault Magnitude 8 (AF8). https://af8.org.nz/, (Accessed 07 2023)

The Impact of CUDA Execution Configuration Parameters on the Performance and Energy of a Seismic Application

Brenda S. Schussler^(✉), Pedro H. C. Rigon, Arthur F. Lorenzon,
Alexandre Carissimi, and Philippe O. A. Navaux

Institute of Informatics, Federal University of Rio Grande do Sul, Porto Alegre, Brazil
{bsschussler,phcrigon,aflorenzon,asc,navaux}@inf.ufrgs.br

Abstract. Simulating the propagation of acoustic waves is the basis of seismic imaging software, widely used by the industry for locating and detecting new oil basins. Due to their complexity, these simulations require a high computational processing power obtained using GPUs. To fully exploit these devices' computing potential, it is necessary to rightly define the configuration of the number of blocks and threads per block that will be assigned to a given kernel. However, as we show in this paper, this task is challenging since the ideal configuration will vary according to the grid size and the target metric (e.g., performance or energy). In this scenario, this paper evaluates different execution configurations for the Fletcher method, a widely used seismic application. When evaluating sixteen different grid sizes over a distinct set of configurations, we show that rightly choosing the number of blocks and threads per block can deliver up to 2 times more performance and save 18% of energy consumption compared to the standard way the Fletcher method is implemented.

Keywords: Seismic application · Performance · Energy efficiency · GPU

1 Introduction

Geophysical exploration methods are fundamental for humanity as they explore essential resources for the economic development of countries, such as oil and gas. However, investigating new oil reservoirs often involves destructive practices, such as drilling in sensitive areas and improper waste disposal. Applications that perform seismic image simulation for oil detection have been developed to reduce these environmental impacts and increase drilling accuracy. Since these applications usually involve the computation of a huge amount of data and are naturally parallel, GPUs (graphics processing units) are widely used to accelerate such applications [Hanindhito et al., 2022].

GPUs are powerful SIMD (single instruction, multiple data) architectures that usually consist of thousands of processing cores [Hennessy and Patterson,

2011]. They are specifically designed as accelerator devices to execute applications that involve array and matrix data structures efficiently. However, despite their high computing performance, GPUs also come with a significant power demand for their operation. For example, the NVIDIA Tesla V100, based on the Volta architecture, has a rated TDP (thermal design power) of 300 W [NVIDIA, 2017]. This high power consumption not only has cost implications but also contributes to environmental impacts.

Therefore, in order to mitigate energy consumption and minimize the environmental and economic impacts, it is essential for software developers to optimize the utilization of the hardware resources available on GPUs [Navaux et al., 2023] [Lorenzon and Beck Filho, 2019]. This involves making efficient use of the GPU's processing cores and memory when executing parallel applications. One of the key ways to optimize the use of hardware resources is by carefully configuring the thread hierarchy when deploying GPU kernels. The thread hierarchy configuration typically involves determining the number of blocks and the number of threads per block. However, finding the optimal thread hierarchy configurations that deliver the best performance while minimizing energy consumption is not a straightforward task.

Firstly, there is a vast number of possible combinations of the number of blocks and threads per block, making it challenging to determine the most efficient configuration. Additionally, the intrinsic characteristics of applications like seismic image simulation can vary dynamically at runtime. Factors such as workload variations and the number of GPU kernels being executed further complicate the task of finding the optimal thread hierarchy configuration. Therefore, software developers face the challenge of striking the right balance between performance and energy consumption. They need to experiment and explore different thread hierarchy configurations to identify the configurations that achieve the best trade-off between performance and energy efficiency. By doing so, developers can reduce energy consumption and minimize the economic and environmental impact associated with GPU-based computations.

Considering the aforementioned scenario, in this paper, we (i) investigate the performance and energy consumption of Fletcher Modeling, a seismic application widely used by oil companies that simulate the propagation of acoustic waves through time with different configurations of the number of blocks and threads per block; and (ii) provide guidelines for software developers to define the execution configuration according to their objectives rightly. Through the execution of the Fletcher modeling with sixteen different input sets, and fifteen configurations of the number of blocks and threads per block on an NVIDIA Tesla V100 SXM2 GPU, we show that:

– There is no unique configuration of the number of blocks and threads per block capable of delivering the best outcome in performance and energy consumption for all input sets at the same time.

- By rightly defining the number of blocks and threads per block, performance can be improved by up to 50% and energy consumption reduced by up to 18% when compared to the standard way the application is executed in the GPU.
- For small grid sizes, a lower number of threads per block is capable of delivering better results because it improves resource utilization, increases SM occupancy, and reduces memory contention. On the other hand, a larger number of threads per block is better as the grid size grows due to the increase in the available parallelism, efficient memory access, and load balancing reasons.

The remainder of this paper is organized as follows. In Sect. 2, we describe the architecture of GPUs, the Fletcher model, and the Related Work. Then, in Sect. 3, we list the methodology employed during the experiments. Performance and energy results are discussed in Sect. 4 while Sect. 5 draws the conclusion.

2 Background

2.1 Graphic Processing Units

NVIDIA GPUs have an internal structure consisting of processing units known as streaming multiprocessors (SMs) [Hennessy and Patterson, 2011. The number of SMs varies depending on the GPU architecture. For example, GPUs based on the Volta architecture, such as the NVIDIA Tesla V100, have 80 SMs, while those based on the Pascal architecture, like the NVIDIA Tesla P100, have 56 SMs. Within each SM, there are processing cores called CUDA cores. These CUDA cores are responsible for executing instructions in parallel. They enable the GPU to perform massively parallel processing and accelerate computations. The fundamental units of execution on GPUs are threads. Each thread executes a specific task or a portion of a computation that can be executed concurrently with other threads.

Threads are logically organized into blocks to facilitate cooperation, communication, and synchronization among them using shared memory regions. This organization into blocks helps manage the execution and coordination of threads within an SM. In this context, each block is assigned to an SM. When the GPU executes a kernel, it maps different blocks to available SMs, distributing the workload across the SMs for parallel execution. The mapping of blocks to SMs is done dynamically by the GPU hardware. Furthermore, each thread within a block is individually assigned to a specific CUDA core within the corresponding SM. This assignment allows the threads to be executed in parallel by utilizing the available CUDA cores within the SM. By leveraging the parallelism offered by the multiple SMs and CUDA cores, GPUs can efficiently execute large-scale computations by dividing the workload into numerous threads, blocks, and SMs, thereby achieving significant acceleration in performance compared to traditional CPU architectures.

Each SM typically contains a group of CUDA cores, caches, warp schedulers, and shared memory. These components work together to enable efficient parallel processing. CUDA cores within an SM are responsible for executing instructions, while CUDA threads are organized into groups called warps, typically consisting of 32 threads. For instance, the NVIDIA Tesla V100 GPU, which was utilized in our experiments, is equipped with 80 SMs. Each SM consists of 64 CUDA cores and possesses an on-chip memory capacity of 128 KB. Additionally, there are four warp schedulers within the GPU [Yuan et al., 2020]. It is worth mentioning that the GPU architecture imposes a limitation of 1024 threads per block.

In CUDA programming [Sanders and Kandrot, 2010], the code segment that is parallelized using CUDA is called a kernel. When the kernel is launched for execution, it is associated with a configuration that determines the number of blocks and the number of threads per block that will be assigned to the available SMs. All the allocated threads are then divided based on the chosen configuration to fit the warp size. When defining a kernel configuration, the number of concurrently executable warps depends on the allocation of registers and shared memory. However, the responsibility for scaling these resources is not directly placed on the programmer, as the GPU automatically manages it. Consequently, setting an appropriate kernel execution configuration becomes essential for effectively utilizing the GPU resources. However, due to the absence of specific directions or guidelines, determining the ideal configuration becomes an empirical process heavily reliant on the characteristics of the application and the specific GPU architecture [PÃ¡ez et al., 2020].

2.2   Fletcher Modeling

The Fletcher method is a well-established technique employed in the field of geophysics for simulating data collection in seismic surveys. This method plays an essential role in modeling subsurface topography and is widely used to obtain detailed information about geological structures, faults, and potential oil reservoirs [Fletcher et al., 2009]. In a seismic survey, various types of equipment, known as seismic sources, are deployed on ships or other platforms. These seismic sources emit sound waves periodically into the subsurface. These sound waves propagate through the different layers of the earth, interacting with the subsurface formations along the way. When these waves reach interfaces between different geological structures or faults, they are partially reflected back to the surface. These reflected waves, also known as seismic signals, carry valuable information about the subsurface.

To capture these seismic signals, receivers are placed at specific locations on the surface, such as on the ship or on land. These receivers are designed to detect the reflected waves and convert them into electrical signals. The electrical signals are then processed and analyzed to extract meaningful information about the subsurface structures. Using the Fletcher method, the collected signals are subjected to computational algorithms that involve sophisticated mathematical techniques and data processing procedures. These algorithms aim to analyze and interpret the seismic data to generate representative images of the subsurface structures being investigated. The resulting images provide valuable insights into the subsurface, enabling geoscientists and engineers to identify geological

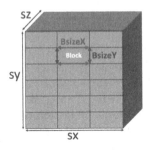

Fig. 1. Example of a three-dimensional grid with dimensions $sx \times sy \times sz$, with 3 blocks in the x direction and 6 blocks in the y direction, totaling 18 blocks in the xy plane.

formations, locate potential oil reservoirs, and assess the viability of hydrocarbon exploration or other geological investigations.

The algorithm Fletcher implements is based on the numerical solution of the wave equation. It is a partial differential equation that considers the environment's elastic properties (e.g., the propagation velocity of the wave) and is represented in a three-dimensional grid. The wave propagation process is iterative, where in each iteration, the algorithm calculates the approximate solution of the wave equation at each grid point, considering the information from previous iterations. During propagation, the wave energy spreads and changes as it interacts with the heterogeneities of the environment, updating the values at each grid point and allowing the algorithm to model seismic waves' reflection, refraction, and diffraction as they propagate underground.

The CUDA implementation of the Fletcher method employs a three-dimensional grid to represent the wave propagation in the environment. The dimensions of this data structure are defined by the inputs of the application (sx, sy, and sz, as shown in Fig. 1 which refer to the size of the x, y, and z-axis of the grid, respectively). The algorithm adds 40 positions on each dimension to this value to help during the computation and edge exchange. In this scenario, a defined input set of $x=y=z=56$ will allocate a grid of 96 elements on each dimension. For this grid to be computed by CUDA threads in parallel throughout the execution of the application, a 2D decomposition of the domain approach is used. It consists of obtaining a two-dimensional plane and making a cut in the volume (for example, in the x and y dimensions of the grid). Then, the algorithm can iterate along the third direction, in this case, represented by the z dimension. In this scenario, this two-dimensional (x,y) plane can be divided into blocks of CUDA threads, where the user in the algorithm defines the number of threads per block in the x and y domains.

Therefore, the total number of threads needed to compute the grid may be determined by dividing the total grid size by the number of blocks of CUDA threads in each dimension. Moreover, the number of threads per block is calculated by multiplying the number of CUDA threads created on each dimension ($BsizeX$, $BsizeY$). For example, for a grid with dimensions $96 \times 96 \times 96$, if the number of CUDA threads in the x and y domains equals 32 and 16, respectively, there will be a total of 18 blocks of threads (*96/32 = 3* in the *x*-domain, and *96/16=6* blocks in the *y*-domain). Furthermore, each block will have 512 CUDA threads. Hence, in the Fletcher algorithm, when a kernel is launched to the GPU, the user must define the number of threads per block in *x* and *y* dimensions, as well as the number of blocks in *x* and *y*.

2.3 Related Work

In this section, we discuss the works that have studied the performance and energy consumption of geophysical applications running on GPU architectures. They are discussed in chronological order.

[Michéa and Komatitsch, 2010] discusses the influence of kernel configuration on the performance of a three-dimensional finite-difference wave propagation code. However, the number of threads per block was fixed while the number of blocks was varied. Different from this work, our research simultaneously varies the number of blocks and threads per block to analyze the impact of this variation as the size of the propagation grid changes.

[PÃ¡ez et al., 2020] evaluate the performance of two strategies (1D and 2D decomposition) for implementing elastic modeling using different kernel configurations. When using the 1D layout, only one big block containing all the processing threads is defined. On the other hand, the 2D layout allows working with larger blocks, while the number of threads per block is a multiple of warp size (e.g., 32). In addition to this work, our research addresses a two-dimensional layout, allowing the software developer to vary the number of threads per block and the number of blocks in each dimension.

[Alkhimenkov et al., 2021] exploit GPUs in the propagation of seismic waves in fluid-saturated porous environments. The research discusses how the number of threads per block in the x, y, and z domains impacts the effective memory transfer rate (MTP) of the numerical application Biot 3D. Fifteen different block combinations were analyzed for a fixed resolution of $576 \times 576 \times 576$. Compared to this proposal, our paper analyzes the influence of the number of threads per block on performance and energy consumption, besides exploring different grid dimensions, as opposed to the fixed resolution of 576 used by [Alkhimenkov et al., 2021].

Sanchez-Noguez et al., 2022] evaluate different block sizes in 3D and 2D kernels to compute 3D and 2D arrays, respectively, aiming to study the impact of shared memory usage on performance. [Serpa and Mishra, 2022] explore the optimization of the Fletcher method with a focus on portability, analyzing the performance and energy consumption of eight code versions. Unlike these two works, our paper addresses the optimization of the Fletcher method by exploring different kernel execution parameters on GPUs and providing guidelines to end-users so they can get better GPU usage regardless of the input set.

Table 1. Characteristics of the target architecture

Processor Specification	
Processor	Intel Xeon E5-2686 v4
Architecture	Broadwell
Processor/GPU	Intel(R) Xeon(R) CPU E5-2686 v4 @ 2.30GHz, 64 VCPUs
Memory	1 MiB L1d, 1 MiB L1i, 8 MiB L2, 90 MiB L3
GPU Specifications	
GPU	NVIDIA Tesla V100-SXM2
Architecture	Volta
Processor/GPU	GV100
Registers	256 KB/SM, 20480 KB/GPU
Memory	4096-bit HBM2, 16 GB, 6144 KB L2 Cache

3 Methodology

The experiments were performed in a heterogeneous architecture as depicted in Table 1. The host is an Intel Xeon CPU E5-2686 with 488 GB of main memory; and the GPU is an NVIDIA Tesla V100 SXM2 with 16GB of main memory, 80 SMs, and 5120 CUDA cores. The Fletcher modeling application was compiled with CUDA version 12.0, driver v.525.85.12, and GCC v.9.4.0. We have considered the following parameters: sixteen different grid dimensions, ranging from $24 \times 24 \times 24$ to $504 \times 504 \times 504$ in intervals of 32 in each axis; fifteen combinations of the number of threads in the x and y dimension, ranging from 4×4 to 32×32.

In the next section, we analyze the performance and energy consumption of all executions. The performance metric considers the number of grid points calculated per second during the execution, represented as *MSamples/s*. Therefore, the higher this value, the better the performance. On the other hand, the energy consumption was obtained directly from the GPU through the NVIDIA SMI (system management interface) command line. In this scenario, the lower the value, the better. Each combination of the input set (grid dimension) and configuration of the number of threads in each dimension was executed ten times, and the results consider the average with a standard deviation lower than 0.5%.

4 Performance and Energy Evaluation

In this section, we discuss the performance and energy results obtained through the execution of Fletcher modeling with all the execution configurations and grid dimensions described in Sect. 3. For that, we start by discussing the results obtained through the design space exploration. Then, we discuss the performance and energy improvements of the ideal configuration when compared to the standard way the Fletcher Method is executed. Finally, we list guidelines for software developers and end-users so they can optimize the execution of the Fletcher Method based on our findings.

4.1 Design Space Exploration

Figure 2 illustrates the performance (y-axis) and energy consumption (x-axis) of six representative grid dimensions: 56, 152, 280, 376, 440, and 504. We have chosen them as they show the heterogeneity of configurations that present better results. The plots are organized as follows: each symbol represents a different combination of block size in the x and y dimensions; the performance of each combination is normalized to the best performance in every grid dimension, so the closer the value to 1.0, the better the performance. On the other hand, energy is normalized to the worst results, and hence, the lower the values, the better the energy consumption. Therefore, the configuration that delivers the best trade-off between performance and energy consumption is the one that is closer to the point $(1,0)$ in the Cartesian plane (x,y).

We start by discussing the results for the execution with the grid dimension $56 \times 56 \times 56$, shown in Fig. 2(a). For this dimension, one can observe that most configurations achieved similar energy consumption. On the other hand, varying the block size in each dimension leads to high variations in the performance. The best scenario for performance is with the configuration 32×4, being 50% better than the default configuration, represented as the baseline (32×16). On top of that, this configuration also delivered the lowest energy consumption, even at lower rates compared to the baseline version. On the other hand, the worst performance and energy consumption were achieved with the 4×16 and 4×4 configurations, respectively.

When it comes to the results for the grid dimension $152 \times 152 \times 152$, shown in Fig. 2(b), the configuration that delivers the best performance is not the same that spends less energy consumption. Although the best performance is achieved with the baseline configuration (32×16), it spent 17% more energy than the configuration with the lowest energy consumption (32×4). In addition, this configuration has a performance loss of 10% compared to the baseline. Therefore, in this situation, it is necessary to analyze the main objectives of the user to define the appropriate configuration. In the end, the worst configuration for performance and energy was 4×16 for both.

For grid dimension $280 \times 280 \times 280$ results, shown in Fig. 2(c), the highest performance is reached with the configuration represented by 32 blocks in the x dimension and 8 blocks in the y dimension. This configuration is about 8% better than the baseline (32×16). On the other hand, the configuration with the lowest energy consumption was 16×8, spending 4% less energy than the baseline. However, this version has a performance loss of 50% compared to the best performance. One can also observe in the plot that the results obtained for the 32×4, 32×8, and 32×16 configurations were very close in energy consumption, varying only 1%.

Considering the results in Fig. 2(d) for the grid size equal to 376, one can observe that the 8×8 configuration is the one that achieves the lowest energy

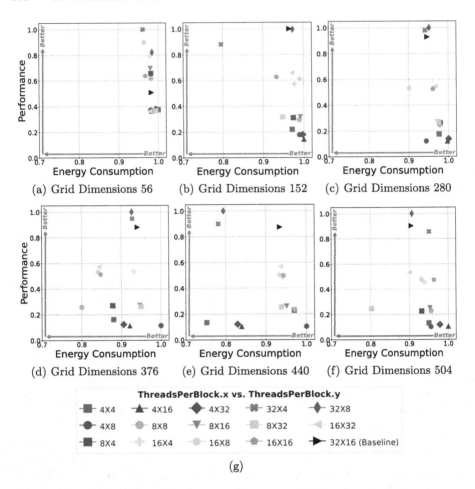

Fig. 2. Performance and Energy Consumption results for each configuration of the number of blocks in x and y.

consumption. However, it also delivers the worst performance. The energy spent by this configuration is about 14% lower than the baseline, but its performance loss is more significant, around 60%. On the other hand, the 32×8 configuration achieved the highest performance, being approximately 12% better than the baseline, with a slight variation concerning energy consumption, around 1%. Compared to the best configuration for energy (8×8), the 32×8 achieved 75% higher performance, spending approximately only 12% more energy.

Three combinations are worth mentioning when considering the results achieved with the grid size equal to $440 \times 440 \times 440$, shown in Fig. 2(e). If the user wants to optimize energy consumption, the 4×4 configuration delivers better results, spending about 18% less energy than the baseline. On the other hand, if the objective is to get the best possible performance, the ideal configuration is 32×8, providing 15% more performance than the baseline. However, if the user wants to optimize the trade-off between performance and energy consumption, the configuration delivers the best results is 32×4. In this scenario, the performance is only 10% lower and spends 3% more energy than each metric's best outcome.

Finally, Fig. 2(f) illustrates the results for the grid size equal to $504 \times 504 \times 504$. In this scenario, if the user wants to prioritize the performance, the ideal configuration is 32×8, which is about 75% better than the configuration that delivers the lowest energy consumption (8×32). On the other hand, if the objective is to reduce energy consumption, the most suitable configuration is the 8×32, which spends 10% less energy than the best performance. When compared to Baseline, the 32×8 configuration presents performance gains of 10%, while the 8×32 configuration spends 11% less energy.

In order to summarize the best configuration found for each grid size, Table 2 depicts the configuration that delivers the best performance and energy consumption for all grid dimensions evaluated in this work. We start by highlighting that there is no unique configuration of block size in the x and y dimensions capable of delivering the best performance and energy consumption results simultaneously for all grid dimensions. For instance, when the grid dimension is $24 \times 24 \times 24$, the best performance is reached with a block size in x equal to 16 and a block size in y equal to 4. On the other hand, for the grid dimension $56 \times 56 \times 56$, the best configuration is 32×4. Furthermore, the configuration that delivers the best performance in most cases differs from the one with the lowest energy consumption. Only in specific grid dimensions (e.g., $248 \times 248 \times 248$), the configuration that delivers the best energy also achieve the highest performance at the same time.

4.2   Performance and Energy Improvements over Baseline

Figure 3 highlights the difference in performance and energy consumption for the best and worst outcome for each grid size. The results are normalized to the baseline (represented by the black line). Hence, for the performance, values above 1.0 mean that the result is better than the baseline. On the other hand, for energy consumption, the lower the value, the better.

We start by discussing the performance results for the smaller grid sizes (from 24 to 120). For these input sets, the best performance is reached with the configurations where the number of threads per block is significantly smaller than the baseline configuration. For instance, while the baseline creates 512 threads per block (32×16), the best performance for a grid dimension equal to 24 creates only 64 threads per block (16×4). In this case, the performance of the ideal configuration is 2 times better than the standard way the application is implemented (baseline). The behavior is very similar for the 56, 88, and 120 grid dimensions, but at different rates. However, when the grid dimension increases, the best performance is either achieved with configurations that create 128 or 256 threads per block in most cases (Table 2). Therefore, the performance difference from the best result to the baseline decreases. On the other hand, the difference from the best to the worst performance increases. This highlights the importance

Table 2. Best configuration found by the DSE for each grid dimension w.r.t. the energy and performance

Grid Dim.	Best Performance	Best Energy Consumption
24	16×4	16×32
56	32×4	32×4
88	32×8	8×16
120	32×4	32×16
152	32×16	32×4
184	32×4	32×16
216	32×8	16×8
248	32×4	32×4
280	32×8	16×8
312	32×4	16×4
344	32×8	32×4
376	32×8	8×8
408	32×8	32×16
440	32×8	4×4
472	32×16	4×16
504	32×8	8×32

of rightly choosing the configurations to execute a given CUDA kernel according to the grid size.

When it comes to energy consumption, the grid dimension starts to play an important role. For larger grids, one can observe that the best configuration is able to save about 20% of energy compared to the baseline (grid size equal to 440). Furthermore, there are many scenarios in which the baseline configuration was not able to deliver the lowest energy consumption. This means that executing the Fletcher method without modifying the number of blocks and threads per block would very likely lead to a waste of energy and power consumption.

In summary, considering the average results of all grid sizes, when the user correctly defines the number of blocks and threads per block, the performance improvement over the baseline is 25%. Furthermore, in a scenario where one compares the average of the best with the worst results, the difference in choosing ideal CUDA kernel configurations is 5.43 times in performance. When considering energy consumption, choosing the best configuration saves 10% of energy compared to the baseline.

4.3   Guidelines for Users and Software Developers

Through the design space exploration performed in the previous section, we discuss some guidelines and directions to help end-users and software developers in the task of defining the number of blocks and threads per block.

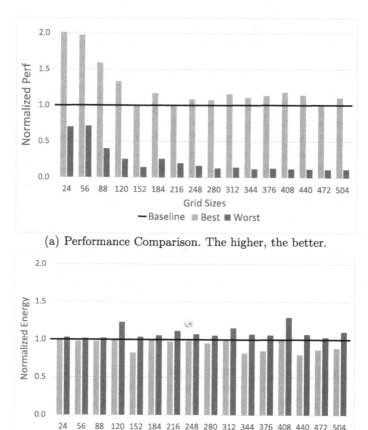

(a) Performance Comparison. The higher, the better.

(b) Energy Comparison. The lower, the better.

Fig. 3. Performance and energy results of the best and worst configuration for each grid size normalized to the baseline.

We have found that for small grid sizes, a small number of threads per block is capable of delivering better performance and energy consumption in most cases. The following reasons can be listed. (*i*) improved resource utilization: with a small input set, using a small number of threads per block allows for better use of registers and shared memory, which reduces the resource contention among threads and enables more threads to be scheduled on an SM simultaneously. (*ii*) increased occupancy (i.e., the ratio of active warps to the maximum possible warps that can be executed concurrently on an SM): with a small number of threads per block, each thread block occupies fewer resources, leaving room for more thread blocks to be launched, allowing the SM to hide memory latency by switching between different thread blocks. (*iii*) reduced memory contention: the memory footprint of the computation is smaller with a small input set. Hence, using a small number of threads per block can reduce memory contention because the threads are accessing a smaller portion of the global memory simultaneously, resulting in fewer memory conflicts and improved memory access efficiency.

On the other hand, a larger number of threads per block may deliver better performance as the grid size increases due to the following reasons. (i) increased parallelism available: Larger grid sizes often require more parallelism to utilize the computational power of the GPU fully. Hence, by using a larger number of threads per block, one can increase the total number of threads running concurrently, enabling more parallel computations. (ii) efficient memory access: by using a larger number of threads per block, one can exploit better memory access patterns. That is, multiple threads can access memory in a coalesced manner, fetching contiguous memory locations efficiently, which may reduce memory latency and improve memory throughput. (iii) load balancing: using a larger number of threads per block allows for finer granularity in workload distribution. In this scenario, each thread can process a smaller portion of the grid, enabling better load balancing among threads. This can help avoid scenarios where a few threads are overloaded while others remain idle, leading to better performance.

5   Conclusions and Future Work

Defining the number of blocks and threads per block according to the CUDA application is challenging, as it directly impacts the performance and energy consumption of the GPU system. Hence, in this work, we have performed extensive experiments over a real-world seismic application to find configurations of blocks and threads per block that optimize its performance and energy consumption. When evaluating different configurations over sixteen distinct grid dimensions, we have shown that no unique configuration can deliver the best outcome for all grid sizes. We have also shown that performance can be improved 2x compared to the default way the application is implemented by carefully selecting the ideal configuration. Furthermore, significant energy reductions were achieved by defining the ideal number of blocks and threads per block.

In summary, it is worth mentioning that the optimal number of threads per block can depend on various factors, such as GPU architecture, memory requirements, and the nature of the computation. Therefore, it is recommended to experiment and profile the application with different thread block sizes to find the optimal configuration for your specific scenario. In this scenario, as future work, we intend to implement a heuristic to automatically define the number of blocks and threads per block according to the grid dimension and optimization objectives (e.g., performance, energy, or the trade-off between them).

Acknowledgment. This work has been partially supported by Petrobras under number 2020/00182-5, by the call CNPq/MCTI/FNDCT - Universal 18/2021 under grants 406182/2021-3, and by the Coordenação de Aperfeiçoamento de Pessoal de Nível Superior - Brazil (CAPES) - Finance Code 001.

References

Alkhimenkov, Y., Räss, L., Khakimova, L., Quintal, B., Podladchikov, Y.Y.: Resolving wave propagation in anisotropic Poroelastic media using graphical processing units (GPUs). J. Geophys. Res. Solid Earth **126**, e2020JB021175 (2021)

Fletcher, R.P., Du, X., Fowler, P.J.: Reverse time migration in tilted transversely isotropic (TTI) media. Geophysics **74**(6), WCA179–WCA187 (2009)

Hanindhito, B., Gourounas, D., Fathi, A., Trenev, D., Gerstlauer, A., John, L.K.: GAPS: GPU-acceleration of PDE solvers for wave simulation. In: Proceedings of the 36th ACM International Conference on Supercomputing, ICS 2022, New York, NY, USA. Association for Computing Machinery (2022)

Hennessy, J.L., Patterson, D.A.: Computer Architecture: A Quantitative Approach. Elsevier (2011)

Francisco Lorenzon, A., Beck Filho, A.C.S.: Parallel Computing Hits the Power Wall. SCS, Springer, Cham (2019). https://doi.org/10.1007/978-3-030-28719-1

Michéa, D., Komatitsch, D.: Accelerating a three-dimensional finite-difference wave propagation code using GPU graphics cards. Geophys. J. Int. **182**(1), 389–402 (2010)

Navaux, P.O.A., Lorenzon, A.F., da Silva Serpa, M.: Challenges in high-performance computing. J. Braz. Comput. Soc. **29**(1), 51–62 (2023)

NVIDIA: Nvidia dgx-1 with tesla v100 system architecture, Technical white paper (2017)

PÃ¡ez, A., SÃ¡nchez, I.J., RamÃrez, A.B.: Computational strategies for implementation of 2D elastic wave modeling in GPU. Entre Ciencia e IngenierÃa **14**, 52–58 (2020)

Sanchez-Noguez, J., Couder-Castañeda, C., Hernández-Gómez, J.J., Navarro-Reyes, I.: Solving the heat transfer equation by a finite difference method using multi-dimensional arrays in CUDA as in standard C. In: Gitler, I., Barrios Hernández, C.J., Meneses, E. (eds.) CARLA 2021. CCIS, vol. 1540, pp. 221–235. Springer, Cham (2022). https://doi.org/10.1007/978-3-031-04209-6_16

Sanders, J., Kandrot, E.: CUDA by Example: An Introduction to General-purpose GPU Programming. Addison-Wesley Professional (2010)

Serpa, M., Mishra, P.: Performance evaluation and enhancement of the fletcher method on multicore architectures. Int. J. Res. Publ. Rev. **3**, 2649–2655 (2022)

Yuan, Y., Shi, F., Kirby, J.T., Yu, F.: FUNWAVE-GPU: multiple-GPU acceleration of a Boussinesq-type wave model. J. Adv. Model. Earth Syst. **12**(5), e2019MS001957 (2020). https://doi.org/10.1029/2019MS001957

High-Performance Computing for Astrophysical Simulations and Astroparticle Observations

L. M. Becerra[1]([✉])(iD), C. Sarmiento-Cano[1](iD), A. Martínez-Méndez[2](iD),
Y. Dominguez[1,3](iD), and L. A. Núñez[1,4](iD)

[1] Escuela de Física, Universidad Industrial de Santander, 680002 Bucaramanga,
Colombia
`laura.becerra7@correo.uis.edu.co`
[2] Escuela de Ingeniería de Sistemas e Informática,
Universidad Industrial de Santander, 680002 Bucaramanga, Colombia
[3] East African Institute for Fundamental Research (ICTP-EAIFR),
University of Rwanda, Kigali, Rwanda
[4] Departamento de Física, Universidad de Los Andes, Mérida, Venezuela

Abstract. Simulations in astrophysics play a crucial role in testing models and comparing them with observational data, for which High-Performance Computing has become indispensable for handling complex scenarios. In this paper, we present two important applications in astrophysical simulations. First, we explore the adaptation of the PENCIL CODE to study the evolution of magnetic field configurations in stratified stars. Second, we highlight the ARTI framework developed to estimate signals at the Latin American Giant Observatory. In addition, we discuss the importance of reproducibility in scientific analysis.

Keywords: HPC · Pencil Code · ARTI · Astrophysics · Astroparticle

1 Introduction

Computers have transformed the practice of science, allowing scientists to tackle problems of exceptional complexity and scale. They have expanded the scope of what can be investigated and have deepened our understanding of the fundamental laws that govern the universe. This, in turn, has led to new research avenues and shaped modern physics's epistemological foundations. The emergence of quantum computing hardware is poised to transfigure physics itself. It can potentially solve problems much faster than classical computers, particularly in quantum physics and materials science.

In Astrophysics, numerical simulations and data visualizations are unprecedented tools to benchmark models and compare them with observations. High-performance computing (HPC) has revolutionized astrophysics simulations by enabling scientists to model complex and diverse astrophysical phenomena with

C. J. Barrios H. et al. (Eds.): CARLA 2023, CCIS 1887, pp. 184–196, 2024.
https://doi.org/10.1007/978-3-031-52186-7_13

remarkable accuracy and detail. This has led to significant advancements in our understanding of the universe, from the smallest particle interactions to the largest scale of cosmic structure and evolution.

Several numerical codes have been developed to model various astrophysical scenarios, ranging from large-scale problems such as galaxy formation to small-scale phenomena such as turbulence in the interstellar medium. These codes can be classified according to their discretisation approach, with grid-based codes (e.g., PENCIL [11], FLASH [6], RAMSES [16], and PLUTO [10]) and particle-based (or N-body) codes (e.g. GADGET [15], PHANTOM [12]) as the two common categories. These codes are often coupled with radiative transfer, gravity, nuclear physics, and general relativity to study a wide range of phenomena, including stellar structure, planet formation, stellar and galactic evolution, and high-energy events such as supernovae, active galactic nuclei (AGN), and gamma-ray bursts (GRBs).

In a recent work [4], we have employed HPC resources to model the evolution of magnetic field configurations in the interior of convective and stratified stars. To do this, we adapted the PENCIL CODE[1] [11], which is a high-level finite-difference numerical code for modelling compressible hydrodynamic fluids with magnetic fields and particles. The code is written primarily in Fortran and runs efficiently in parallel on shared or distributed memory computers. Its modular structure allows it to easily adapt to simulate different problems, supporting Cartesian, cylindrical and spherical geometries.

On the other hand, by analysing astroparticle observations, scientists can refine and validate the accuracy of astrophysical simulations, leading to a deeper understanding of cosmic phenomena and enabling more accurate predictions of astroparticle processes. For example, ground-based detection of secondary particles allows the study of transient events such as GRBs and/or Forbush decays [17], as well as practical applications such as muography [8]. These studies require a detailed understanding of how secondary particles are produced in the atmosphere and reach specific locations.

The Latin American Giant Observatory (LAGO) focuses on detecting background radiation for studying astroparticles and geophysical phenomena. LAGO comprises an extended network of Water Cherenkov Detectors across the continent, covering a wide range of geomagnetic rigidity cutoffs and atmospheric absorption depths. A comprehensive computational framework that considers the influence of the geomagnetic field on the propagation of Galactic Cosmic Rays (GCRs) has been developed to estimate the expected signals at the LAGO detector sites. This framework consists of a collection of individual tools, collectively known as the ARTI[2].

In this article, we present a comprehensive overview of the main applications developed by our group using HPC resources. Section 2 is dedicated to stellar simulations with the PENCIL CODE, while Sect. 3 is dedicated to astroparticle

---

[1] https://github.com/pencil-code/pencil-code.git.
[2] https://github.com/lagoproject/arti.

simulations with ARTI. Section 4 describes the measures taken to improve the reproducibility of our analyses. Finally, in Sect. 5, we give some final remarks.

2 Stellar Astrophysics Applications

2.1 Star-in-a-Box Simulation

Large and stable magnetic fields have been observed on the surface of chemically peculiar stars of spectral type A and B (Ap/Bp stars), some white dwarfs and neutron stars. These magnetic fields will likely be in magnetohydrodynamic equilibrium in the stellar interior since neither their properties nor the physical conditions inside these stars are compatible with dynamo action. Yet, our understanding of the conditions that enable this equilibrium and its implications for stellar structure and evolution remains limited. The complexity of this problem required the use of numerical simulations.

To evolve the magnetic field inside the star, we solve the magneto-hydrodynamic equations using the PENCIL CODE:

$$\frac{\partial \rho}{\partial t} = \boldsymbol{\nabla}(\rho \boldsymbol{v}) \tag{1}$$

$$\frac{\partial \rho \boldsymbol{v}}{\partial t} = -\boldsymbol{\nabla}(\rho \boldsymbol{v} \cdot \boldsymbol{v}) - \boldsymbol{\nabla}P - \rho \boldsymbol{\nabla}\Phi + \boldsymbol{j} \times \boldsymbol{B} - \frac{\boldsymbol{\nabla}(2\rho \nu \boldsymbol{S})}{\rho} \tag{2}$$

$$\frac{\partial s}{\partial t} = -\boldsymbol{v} \cdot \boldsymbol{\nabla}s + \frac{\eta j^2}{\rho T} + \frac{2\nu \boldsymbol{S}^2}{T} \tag{3}$$

$$\frac{\partial \boldsymbol{A}}{\partial t} = \boldsymbol{v} \times \boldsymbol{B} - \eta \boldsymbol{j}, \tag{4}$$

where ρ, p, $\boldsymbol{v}$, T and s are the fluid mass density, pressure, velocity, temperature and entropy, respectively; Φ is the gravitational potential; $\boldsymbol{S}$ is the viscous stress tensor; $\boldsymbol{A}$, $\boldsymbol{B}$ and $\boldsymbol{j}$ are the magnetic vector potential, magnetic field, and current density, respectively; η is the magnetic diffusivity and ν is the fluid viscosity. The magneto-hydrodynamic equations regarding the vector potential are solved, ensuring that the magnetic field remains divergence-free.

We used an equally spaced Cartesian grid to model the star and its dynamics. In this approach, the star with radius R is placed in the centre of a cubic box with side length L (star-in-a-box). The advantage of using Cartesian coordinates over spherical ones is twofold. First, it allows us to model the entire star, including its centre, which is not defined in spherical coordinates. Second, it is computationally simpler to work with Cartesian coordinates. The trade-off, however, is that the resolution of the star is lower compared to a corresponding simulation in spherical coordinates.

In all the simulations presented here, we used a computational box of $L = 4.5$ (arbitrary units) and employed a Cartesian grid with periodic boundary conditions in all directions. The star is at the centre of the box and has a radius of $R = 1.0$ (arbitrary units). Outside the star, we typically assume a complete vacuum with no currents ($\boldsymbol{B} = \boldsymbol{\nabla}\Psi$). To simulate this condition numerically,

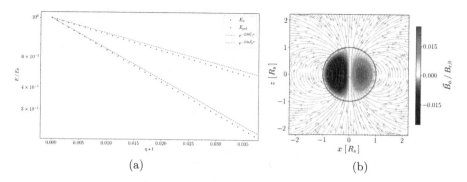

Fig. 1. Left: Magnetic energy decay of a purely Ohmic mode ($l = 1$ and $n = 1$). Right: Snapshot of the magnetic field at the end of the simulation. The field lines correspond to the poloidal component of the magnetic field, and the surface contours to the toroidal one. We simulate with the PENCIL CODE in a Cartesian box with an equally-spaced grid.

we add an atmosphere of low electrical conductivity in which the magnetic field relaxes into a potential field:

$$\eta = \begin{cases} \eta_i & \text{if } r < R, \\ \frac{\eta_o - \eta_i}{\Delta_r}(r - R) + \eta_i & \text{if } R < r < R + \Delta_r \\ \eta_o, & \text{if } r > R + \Delta_r. \end{cases} \tag{5}$$

The outer diffusivity, η_o, is 10^3 times greater than the inner one, η_i. The transition zone connecting the star's interior with the atmosphere has a width of $\Delta_r \approx 0.3R$.

To test the PENCIL CODE for star-in-a-box simulations and the performance of the magnetic diffusivity given in Eq. (5), we first solve the induction equation neglecting the advection term:

$$\frac{\partial \boldsymbol{B}}{\partial \tau} = -\boldsymbol{\nabla} \times \boldsymbol{j} = \boldsymbol{\nabla}^2 \boldsymbol{B} \tag{6}$$

with $\tau = \eta t$. This equation has an analytical solution, which is:

$$\boldsymbol{B}(\boldsymbol{r}) = B_\phi(\boldsymbol{r})\hat{\phi} + \boldsymbol{\nabla} \times (A_\phi(\boldsymbol{r})\hat{\phi}), \tag{7}$$

with

$$B_\phi(\boldsymbol{r}) = \sum_{l,n=1} (A_{ln}j_l(k_{ln}r) + B_{ln}y_l(k_{ln}r)) \, P_l^1(\cos\theta)e^{-k_{ln}^2\tau} \tag{8}$$

$$A_\phi(\boldsymbol{r}) = \sum_{l,n=1} (C_{ln}j_l(\omega_{ln}r) + D_{ln}y_l(\omega_{ln}r)) \, P_l^1(\cos\theta)e^{-\omega_{ln}^2\tau}, \tag{9}$$

where j_l and y_l are the spherical Bessel functions of the first and second kind, respectively, and P_l^1 are the associated Legendre polynomials. The constants

Table 1. Hypatia cluster timing for the Pencil Codel evolving stellar magnetic fields

p	$\frac{\text{time step}[\mu s]}{N \times p}$	N	Layout	p	$\frac{\text{time step}[\mu s]}{N \times p}$	N	Layout
1	12.312	128^3	$1 \times 1 \times 1$	1	63.279	256^3	$1 \times 1 \times 1$
4	1.761	128^3	$1 \times 1 \times 4$	16	0.049	256^3	$1 \times 1 \times 16$
4	0.575	128^3	$1 \times 2 \times 2$	16	0.075	256^3	$1 \times 2 \times 8$
8	0.160	128^3	$1 \times 1 \times 8$	16	0.072	256^3	$1 \times 4 \times 4$
8	0.537	128^3	$1 \times 2 \times 4$	16	0.082	256^3	$2 \times 2 \times 4$
8	0.573	128^3	$2 \times 2 \times 2$	32	0.049	256^3	$1 \times 1 \times 32$
16	0.178	128^3	$1 \times 1 \times 16$	32	0.153	256^3	$1 \times 2 \times 16$
16	0.171	128^3	$1 \times 2 \times 8$	32	0.022	256^3	$1 \times 4 \times 8$
16	0.122	128^3	$1 \times 4 \times 4$	32	0.017	256^3	$2 \times 2 \times 8$
16	0.041	128^3	$2 \times 2 \times 4$	32	0.026	256^3	$2 \times 4 \times 4$
32	0.055	128^3	$1 \times 1 \times 32$	64	0.038	256^3	$1 \times 1 \times 64$
32	0.036	128^3	$1 \times 2 \times 16$	64	0.032	256^3	$1 \times 2 \times 32$
32	0.052	128^3	$1 \times 4 \times 8$	64	0.032	256^3	$1 \times 4 \times 16$
32	0.075	128^3	$2 \times 2 \times 8$	64	0.031	256^3	$1 \times 8 \times 8$
32	0.025	128^3	$2 \times 4 \times 4$	64	0.037	256^3	$2 \times 4 \times 8$
				64	0.041	256^3	$2 \times 2 \times 16$
				64	0.029	256^3	$4 \times 4 \times 4$

A_{ln}, B_{ln}, C_{ln}, D_{ln}, k_{ln} and ω_{ln} are determined by the boundary conditions: regular conditions in the centre of the star make $B_{ln} = D_{nl} = 0$. In contrast, the continuity condition of the magnetic field across the star's surface gives $\omega_{11} = 3.14$ and $k_{11} = 4.49$ for the $n = 1$, $l = 1$ mode.

We follow the evolution of the magnetic field for about one τ time. From the analytical solution, the magnetic energy of the toroidal component scales with $e^{-2.0k_{11}^2\tau}$ and the poloidal with $e^{-2.0\omega_{11}^2\tau}$. Figure 1 shows a good agreement between the simulated and the analytical model over time. This confirms the validity and effectiveness of employing the high magnetic conductivity atmosphere in star-in-box simulations. Additionally, Becerra et al. [4] confirmed that for sufficiently large box sizes $(L > 3R_s)$, the evolution of the magnetic field in the stellar interior remains unaffected by the periodic boundary conditions at the box's sides.

2.2 Code Performance: Stably Stratified Stars

We now evaluate the parallelization performance of the Pencil Code on the Hypatia cluster[3]. For this, we run simulations solving the full set of Eqs. (1)–(4) to track the evolution of magnetic field configurations inside the star. As

---

[3] https://exacore.uniandes.edu.co/es/que-hacemos/procesamiento.

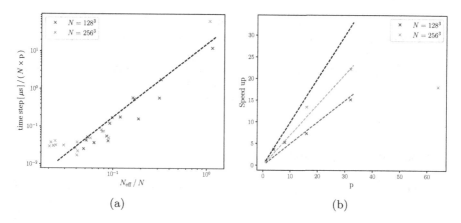

Fig. 2. Left: Mean time spent in each time step per number of points and processors as a function of the fraction of more effective points in each processor over the total points of the simulation. Right: Speed up of parallelization of the PENCIL CODE in Hypatia cluster.

an initial condition, we assume a polytropic relationship between the gas pressure and density within the star, where the radial dependence of the entropy determines the star's stable stratification. The stellar interior is also connected with a uniform-temperature atmosphere outside the star. The simulations start with a random magnetic field in the star's centre. In stably stratified stars, this configuration is expected to evolve toward an equilibrium configuration [4,5]. Throughout the simulation, we assume an ideal gas law for the fluid matter: $P = \mathcal{R}\rho T$, where $\mathcal{R}$ is the universal gas constant.

The PENCIL CODE is a finite-difference code, and it efficiently employs Message Passing Interface (MPI) for parallelization. A mesh size of $N = N_x \times N_y \times N_z$ points is distributed in a layout of $p = p_x \times p_y \times p_z$ processors. To compute the spatial derivatives, the PENCIL CODE uses a sixth-order finite difference scheme, requiring an additional 6 ghost zones in each processor. The points in these zones are communicated with neighbouring processors at each time step. The total number of points in each processor is:

$$N_{\text{eff}} = \left(\frac{N_x}{p_x} + 6\right) \times \left(\frac{N_y}{p_y} + 6\right) \times \left(\frac{N_z}{p_z} + 6\right) \qquad (10)$$

We run simulations with two different resolutions: 128^3 and 256^3. Table 1 summarises the simulations performed for this test. Each simulation gives the number of processors used, p, the number of points in the grid, N, the layout, and the mean time spent in each time step per number of points and processors. The left panel of Fig. 2 clearly shows that the code's performance improves as the fraction between the number of points per processor and the total points of the simulation decreases when the resolution is 128^3, even when up to 32 processors are utilized. This trend seems to be the same for the 256^3 resolution, but when 64 processors were employed, the code's performance did not improve.

The right panel of Fig. 2 shows the speed-up achieved through parallelization as a function of the number of processors. This quantity is calculated as the time the code takes to complete 100 interactions on a single processor over the time taken when using multiple processors. For both resolutions, the code exhibits speedup benefits up to the utilization of 32 processors.

3   Astroparticle Applications

Atmospheric particle flux simulations require a significant number of simulated particles. This number increases as the simulation progresses. For example, simulating just one minute of flux introduces about 100,000 primary protons into the atmosphere. As these primary particles interact with the atmosphere, they create hundreds of millions of secondary particles. To get a realistic and statistically meaningful representation, we must simulate at least 40 million primary protons, equivalent to five hours of flux. In this case, high-performance computing (HPC) is the only viable option for these simulations.

We used the ARTI [14] code to estimate the secondary particle flux at each LAGO site and to simulate the neutron flux. ARTI is a complete framework designed to simulate the signals produced by the secondary particles emerging from the interaction of single, multiple, and even from the complete flux of primary cosmic rays with the atmosphere. These signals are simulated for any particle detector located anywhere (latitude, longitude and altitude), including the real-time atmospheric, geomagnetic and detector conditions. Formulated through a sequence of codes written in C++, Fortran, Bash and Perl, it provides an easy-to-use integration of standard astroparticle simulation environments. ARTI supports different cluster architectures and distributed computing solutions, such as those based on grid and federated or public clouds implementations [13]. In the following section, we present the results for both applications.

3.1   Estimation of Cosmic Background Radiation at the Ground Level

We used ARTI to calculate the expected flux and spectrum of secondary particles at each LAGO detector site. It follows the procedure described in [2,3]. Here, the primary injected particle flux, Φ, at an altitude of 112 km a.s.l. is given by:

$$\Phi(E_p, Z, A, \Omega) \simeq j_0(Z, A) \left(\frac{E_p}{E_0}\right)^{\alpha(E_p, Z, A)}, \tag{11}$$

where E_p is the energy of the primary particle, $\alpha(E_p, Z, A)$ is its spectral index, which can be considered constant ($\alpha \equiv \alpha(Z, A)$) in the energy range, from a few GeV to 10^6 GeV. Each kind of GCR considered is characterized by its mass number (A) and atomic number (Z), and $j_0(Z, A)$ is the measured flux in the top of the atmosphere at the reference energy $E_0 = 10^3$ GeV.

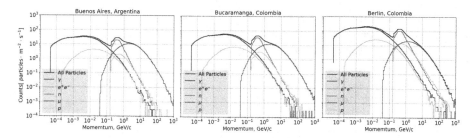

Fig. 3. Energy spectrum of secondary particles at three different study sites: Buenos Aires (19 m a.s.l), Bucaramanga (956 m a.s.l), and Berlin (3450 m a.s.l.). The total spectrum of particles produced as they reach the ground is shown in black. The electromagnetic component comprises gamma photons (blue), electrons, and positrons (yellow). The muon component is shown in green, and the protons in purple. The neutrons, which have a cut of about 300 MeV applied by CORSIKA to optimize the computation time, are shown in magenta.

ARTI uses CORSIKA [7] to evaluate the particles produced by the interaction of each GCR with the atmosphere. In these simulations, each secondary particle is tracked up to the lowest energy threshold (E_s) allowed by CORSIKA, which depends on the type of the secondary particle. Currently, these thresholds are $E_s \geq 5$ MeV for muons and hadrons (excluding pions) and $E_s \geq 5$ KeV for electrons, pions and gammas photons. As the atmospheric profile is a key factor for the production of secondary particles and a parameter for CORSIKA, we set atmospheric MODTRAN profiles models [9] according to the geographical position of the LAGO sites (see [14] and references therein for a detailed description of this method).

Figure 3 shows examples of the results for the obtained spectra of each type of secondary particle at Buenos Aires, Argentina (19 m a.s.l), Bucaramanga, Colombia (956 m a.s.l) and Berlin, Colombia (3450 m a.s.l.). These sites are located at different altitudes, with a difference of up to 2,000 m. These altitude variations are reflected in the total flux, with the difference between Buenos Aires and Berlin being almost one order of magnitude. The neutron component in these spectra is shown in magenta, and as can be seen, CORSIKA imposes a cutoff of about 300 MeV to optimize computational time. We use Geant4 [1] to simulate the last 2 km of particle trajectories to capture the low-energy neutron component. Geant4 is a software package that simulates the interaction between radiation and matter. A more detailed discussion of this phase follows in the next section.

As shown in [13], the generation of such simulations, when stored, transforms into synthetic data with versatile applications for various research objectives. A machine with 128 cores and 1 TB of RAM generated the spectra shown in Fig. 3. ARTI, a software optimized for parallel processing, efficiently divides these simulations among up to 120 cores, generating 120 binary files. Under these conditions, simulating one hour of cosmic ray flux takes 1.5 h of computing time. In contrast, using a desktop machine with eight cores and 16 GB of RAM, the simulation time increases to approximately 24 h. We simulated 12 h of cosmic ray flux for each site in this case.

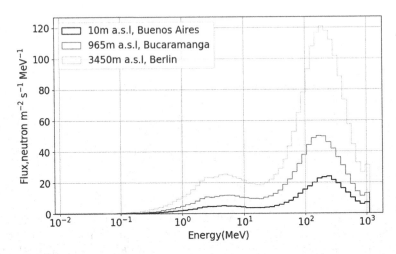

Fig. 4. Energy spectrum of neutrons produced by the interaction of cosmic rays within the atmosphere or three locations in South America. This spectrum was generated in Geant4.

3.2   Neutron Flux Simulation

As emphasized in the previous section, ARTI calculates the flux of secondary particles reaching a given observation point. However, our interest is focused on low-energy neutrons produced in the atmosphere, which are interesting for research applications in smart agriculture. CORSIKA excludes these since this software is designed for particles with energies greater than GeV. To solve this problem, we extended our simulations by including the last 2 km of the atmosphere using Geant4.

Figure 4 shows the resulting spectra after propagating the flux through the new atmospheric segment. The initial particles injected into Geant4 are the output of ARTI. These spectra were generated specifically for three locations in South America: Buenos Aires, Bucaramanga, and Berlin, containing only the neutron component. As can be seen, there is a significant difference in the neutron flux at the surface as the altitude changes. In addition, the shape of the spectrum and the ratio between the two prominent peaks remain consistent for each altitude.

The total neutron flux at the different altitudes is shown in Table 2. This summarises the flux variation with altitude, highlighting significant changes in flux levels. Furthermore, Table 2 shows the ratio $flux_i/flux_0$ for each altitude, where we have considered the Buenos Aires flux as the sea level reference, $flux_0$.

3.3   Simulation Time

GEANT4 approach is based on the sequential injection of particles, which means that by default, it uses a single processing core to perform a simulation. To overcome this limitation, we have developed a parallelization strategy that divides the input file, where each row represents a particle, into as many processing cores as possible. This approach is feasible because no information exchange is required between the jobs, guaranteeing that the resulting total file is the sum of all the individual files generated.

Table 2. Ratio of the flux per altitude according to the *see level* flux as reference.

Altitude	$flux_i$	$flux_i/flux_0$
10 m a.s.l	445	1
956 m a.s.l	986	2.21
3450 m a.s.l	2339	5.24

The simulations, which included 65 million events, each representing one particle emitted by a source located 2 km above the surface, were planned by calculating the average time per event. This was done by running four simulations with 100, 1000, 5000, and 10000 events each. Each event took approximately 0.26 s on a single CPU core. The simulations were run in parallel using 100 CPU cores, and the task took almost 48 h to complete.

4   Reproducibility Considerations

To improve the reproducibility of our analyses, we employ several strategies, including the use of Docker[4] and Singularity containers to preserve the computational environment. By encapsulating our software, dependencies and configurations within these containers, we ensure that the exact same environment can be replicated regardless of the underlying operating system or computing infrastructure. This eliminates compatibility issues and minimises the risk of software version conflicts, allowing other researchers to reproduce our simulations easily.

We also emphasise using open-source software tools based on version control systems. For example, the PENCIL CODE we use for stellar simulations is licensed under the GENERAL PUBLIC LICENSE version 2. In contrast, ARTI, our astroparticle simulation framework, is licensed under the 3-Clause BSD. These open licences promote transparency and allow researchers to access, study, modify and redistribute the software, facilitating the replication and validation of our analyses.

In addition to containerisation and open software, our approach also aims to facilitate the findability, accessibility, interoperability and reuse (FAIR) [18] of

---

[4] https://hub.docker.com/u/lagocollaboration.

our digital assets[5]. We assign persistent identifiers, such as DOIs, to our datasets and code repositories, making them easy to find. Our open-access policy ensures the accessibility of our research results, allowing other researchers to reproduce and build on our work. By adhering to standard file formats, data structures and interfaces, we promote interoperability with other tools and facilitate the integration of our analyses into larger scientific workflows. Finally, by openly sharing our data, code and methods, we encourage their reuse, enabling other researchers to validate our findings and explore new research directions.

Overall, our comprehensive approach to reproducibility, which includes containerisation, open software and adherence to the FAIR principles, ensures that our analyses can be accurately replicated, validated and extended by the scientific community. By promoting transparency, accessibility and compatibility, we contribute to the robustness and reliability of scientific research, foster collaboration and advance knowledge in our field.

5   Remarks

In this paper, we have discussed two particular cases of study of HPC in astrophysical and astroparticle simulations. HPC provides the computational power to model complex astrophysical systems and validate theoretical models against observational data.

In the first application, we used the PENCIL CODE, a high-level finite-difference numerical code, to simulate the evolution of magnetic field configurations in convective and stratified stars. We test the performance of these simulations on the Hypatia Cluster and conclude that the code demonstrates improved speedup performance when utilizing up to 32 processors.

We also discussed the importance of astroparticle observations in refining and validating astrophysical simulations. Ground-based detection of secondary particles is crucial in studying transient events and applications such as muon radiography. Collaboration between astrophysicists, computational scientists and observational researchers is essential to advance our knowledge of the Universe. HPC resources and sophisticated numerical codes and astroparticle observations enable us to tackle challenging problems and significantly advance astrophysics[6].

In the future, we aim to refine our simulations by incorporating additional physics and considering more complex astrophysical scenarios[7]. We also look forward to exploring new avenues of research that harness the power of HPC and astroparticle observations to deepen our understanding of cosmic phenomena[8].

Acknowledgement. L. M. B is supported by the Vicerrectoría de Investigación y Extensión - Universidad Industrial de Santander Postdoctoral Fellowship Programme No. 2023000359. MINCIENCIAS has partially founded this work under project 82242 of

---

[5] https://lagoproject.github.io/DMP/.

[6] https://exacore.uniandes.edu.co/es/que-hacemos/procesamiento.

[7] http://wiki.sc3.uis.edu.co/index.php/Cluster_Guane.

[8] https://www.renata.edu.co/.

call 890 of 2020, managed through the ICETEX contract 2022-0718. The computations presented in this paper were performed on the Hypatia cluster at the Universidad de los Andes and the Guane cluster at the Universidad Industrial de Santander, both located in Colombia. These HPC clusters were accessed through the LaRedCCA initiative of the National Academic Network of Advanced Technology, RENATA.

References

1. Agostinelli, S., Allison, J., Amako, K., Apostolakis, J., et al.: Geant4 - a simulation toolkit. Nucl. Instrum. Methods Phys. Res. Sect. A: Acceler. Spectromet. Detect. Associat. Equip. **506**(3), 250–303 (2003). https://doi.org/10.1016/S0168-9002(03)01368-8
2. Asorey, H., Dasso, S., Núñez, L.A., Pérez, Y., Sarmiento-Cano, C., Suárez-Durán, M., the LAGO Collaboration: The LAGO space weather program: drectional geomagnetic effects, background fluence calculations and multi-spectral data analysis. In: The 34th International Cosmic Ray Conference, vol. PoS(ICRC2015), p. 142 (2015)
3. Asorey, H., Núñez, L., Suárez-Durán, M.: Preliminary results from the Latin American giant observatory space weather simulation chain. Space Weather **16**(5), 461–475 (2018)
4. Becerra, L., Reisenegger, A., Valdivia, J.A., Gusakov, M.E.: Evolution of random initial magnetic fields in stably stratified and barotropic stars. Mon. Not. R. Astron. Soc. **511**(1), 732–745 (2022). https://doi.org/10.1093/mnras/stac102
5. Braithwaite, J., Nordlund, Å.: Stable magnetic fields in stellar interiors. Astron. Astrophys. **450**(3), 1077–1095 (2006). https://doi.org/10.1051/0004-6361:20041980
6. Fryxell, B., et al.: FLASH: an adaptive mesh hydrodynamics code for modeling astrophysical thermonuclear flashes. Astrophys. J. Suppl. **131**(1), 273–334 (2000). https://doi.org/10.1086/317361
7. Heck, D., Knapp, J., Capdevielle, J.N., Schatz, G., Thouw, T.: CORSIKA: a Monte Carlo code to simulate extensive air showers (1998)
8. Jourde, K., et al.: Monitoring temporal opacity fluctuations of large structures with muon radiography: a calibration experiment using a water tower. Sci. Rep. **6**(23054) (2016). https://doi.org/10.1038/srep23054
9. Kneizys, F.X., Abreu, L.W., Anderson, G.P., Chetwynd, J.H., et al.: The MODTRAN 2/3 report and LOWTRAN 7 model. Tech. Rep. (1996). https://web.gps.caltech.edu/~vijay/pdf/modrept.pdf
10. Mignone, A., et al.: PLUTO: a numerical code for computational astrophysics. Astrophys. J. Suppl. **170**(1), 228–242 (2007). https://doi.org/10.1086/513316
11. Pencil Code Collaboration, Brandenburg, A., et al.: The Pencil Code, a modular MPI code for partial differential equations and particles: multipurpose and multiuser-maintained. J. Open Source Softw. **6**(58), 2807 (2021). https://doi.org/10.21105/joss.02807
12. Price, D.J., et al.: Phantom: a smoothed particle hydrodynamics and magnetohydrodynamics code for astrophysics. Publ. Astron. Soc. Austral. **35**, e031 (2018). https://doi.org/10.1017/pasa.2018.25
13. Rubio-Montero, A.J., Pagán-Muñoz, R., Mayo-García, R., Pardo-Diaz, A., Sidelnik, I., Asorey, H.: The EOSC-synergy cloud services implementation for the Latin American giant observatory (LAGO). arXiv preprint arXiv:2111.11190 (2021)

14. Sarmiento-Cano, C., et al.: The arti framework: cosmic rays atmospheric background simulations. Eur. Phys. J. C **82**, 1019 (2022). https://doi.org/10.1140/epjc/s10052-022-10883-z

15. Springel, V., Pakmor, R., Zier, O., Reinecke, M.: Simulating cosmic structure formation with the GADGET-4 code. Mon. Not. R. Astron. Soc. **506**(2), 2871–2949 (2021). https://doi.org/10.1093/mnras/stab1855

16. Teyssier, R.: Cosmological hydrodynamics with adaptive mesh refinement. A new high resolution code called RAMSES. Astron. Astrophys. **385**, 337–364 (2002). https://doi.org/10.1051/0004-6361:20011817

17. Usoskin, I.G., et al.: Forbush decreases of cosmic rays: energy dependence of the recovery phase. J. Geophys. Res.: Space Phys. **113**(A7) (2008). https://doi.org/10.1029/2007JA012955

18. Wilkinson, M.D., et al.: The FAIR guiding principles for scientific data management and stewardship. Sci. Data **3**(1), 160018 (2016). https://doi.org/10.1038/sdata.2016.18

Improvement of the Simulation of the Degradation of Reinforced Concrete in Saltwater Environments Using Directives

Félix A. Mejía[1,2,3(✉)] ⓘ, Carlos J. Barrios H.[1,2,3] ⓘ, and Darío Y. Peña B.[1,2,4] ⓘ

[1] Universidad Industrial de Santander (UIS), Bucaramanga, Santander, Colombia
felix2067165@correo.uis.edu.co
[2] High Performance and Scientific Computing UIS (SC3UIS), Bucaramanga, Colombia
[3] Large Scale and Advanced Computing Research Group UIS (CAGE), Bucaramanga, Colombia
[4] Corrosion Research Group (GICUIS), Santander, Colombia

Abstract. High-performance computers are now essential in scientific and technological research and development because of their high processing capacity and extensive memory; they allow us to simulate phenomena where processing and handling such information is necessary. The simulation of physicochemical problems involves the inherent analysis and processing of large volumes of data. For this, a large computing capacity is required. Therefore, it is necessary to apply a parallel processing scheme using GPUs that allows an efficient way of obtaining the simulation results. This work presents a simulated diffusion model, considering the factors that affect the corrosion initiation rate of the reinforcement structure, such as the water-cement ratio, temperature, density, and chloride binding capacity of concrete since all these variables are handled. A significant amount of information becomes necessary to use computational architectures based on multiple GPUs to obtain better results in shorter times and thus minimize this phenomenon by changing specific design and manufacturing parameters [1, 2].

Keywords: GPGPU Computing · Advanced Computing Materials · Simulation

1 Introduction

The simulation of physicochemical problems is inherent in analyzing and processing large volumes of information. For this, it requires a large capacity of computation. It is necessary to apply a parallel processing scheme using GPU that efficiently obtains the simulation results. Multi-GPU systems use multiple GPUs [3] to shorten simulation times and eliminate any obstacle that slows down productivity. This achieves much higher simulation speeds in their systems and generates models with a fidelity that was not possible before so that more variations in the design can be produced in a shorter time.

© The Author(s), under exclusive license to Springer Nature Switzerland AG 2024
C. J. Barrios H. et al. (Eds.): CARLA 2023, CCIS 1887, pp. 212–225, 2024.
https://doi.org/10.1007/978-3-031-52186-7_14

1.1 Physicochemical Phenomenon

The corrosion phenomenon of the steel structures that are part of the reinforced concrete is caused by oxygen and humidity, in addition to the existence of free chlorides in the surrounding environment. Seawater has a high concentration of dissolved salts that represents a severe threat to reinforced concrete because it promotes and accelerates corrosion.

In coastal areas, the sea breeze carries with it actual moisture contents that, in one way or another, take chlorides, so structures that are not in direct contact with the sea begin to suffer from the action of chlorides.

Reinforced concrete is one of the most used materials in construction today due to its structural properties, low cost, and outstanding durability. The alkaline character present in the pores of the concrete allows the reinforcement steel to be in a passive state in terms of corrosion, its speed being almost nil. However, this speed increases due to the entry of aggressive agents into the environment, such as chloride ions and carbon dioxide. This leads to the corrosion of the steel structures that reinforce the concrete.

In a marine environment, the leading cause of deterioration of reinforced concrete structures is corrosion, which is initiated by chloride ions due to the exposure of these structures to seawater, sea breezes, or the use of aggregates contaminated with salts. Once the chloride ions reach a critical concentration on the surface of the steel, the passive protection layer loses its stability and initiates corrosion. Due to the outstanding deficiencies of concrete, such as low tensile strength and porosity, the latter is the product of the hydration processes of the reaction between cement and water. Once hardened, these remains of water will become pores of different sizes, which will be interconnected with each other, facilitating the transport of fluids, gases, and other chemical substances that are highly detrimental to reinforced concrete since it allows the beginning of the process of deterioration of the steel structures that comprise it (Fig. 1).

Fig. 1. Corrosion of reinforced concrete exposed to a marine environment. (Authors Photo)

Through this simulation, it is possible to analyze and experiment with what happens inside the reinforced concrete, thus minimizing this corrosion phenomenon by changing specific design and manufacturing parameters. Given that many variables and a large amount of information are handled in this simulation, it is necessary to use multiple GPU architectures to provide the researcher with the best results in the shortest possible time.

Corrosion. It is the chemical reaction product of the union of the metal with oxygen. it is a deterioration observed in a metallic object due to a high electrochemical impact of the oxidative character, and the degenerative speed of said material will depend on the ex-position to the oxidizing agent, the temperature presented if it is exposed to saline solutions and the chemical properties of these metallic agents, this process is spontaneous, and this can occur in materials that are not metallic [4].

Reinforced Concrete: Also called reinforced concrete, it consists of the use of reinforced concrete with steel bars or meshes, although it also uses plastic fibers, fiberglass, steel fibers, or combinations of steel bars with fibers depending on the requirements to which will be submitted. It is used in all types of buildings, such as bridges, dams, tunnels, and industrial works [5].

Durability of Concrete: It is defined as the ability to resist weathering, chemical attack, abrasion, or any other process or service condition of structures that produce the concrete deterioration. Several factors affect the durability of reinforced construction, such as the quality of its components, dosage of each part, mix for a sufficient time to obtain a homogeneous material, correct placement of steel structures, and suitable compaction to avoid segregation and porosity [6].

Deterioration of Concrete: Physical, chemical, or physicochemical factors lead to the reinforcements' corrosion. In any of these categories, the influence of the components of the concrete and its geographical location on the structure's useful life is recognized. The physical mechanisms of deterioration are associated with the dissolution of pulp compounds in the medium, with loss of mass, increased porosity, and a drop in resistance. The chemical mechanisms correspond to the exchange of ions of the pulp with the medium, giving rise to compounds that are soluble or not but of a non-expansive nature that eventually cause similar effects to the physical ones. The physicochemical combines the two concepts, giving rise to the formation of expansive-type compounds that cause internal tensions and lead to cracking and possible component disintegration [7].

Attack by Chlorides: Chloride can penetrate the reinforced concrete from the external environment to the interior, generating corrosion in the reinforcements by combining various transport mechanisms such as ionic diffusion, water absorption, water flow, and chloride ion dispersion, or by an effect of external electric potential.

Carbonation of Concrete: Concrete is a very porous material, which allows penetration into the interior of the CO_2 from the air. When this happens, the CO_2 reaction occurs with the calcium hydroxide of the concrete and the hydrated compounds of the cement, calcium carbonate formed by which the pH decreases, reaching values lower than nine [8].

This paper presents a diffusion model simulated considering the different factors that affect the corrosion initiation rate of the reinforcement structure, such as the water-cement ratio, temperature, density, and chloride binding capacity of concrete since all these variables are handled. A significant amount of information becomes necessary to use computational architectures based on multiple GPUs to obtain better results in shorter times. This section presents the physical problem from the material's point of view. The second section shows the mathematical model, the simulation, and the results. Finally, a conclusion and further work are presented.

2   Simulations and Results

2.1   Mathematical Model

Simulation of the Prediction of the Useful life of Concrete: The corrosion of the reinforcement due to the penetration of chloride ions and the carbonation of concrete is a major problem that reduces the durability of reinforced concrete structures. Once the chloride concentration around the surface of the steel reinforcement exceeds a certain limit concentration or the pH value of the concrete pore solution decreases to a threshold value due to the carbonation reaction, the steel reinforcement will undergo the *depassivation* process, and then the metallic corrosion. [10, 11, 12].

Carbonation Process: Concrete carbonation is a complex physical and chemical process. In our model, this process is divided into four parts: (1) carbon dioxide transport, (2) dissolved calcium hydroxide mass balance, (3) solid calcium hydroxide solution in concrete pore solution, and (4) Chemical reaction of CSH with carbon dioxide. The governing equations can be given by:

$$\frac{\partial (\emptyset - \emptyset_{we}) C_{co_2}}{\partial t} + \nabla . J_{co_2} = -I_{ch} - I_{CSH} \tag{1}$$

$$\frac{\partial \emptyset_{we} C_{ch,d}}{\partial t} + \nabla . J_{ch,d} = -I_{ch} + I_d \tag{2}$$

$$\frac{\partial C_{ch,s}}{\partial t} = -I_d \tag{3}$$

$$\frac{\partial C_{CSH}}{\partial t} = -r_{CSH} \tag{4}$$

where C_{CO_2} is the molar concentration of carbon dioxide in the gaseous phase of the pores (mol/m^3 of porous air), $\emptyset$ is the current porosity of the concrete, $\emptyset_{we}$ is the fraction of water volume in the evaporable pore (m^3 of solution/m^3 of concrete), J_{co_2} is the flow of carbon dioxide I_{ch}, and I_{CSH} is the rate of carbon dioxide consumption due to its chemical reaction with Ca (OH)$_2$ and CSH, respectively.

$C_{ch,d}$ is the molar concentration of dissolved calcium hydroxide (mol/m^3 of solution). $J_{ch,d}$ is the flow of hydroxide ions, I_d is the dissolved velocity of solid calcium hydroxide to the pore water. $C_{ch,s}$ is the molar concentration of solid calcium hydroxide (mol/m^3

of concrete), C_{CSH} is the molar concentration of CSH in concrete (mol / m^3 of concrete), r_{CSH} is the reaction rate of CSH with carbon dioxide. The right sides in Eqs. (1)–(4) are determined by the Papadakis carbonation model [13, 14, 15]. The relationship between $\varnothing_{w_e}$ and h can be estimated according to the BSB model [16]. Several carbon dioxide diffusion coefficient estimation methods are used $D_{CO_2}^{car}$ are available in the literature [15, 16] [17].

Transport of Chloride Ions with Carbonation: It is assumed that the transport equation of chloride ions after carbonation still complies with Fick's second law of diffusion. The total amount of chloride in a unit volume of concrete consists of the free chloride present in the pore solution and the bound chloride of the Friedel salt.

$$C_{tc} = \varnothing_{w_e} C_{fc} + C_{bc} \qquad (5)$$

where C_{tc} is the total chloride content in a unit of concrete volume (mol/m^3 of concrete) and C_{fc} is the content of free chloride ions (mol / m^3 of pore solution). C_{bc} is the content of bound chloride (mol/m^3 of concrete). A part of the bound chloride can participate in the chemical reaction shown in Eq. (3), releasing free chloride ions.

The amount of chloride attached depends on the concentration of free chloride in the pore solution and the degree of carbonation because we consider carbonation. Therefore, the instantaneous variation of the total chloride can be expressed as:

$$\frac{\partial C_{tc}}{\partial t} = \frac{\partial \varnothing_{w_e} C_{fc}}{\partial t} + \frac{\partial C_{bc}}{\partial C_{fc}} \frac{\partial C_{fc}}{\partial t} + \frac{\partial C_{bc}}{\partial \alpha_c} \frac{\partial \alpha_c}{\partial t} \qquad (6)$$

where $\frac{\partial C_{bc}}{\partial C_{fc}}$ is an isotherm between the bound chloride and the free chloride $\frac{\partial C_{bc}}{\partial \alpha_c}$ can also be described with an isotherm in which carbonation should be considered.

Presented the mathematical model to describe the degradation of reinforced concrete in saltwater environments, proposing an algorithm to be implemented is possible, as shown in the following section.

2.2 Simulation Algorithm

The algorithm's first part is loading input variables and initializing the data structures with the initial values. Subsequently, it starts the iterations where the time variable varies. The concentrations in current carbonates and chlorides are calculated simultaneously with the transfer of temperatures and humidity in the concrete. The chloride concentrations are stored in a VTK file to visualize the chloride entry in the reinforced concrete block. Afterward, it is verified that the chloride concentrations do not reach their limit value and continue until reaching the limit value, thus estimating the valuable lifetime of reinforced concrete. (See Fig. 2).

Using the parallelization techniques and the OpenACC libraries [9], and the compiler since it is the most robust one currently available, as well as being installed on the GUANE-1 cluster of the High-Performance and Scientific Computing Center, SC3UIS (from Spanish acronym of Supercomputación and Cálculo Científico) at Universidad Industrial de Santander in Bucaramanga, Colombia [18]. The process of implementing the codes using parallelization techniques of the simulation algorithm based on the chlorides diffusion model combined with the diffusion of carbonates in reinforced concrete exposed to a marine environment for their respective execution in architectures based on multiple GPUs. Code development is performed by scientists of the Advanced Computing and Large Scale Group, CAGE (from Spanish acronym of Computación Avanzada y de Gran Èscala), and Corrosion Research Group, GIC (from Spanish acronym of Grupo de Investigación en Corrosión).

The algorithm in Fig. 2 shows the parallel regions in the workflow after the data input, calculating the current chloride and carbonate concentration and verifying the concentrations. In the workflow, visualization is also presented, and, using some specific functions with the directives, the simulation provides information about the process, as seen later in Fig. 4.

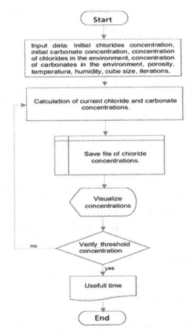

Fig. 2. Algorithm workflow diagram

The main function that calculates the diffusion of the chloride ion in the reinforced concrete using the second law of Fick was parallelized; for this purpose, the "pragma acc kernels" directive was used, which tells the compiler to generate parallel accelerator cores (CUDA cores in our case) for the loop nests that follow the directive. (See Fig. 3). Obviously, the algorithm is independent of the implementation mechanism and execution support. Still, contemplating the need to accelerate the execution of the simulation as the mathematical properties of the algorithm, we will concentrate on the implementation thought towards massively paralleled machines based on Purpose General platforms based in CPUs/GPUs.

An important aspect to consider is that for this project, and as the proposed algorithm is seen, we seek to accelerate the visualization of the phenomenon; in this case, the concentration of the chloride ion advances in reinforced concrete, then the visualization of the concentrations is critical[1].

The implementation mechanism of the algorithm mainly used C and directives using OpenACC in a homogeneous code. All functions and open-source code are available in a open repository in [18].

```c
float *fd3d_difussion_2Fick_3D ( int x_num, float x[], int y_num, float y[], int z_num, float z[], float t, float dt,
                float cflx, float cfly, float cflz, float * Coeff_Diff, float *V, float valueBond,
                void bc ( int x_num, int y_num, int z_num, float *V, float value  ) )
{
    float *V_new;
    int j, i, k;
    long index_ijk, index_ijpk, index_ijnk;
    long index_injk, index_ipjk;
    long index_ijkn, index_ijkn2, index_ijkp, index_ijkp2;
    V_new = ( float * ) malloc ( x_num * y_num * (z_num) *sizeof ( float ) );
    k=0;
    #pragma acc kernels copyin(V[0:x_num * y_num * z_num], Coeff_Diff[0:x_num * y_num * z_num]) copyout(V_new[0:x_num * y_num * z_num])
    #pragma acc loop independent
    for(i = 1; i < x_num - 1; i++ )
    {[...]
    }
    #pragma acc loop independent collapse(2) gang
    for(k = 1; k < z_num -1; k++ )
    {
        for(i = 1; i < x_num - 1; i++ )
        {
            #pragma acc loop independent vector
            for ( j = 1; j < y_num - 1; j++ )
            {[...]
            }
        }
    }
    k=z_num-1;
    #pragma acc loop independent
    for(i = 1; i < x_num - 1; i++ )
    {
        #pragma acc loop independent
        for ( j = 1; j < y_num - 1; j++ )
        {[...]
        }
    }
    bc ( x_num, y_num, z_num, V_new, valueBond );
    return V_new;
}
```

Fig. 3. Parallel code of the function

Figure 3 shows a fragment of the parallel code of the function to highlight the use of the pragmas and the placement in the structure of the code. It is important to note the use of collapse on the loop level since this will allow the compiler to use multi-dimensional blocks.

Considering that about five to seven runs were performed for the simulation for each of the thirteen simulations presented (and obtain the respective values), a very good standard deviation was obtained (with very little variability, between 0,3 and 0,5). However, as explained below, we must not confuse the runs with the interactions made.

---

[1] Another important aspect to observe, but more for computational reasons, was the performance measures around the resources balancing, the acceleration, and time used in the execution, visible in the proposed algorithm in Fig. 2.

The visualization of the *vtk* files generated by the algorithm can be seen as a movie using the Paraview software,[2] as seen in Fig. 4. Fundamentally, it is visualized by highlighting the colors according to key information needed to observe the phenomenon and understand the degradation. Then, the color difference provides information about the concentration of the chloride ion advance in reinforced concrete.

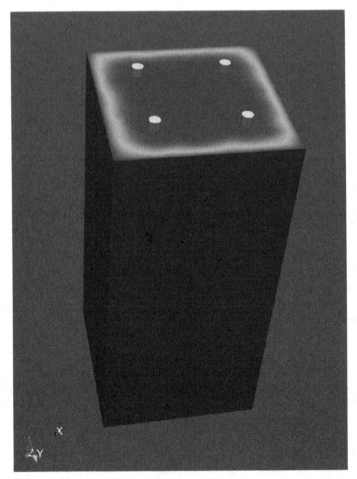

Fig. 4. Visualization of the chloride ion advance in reinforced concrete.

The simulation was executed in sequential solution using only CPUs and in a parallel solution on a CPU/GPU platform using initially one GPU and after with two GPUs, obtaining the results shown in Table 1. This usage configuration corresponds to one of the GUANE-1 Supercomputer node types. The presented results are in terms of processing

---

[2] ParaView is an open-source, multi-platform data analysis and visualization tool. It is widely used in various fields, including the materials and condensed physics community. More information about Paraview in: https://www.paraview.org/

time in seconds for each of the solutions, considering the next computer architecture elements:

Sequential Running: Intel Xeon CPU E5645 @ 2.40GHz (12 Cores), RAM 104 GB. Linux operating system, CENTOS distribution. Compiled in GCC.

Parallel CPU/GPU: Intel Xeon CPU E5645 @ 2.40 GHz (12 Cores), RAM 104 GB, NVIDIA GPU Tesla 12 GB GDDR5. Linux operating system, CENTOS Distribution. Compiled in NVIDIA NVC (to exploit OpenACC directives suite).

Table 1 shows in the first column the size of the cube for the analysis is varied (256 × 256 × 400, 512 × 512 × 400, and 1024 × 1024 × 400). The second column presents the number of iterations of the simulation (8000, 16000, 32000, and 64000) and obtains results from an average of executions (five to seven executions). The last three columns organize the results for the performed simulations, the third column only for results using the CPU, and the fourth and last columns the results using one GPU and two GPUs.

Table 1. Execution times (seconds) of the simulation

Cube size	Iterations	Sequential (seg)	GPU (sec)	2XGPU (sec)
256x256x400	8000	57600	32000	17297
256x256x400	16000	115200	65455	34898
256x256x400	32000	230400	137143	73555
256x256x400	64000	460800	263314	142665
512x512x400	8000	268800	76800	40394
512x512x400	16000	537600	145297	75991
512x512x400	32000	1075200	303729	159500
512x512x400	64000	2150400	627854	331192
1024x1024x400	8000	1084800	166892	86473
1024x1024x400	16000	2169600	335332	173523
1024x1024x400	32000	4339200	666544	344544
1024x1024x400	64000	8678400	1329005	683203

In Table 1. is interesting to observe the increase of base time in the execution by increasing the dimensions of the simulation. However, very quickly to associate these dimensions to threads of support of the execution obtains a significant reduction in time, which requires an analysis of the acceleration. According to the obtained data, the simulation implementation using GPU parallelization achieves much shorter times than the sequential implementation, achieving accelerations close to seven times compared to the sequential algorithm, as shown in Fig. 5.

Looking for more complexity, resolution, and acceleration, two GPUs were used in a new implementation. Thenceforward, employing the parallel algorithm in a hybrid version that combines OpenMP with OpenACC over a multi-GPU architecture of two

GPUs, results were almost equal to twice the acceleration obtained for its version for a single GPU analyzed previously. Hence, it determines that the algorithm is scalable and accelerates the processing by increasing the number of GPUs used.

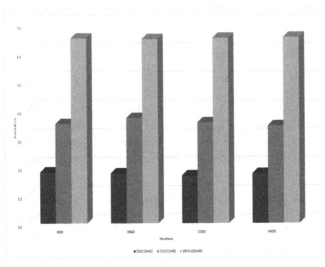

Fig. 5. Acceleration for the simulation in 1XGPU.

The acceleration obtained for each cube size analyzed for the MultiGPU algorithm is shown in Fig. 6. Comparing the results of both Figs. 5 and 6, we observe that linear acceleration that is visible, independent of the change in dimension, is sustained by scaling, as stated above. In the case of using one GPU, the attended acceleration is the 7X, and in the case of the two GPUs is the 12X.

However, the presented results, it's important to note that not all code can be easily parallelized and accelerated on a GPU using directives. Some algorithms and computations may require more fine-grained control and optimization using low-level GPU programming techniques. Furthermore, the performance benefits of GPU acceleration using directives may vary depending on the specific code and hardware configuration. It's important to profile and optimize the code to achieve the best performance on the target GPU architecture. For this simulation, the configuration of the support platform and different elements organized in the compute node allow to focus on processing acceleration. As can be seen, for example, the RAM memory used allows the dimensions of the experiment to be increased easily and the limitation used was due to the detail characteristics required by the experiment of the degradation of armored concrete in saltwater locations, as the columns on a pier.

In Fig. 7, the execution times obtained for the sequential version as the parallel version using OpenACC directives are shown, with the values of the parallel version being much smaller, and its difference concerning the serial version increases as the size of the data increases cube to simulate.

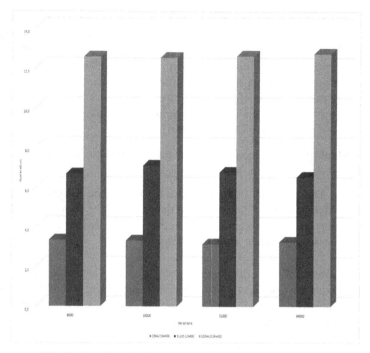

Fig. 6. Acceleration obtained for the simulation in 2XGPU.

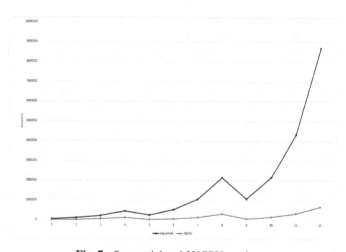

Fig. 7. Sequential and 2XGPU runtimes

2.3 2.3. OpenACC Directives

The OpenACC directives facilitate the programming of the GPU since employing a few lines of code without worrying about the location of the data allows for parallelizing in the GPU program. These directives are added to the code reasonably easily and quickly. Still, it does not allow the programmer to control the hardware in which it is executed directly, so the program can behave differently than expected; besides, not directly allowing handling the details of the communication between CPU-GPU can cause software optimization to deteriorate performance. [9] The OpenACC directives are based on the use of #pragma compiler instructions following the syntax:

#pragma acc directive-name [clause-list] new-line.

These directives apply to the code block immediately following the #pragma tag. PGI now supports the following OpenACC directives:

Kernels Construct. Defines the program region that must be compiled in a sequence of kernels for execution in the accelerator device.

Data Directive. Defines data, usually matrices that must be assigned in the device memory for the duration of the data region, if the data must be copied from the host to the memory of the device when entering the region and copied from the device to the memory of the device host when leaving the region.

- **Host Data Construct.** It makes the device's data address available on the host.
- **Loop Directive.** Describe the type of parallelism to run the cycle and declare variables, private reduct, and arrangements within the cycle. It applies to the cycle that should appear in the following line of the directive.

Combined Parallel and Loop Directive. *Specifying a Loop Directive nested immediately within a Kernel Directive is a shortcut.* The meaning is identical to the explicit kernel specification that contains a Loop Directive.

Cache Directive. Specifies the matrix elements or sub-arrays to be searched at the highest level of the cache for the body of a Loop. It should appear at the top inside the Loop.

Declare Directive. Specifies that a matrix or arrays should be allocated in the device's memory for the duration of the implicit data region of a function, subroutine, or program. Specifies whether the data values will be transferred from the host to the device memory when entering the implicit data region and from the device to the host memory when exiting the implicit data region.

Update Directive. They were used during the validity of the accelerator data to update all or a part of the host memory array with the corresponding array values in the device's memory or to update all or part of the memory array of the device with the corresponding array values in the host memory.

Routine Directive. It tells the compiler to compile a procedure for an accelerator and the host. In a file or routine with a procedure call, the Routine Directive describes the implementation of the attributes of the process when it is called over the accelerator.

The detailed used directives are available and documented in the provided code via the site [18]. In these experiments to improve the simulation of the degradation of reinforced concrete in saltwater environments, achieving the GPU acceleration using directives simplifies the coding. The used directives provide a high-level approach to

GPU programming, allowing developers to offload computationally intensive tasks to the GPU without having to write low-level GPU-specific code and obtain a good acceleration to take advantage of the available architecture.

3   Conclusions and Further Work

The application of high-performance computing techniques allows for obtaining results of estimating the advance of the chloride ion within a concrete structure faster and more accurately. Since it enables it to handle many more factors that affect it and is more meshing-dense, it allows for much more accurate results. In the case of materials, developing techniques, algorithms, and implementation mechanisms, as the use of directives, is crucial to obtain good results in measured times.

The model proposed in this project is a convenient tool that allows evaluating the progress of the Cl- ion through the concrete structures. Thus, if the necessary concentration has been reached for the start of *depassivation* of the reinforcing steel or the approximate time for this to happen, before this work, the simulations performed using sequential solutions were very costly in time and with little precision.

Using the OpenACC directives simplified the implementation of the parallel version simulation algorithm using architectures based on multiple GPUs. Today, other projects collaborate are in progress with materials engineers, physicists, and computer developers working on open-source codes to perform simulations. These codes and documentation are available in [18].

Acknowledgment. All experiments were supported by the Supercomputación y Cálculo Científico UIS (SC3UIS), a special support unit for advanced computing of the vice-rector for research and extension of the Universidad Industrial de Santander (UIS).

References

1. Li, L., Page, C., Wang, Y.: Modelling of chloride ingress into concrete from the saline environment, pp. 1573–1582 (2005)
2. Velázquez Gonzalez, R.: Electrochemical evaluation of the corrosion in grade in reinforced steel in the presence of admixtures. Portugaliae Electrochimica **23**, 179–194 (2005)
3. Nvidia Corporation. ¿Qué es el GPU Computing acelerado?. http://www.nvidia.es/object/gpu computing-es.html
4. Mejía de Gutiérrez, R.: Durabilidad y Corrosión en Materiales Cementicios. Universidad del Valle, Cali, Colombia. Cyted, pp. 85–115 (1999)
5. Del Valle Moreno, A., Pérez López, T., y Maerínez Madrid, M.: El Fenómeno de la Corrosión en Estructuras de Concreto Reforzado. Publicación Técnica No. 182 Sanfandila, Qro, pp. 33–50 (2001)
6. Fontana, M.G.: de Corrosion engineering, Nueva York, Mc GrawHill, 556 (1986)
7. Mindess, S.a.Y.J.: Concrete. Prentice Hall, Nueva Jersey (1981)
8. G. d. I. d. c. UIS, Desarrollo metodológico electroquímico de la corrosividad de estructuras de concreto sometidas a los ambientes marinos de las costas del pacífico colombiano, Bucaramanga, Colombia, pp. 15–18 (2009)

9. OpenACC, Homepage. https://www.openacc.org/sites/default/files/inline-files/OpenACC_P rogramming_Guide_0.pdf
10. Bazant, Z.: Physical model for steel corrosion in concrete sea structures theory, de. J. Struct. Div. ASCE **105**, 1137–1153 (1979)
11. Caims,J.: State of the art report on bond of corroded reinforcement (1998)
12. Ho, R.L.D.W.S.: Carbonation of concrete and its prediction, pp. 489–504 (1987)
13. Papadakis, C.V.M.F.V.: Fundamental modeling and experimental investigation of concrete carbonation. ACI Mater. J. **88**(4), 363–373 (1991)
14. Papadakis, C.V.M.F.V.: A reaction engineering approach to the problem of concrete carbonation. J. Am. Inst. Chem. Eng. **35**(10), 1639–1650 (1989)
15. Papadakis, C.V.M.F.V.: Physical and chemical characteristics affecting the durability of concrete. ACI Mater. J. **88**(2) 186–196 (1991)
16. Brunauer, J.S.E.B.S.: Adsorption on non-porous solids,» J. Colloid Interface Sci. 30 (4), p. 546–552, (1969); Saetta, R. V. A.: Experimental investigation and numerical modeling of carbonation process in reinforced concrete structures. Part I. Theoretical Formulation, pp. 571–579 (2004)
17. Saetta, R.S.R.V.A.: Mechanical behavior of concrete under physical–chemical attacks. J. Eng. Mech. ASCE **124**(10), 1100–1109 (1998)
18. Supercomputación y Cálculo Científico, Homepage. http://www.sc3.uis.edu.co/

Parallel Hybrid-Heterogeneous Single Value Decomposition Factorization

Juan C. Hernández-Cortés[1] , Amilcar Meneses Viveros[2,3] ,
Liliana Ibeth Barbosa-Santillán[3(✉)] , Erika Hernández-Rubio[3] ,
and Juan J. Sánchez-Escobar[3]

[1] Department of Computer Science, Cinvestav -IPN, Mexico City, Mexico
ameneses@cs.cinvestav.mx
[2] Universidad de Guadalajara, Guadalajara, Mexico
[3] SEPI -ESCOM and CETI, Mexico City, Mexico
ibarbosa@cucea.udg.mx

Abstract. SVD factorization is a fundamental operation to solve problems in chemistry, biology, physics, and engineering. These problems are image processing, data mining, and big data, among others. There are several methods to get SVD factorization. One of these methods involve the use of Householder transformation, so it is possible to parallelize this task. Furthermore, novel computer architectures are oriented to use heterogeneous computing, such as CPUs and GPUs, in order to increase the performance and reduce the energy consumption. In this work, an heterogeneous parallel implementation of SVD based on Householder transformation is presented. Some strategies for matrix partition are presented in order to scale the program in the use of GPU cards. The speedup is increased when several GPU cards are used.

Keywords: SVD · Heterogeneous parallel programming · Householder Transformation

1 Introduction

Engineering and science problems use matrix operators or large matrices that are usually symmetric. The main transformations that apply to these operators are QR factorization for the resolution of systems of equations (which are generally LU, Givens, Householder or Cholesky factorization) (Sameh and Kuck 1978; Cosnard et al. 1986).

Bowgen and Modi (1985) QR factorization is a basis for solving equations and is also very useful for calculating other operations such as the determinant or inverse of a matrix (Choi et al. 1996). Factorization can be carried out by various methods, including LU, Cholesky, Householder or Givens rotations (Householder 1958; Sameh and Kuck 1978; Chen et al. 2008). The Householder transformation H is a reflection of a vector v on a plane. It allows many elements of v to be zero in a single transformation. The Householder transformation is characterized by its low complexity and the properties that have its transformation because it allows rebuilding in an appropriate way to the matrix Q while building R.

C. J. Barrios H. et al. (Eds.): CARLA 2023, CCIS 1887, pp. 197–211, 2024.
https://doi.org/10.1007/978-3-031-52186-7_15

Bifactorization is an essential step in several processes such as diagonalization, SVD factorization, or solving low-rank matrix recovering problems.

The problem runs on supercomputers due to the high complexity and the large size of the matrices. The diagonalization of a matrix normally takes a few hours or days (Sunderland 2009) (Leininger et al. 2001) do it in less time. In several cases, the SVD factorization must be calculated in real-time, for example, in Internet search engines such as Google. The diagonalization and SVD factorization therefore needs to be done within a short time (Osinski and Weiss 2005; Liu et al. 2002).

Many of the current supercomputers are computer nodes connected to high-speed networks that share a mass storage system. Each node may have one or more multicore processors or an accelerator such as a GPU or Xeon-Phi. This diversity of processing units means that only one node must have programs other than the multicore processors. Based on GPUs' use, it is possible to coordinate between them and with other processes to obtain the maximum performance of a node. Hence, it is necessary to apply various parallel programming paradigms, such as shared memory, distributed memory, hybrid memory, and heterogeneous computing. We require programs that combine paradigms, such as hybrid-heterogeneous parallel programs. This type of program can combine MPI with OpenMP and CUDA, or MPI with OpenCL, allowing us to use the different processing units.

The diversity of execution types units to execute processes in parallel. It forces us to ask ourselves which option of execution in parallel is the most appropriate. It is not the same to send the task to a server with some GPU and multicore processors than to diverse nodes in a supercomputer. Therefore, are several parallel implementations to use the most convenient one. In this work, we present various parallelization strategies for the Householder transformation depending on their application to other algebraic operations. These strategies are oriented towards parallelization with GPUs using CUDA, multicore processors using OpenMP and, distributed memory using MPI. The main idea is to present how Householder's transformation has various parallelization strategies that depend on the matrix operation. That is a fundamental operation. Its best performance varies from implementations in heterogeneous hybrid environments.

A householder in 1958, (Householder 1958), proposed a transformation to solve a system of equations using a point reflection on the plane. The reflection is defined by a unit vector $\mathbf{v}$ that is orthogonal to the plane such that the reflection of a point $\mathbf{x}$ in the plane is the linear transformation:

$$\mathbf{x} - 2\langle \mathbf{x}, \mathbf{v} \rangle = \mathbf{x} - 2\mathbf{v}\mathbf{v}^T\mathbf{x}.$$

We can also write this transformation in matrix form, as follows:

$$\mathbf{P} = \mathbf{I} - \frac{\mathbf{v}\mathbf{v}^T}{H}, \tag{1}$$

where $H = \frac{1}{2}|\mathbf{v}|^2$ and $\mathbf{v}$ is a real vector. The Householder transformation matrix has the property of being symmetrical or orthogonal. The main idea of

Householder transformation is that by applying it to a vector x, the result will be:

$$\mathbf{Px} = ||\mathbf{x}||e_0.$$

where e_0 is the first vector of the canonical base. To achieve this, the vector $\mathbf{v}$ in Eq. (1) must be $\mathbf{v} = \mathbf{x} \pm |\mathbf{x}|e_0$.

In 1992, (Press et al. 1992), discussed how to use the Householder transformation for the tridiagonalization of a symmetrical matrix. $\mathbf{A}$ is a non-singular symmetrical matrix used to find the tridiagonal matrix $\mathbf{T}$ similar to $\mathbf{A}$. Then, we are looking for an invertible matrix $\mathbf{P}$ for which:

$$\mathbf{T} = \mathbf{PAP}^{-1} \tag{2}$$

The matrix $\mathbf{P}$ is a multiplication of k matrices of the form $\mathbf{P}_K\mathbf{P}_{k-1}\ldots\mathbf{P}_1$, where a matrix $\mathbf{P}_J$ is a transformation of Householder, and $\mathbf{P}^{-1} = \mathbf{P}_1\ldots\mathbf{P}_{k-1}\mathbf{P}_K$.

Then $\mathbf{P}_1$ is such that

$$
\mathbf{P}_1\mathbf{A} =
\begin{bmatrix}
1 & 0 & 0 & \cdots & 0 \\
0 & & & & \\
0 & & & & \\
\vdots & & {}^{(n-1)}\mathbf{P}_1 & & \\
0 & & & &
\end{bmatrix}
\begin{bmatrix}
a_{00} & a_{01}\ a_{02} & \cdots & a_{0n-1} \\
a_{10} & & & \\
a_{20} & & & \\
\vdots & & \text{irrelevant} & \\
a_{n-1,0} & & &
\end{bmatrix}
$$

$$
=
\begin{bmatrix}
a_{00} & a_{01}\ a_{02} & \cdots & a_{0n-1} \\
k & & & \\
0 & & & \\
\vdots & & \text{irrelevant} & \\
0 & & &
\end{bmatrix}.
$$

Where ${}^{(n-1)}\mathbf{P}_1$ is a Householder matrix with dimension $(n-1) \times (n-1)$. Then computing a a bifactorization for $\mathbf{P}_1$ applied to $\mathbf{A}$ we get

$$
\mathbf{P}_1\mathbf{A}\mathbf{P}_1 =
\begin{bmatrix}
a_{00} & k & 0 & \cdots & 0 \\
k & & & & \\
0 & & & & \\
\vdots & & \text{irrelevant} & & \\
0 & & & &
\end{bmatrix}.
$$

This process is repeated $k - 1$ times, to obtain the tridiagonal matrix. And for each $\mathbf{P}_i$, the dimension of the Householder matrix is decreased.

From the original paper of Householder (Householder 1958), the complexity in QR factorization is

$$O(n^3).$$

The main problem addressed in this work is to carry out the bifactorization of large matrices in different GPU cards, such that the acceleration advantages of these devices are.

Section 2 shows the related work. Section 3 discusses the parallelization strategies. Section 4 shows the results of the experiments. Finally, we conclude with the conclusions and the future work.

2 Related Work

In the last decades, parallel algorithms developed for bifactoriazacion; many of them do not use Householder transformation. Several papers have been published on the parallelization of the Householder transformation in CUDA for bifactorization and other transformations.

Cosnuau in 2014, (Cosnuau 2014), implemented Householder bifactorization in order to perform the tridiagonalization of matrices. Here, small matrices of 128×128 used to solve eigenvalues and eigenvectors problems since the author had the idea that it was more efficient to perform for small instances of the problem the calculations on CPU. Lahabar and Narayanan (2009) implemented an algorithm to carry out SVD array decomposition on a GPU. In order to perform the decomposition, it was necessary to apply bifactoring to diagonalize the matrix later. The next step of bifactorization is carried out with the Householder method of reflection.

Sachdev et al. (2010) implemented SVD using bidiagonalization followed by diagonalization. This procedure was the first to be deployed on a GPU. Bidiagonalization implemented using Householder transformations that were closely related to BLAS operations. The QR algorithm is applied for diagonalization. This work outperformed an implementation using MATLAB and Intel Math Kernel Library (MKL) LAPAC on the CPU.

3 Parallelization Strategies of PahHousholder Architecture

In this work, we consider MPI, OpenMP and CUDA programming models. The use of several programming models allows us to build hybrid-heterogeneous parallel programs that can be executed on clusters with nodes based on multicore processors and GPUs.

MPI is used for communication between the different processes to give a distributed memory model. OpenMP is used to perform some operations in parallel, using multithreading in a shared-memory scheme, and CUDA is used to accelerate the GPU computations.

Figure 1 shows that communication is an essential aspect of hybrid-heterogeneous parallel programs to obtain good performance. The transfer times between the different execution units must be reduced, and memory access must be efficient. A good data partitioning strategy is to minimize the number of communication operations. Also, the exchange of information between the CPU and GPU consider since the stored data operates in the host memory. One feature of the strategies we present here is that they try to minimize information transfer between the host and the GPU.

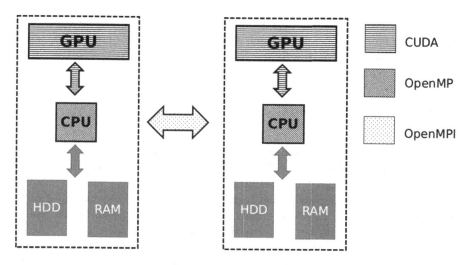

Fig. 1. Use of MPI, OpenMP and, CUDA functions in parallel implementations.

The iterative method calculates the Householder matrix based on the tridiagonal form of a symmetric matrix.

Symmetric matrix A multiplied by this matrix. The elements below the i-th row and the elements to the right of the i-th column become zero.

Several different implementations of this method are described in the following sections.

3.1   Sequential Implementation

This implementation used the C language to realize the algorithm of (Householder 1958) (Golub and Loan 2012; Press et al. 1992). The main tasks in this implementation are the computation of the 2-norm of a vector, the vector inner and outer products, submatrix multiplication, the sum of matrices, and scalar and matrix multiplication. The data structures used to store the input, Householder matrix, and the resulting matrices are double type arrays of size $n \times n$. Since the size of the Householder matrix decreases by one row and one column at each iteration, the operations between submatrices were implemented by traversing the indexes in the original array of size $n \times n$.

3.2   OpenMP Implementation

The parallelization of OpenMP programs is straightforward, and since the Householder transformation uses matrix and vector operations, then quickly parallelized. The tasks parallelized with OpenMP were the computation of the 2-norm of a vector, the vector inner and outer products, submatrix multiplication, the sum of matrices, and scalar and matrix multiplication.

A critical point to bear in mind with this implementation is that the threads created to execute the tasks in parallel are managed by the operating system, meaning that parallelization with this tool can result in excessive operations involving the creation and destruction of threads, which can create difficulties for massive instances of the problem. To take advantage of parallelization with OpenMP is the parallelized tasks must be of coarse granularity.

3.3   GPU Implementation

Implementing an algorithm in a GPU can represent a great advantage because this type of device has high computing power. Depending on the programming tool used, parallelization can be fast (with OpenAcc) or may take more time (with CUDA). However, a CUDA implementation is beneficial since it raises a better performance. The parallelized tasks with CUDA were the computation of the 2-norm of a vector, the vector inner and outer products, submatrix multiplication, the sum of matrices, and scalar and matrix multiplication.

Due to the GPUs' architectural features, the arrays' data structure was a double array of size $n \times n$. A critical aspect of this implementation is the data exchange operations between the host memory and the GPU memory. Since the application matrices are in host memory, they must be copied to the GPU memory, as shown in Fig. 2. Since this method requires $n1$ iterations, the implementation performs the smallest possible number of this type of operation.

3.4   Hybrid-Heterogeneous Implementation

The bifactorization of a matrix is necessary to perform two matrix multiplications in each method's iteration. We also have vector operations, the addition of matrices, and the multiplication of a scalar by a matrix. All of these operations

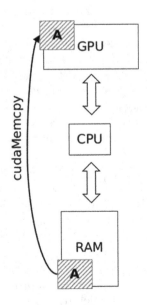

Fig. 2. Copy matrix from host memory to GPU memory.

are performed in the GPU, while operations involving sending and receiving data in the CPU.

Figure 3 shows the bifactorization process in the hybrid-heterogeneous implementation. From Fig. 3, In the first stage, the vector u is sent to all processes using a *broadcast* operation. The vector **u** is the i-th row of the matrix **A**. The slave and master nodes calculate the part of the Householder matrix (**H**); the part that is calculated by each node depends on the *range* of the node and the total number of processes that are running. It is important to note that although MPI balances the nodes' loads, this implementation assumes that all GPUs have the same capabilities.

As shown in Fig. 3, Stage 2 starts when each process receives the vector **u**. The calculation of the 2-norm of the vector is done, and the product point and a scalar. All these operations are performed on the CPU using OpenMP, since reduction operations (i.e., of a vector) we obtain one scale. It is better to perform this type of operation on the CPU, as the GPU would require too many synchronizations between the threads. At this stage, when each process has calculated the corresponding part of the Householder matrix, the master process sends the columns of the original matrix to each node to perform partial multiplication with the Householder matrix.

In Stage 3, the slave processes send the solutions to the master process, which combines them to give the matrix resulting from the multiplication of the matrix **H** and **A**. The combined solution is sent to all nodes as the rows of the matrix **HA**.

In Stage 4, as shown in Fig. 3, each process receives the rows of the matrix **HA** and performs a partial multiplication of the matrices **HA** and **H**. When these processes have generated the partial results, they go to the master process.

In the last stage, the master process unifies the partial solutions to form the matrix **HAH**. If the number of iterations is less than $n-1$, iterating until the tridiagonal matrix is obtained.

3.5 Considerations

The following considerations are :

- The matrices are symmetric; the rows sent since rows store the matrices. When the columns are sent to the nodes to perform the **HA** multiplication,
- In each iteration, no ones are added to the main diagonal of the reflection matrix as indicated by (Householder 1958), but the indices of the multiplying matrices traversed.
- At the end of the iteration, a reordering of the matrix **HAH** is carried out, because in this last multiplication columns in the different nodes divide the matrix.

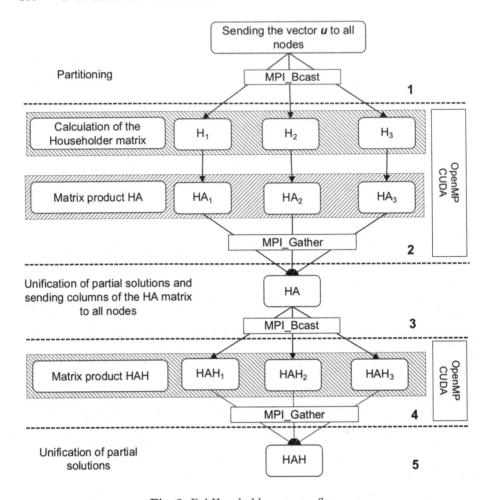

Fig. 3. PahHousholder process flow.

4 Experiments and Results

In order to test parallel strategies implemented we have conduce several experiments. Dense matrices up to 4000×4000 are used as input and the execution times, communication times and information exchange time between GPU and CPU are analyzed.

The infrastructure is two computers for these experiments are used: a server and a laptop, which used CentOS and Ubuntu Linux distributions, respectively.

The server has:

- **CPU**
  - **Model:** Intel Xeon X5675
  - **Socket number: 2**

- **Frequency:** 3.07 GHz
- **Cache Memory:** 12 MB
- **Core number:** 6 physics, 6 virtual per socket. 12 physics and 12 virtual in total.
- **RAM Memory:** 23 GB.

The server also had three nVidia GPU cards, as shown in Table 1:

Table 1. GPU cards characteristics.

GPU	Memory (MB)	Threads Maximum by bloc	CUDA Cores	Memory Velocity (MHz)	GPU (MHz) Velocity
Tesla C2070	5375	1024	448	1494	1147
GeForce GTX 460	1024	1024	336	1850	1530
Quadro K2000	2048	1024	384	2000	954

The Laptop had the following characteristics:

- **CPU**
  - **Model:** Intel i7 6700HQ
  - **Frequency:** 3.5 GHz
  - **Cache Memory:** 6 MB
  - **Cores numbers:** 4 Physics, 4 virtual
- **RAM memory:** 8 GB

This laptop has a nVidia GTX 960M, Table 2:

Table 2. Characteristic of GTX 960M.

GPU	Memory (MB)	Max Threads per block	CUDA Cores	Memory Velocity (MHz)	GPU Frequency (MHz)
GeForce GTX 960M	4044	1024	640	2505	1176

The programming language is C with the following libraries: CUDA (version 6.5), OpenMP (version 4.4.7), and OpenMPI (version 1.4).

The bifactorization implementations were tested on square random symmetric matrices of different dimensions were generated, and the following programs executed: the sequential program, parallel with OpenMP, heterogeneous using CPU and GPU devices, and finally a hybrid- heterogeneous implementation using heterogeneous MPI processes to scale up to two and three GPUs.

Table 3. Execution time for OpenMP implementation of bifactorization process shows.

n	Time (ms)			
	One Thread	Two Threads	Four Threads	Six Threads
128	819	413	214	150
256	19325 4	9755	4997	3514
512	330515	165750	84017	57793
1000	17046837	8482279	4137022	2761388
n	Speedup (ms)			
	One Thread	Two Threads	Four Threads	Six Threads
128	1	1.98	3.82	5.46
256	1	2.25	4.42	4.98
512	1	2.17	4.25	5.19
1000	1	2.009	4.12	6.17

4.1 Sequential Execution

In order to get a reference execution time to compare the different parallel implementations. This experiments are shows in column "*One Thread*" in Table 3. The behavior of the complexity of the algorithm observes in these results.

4.2 OpenMP Experiments

Table 3 shows the execution times for one, two, four and six threads for square matrices of size 128×128, 256×256, 512×512 and 1000×1000. We can observe that the speedup is close to the number of threads used, meaning that the speedup is close to four for four threads. Table 3 present the execution time and speedup obtained using several cores in the multi-core processor. In several cases, the acceleration achieved is greater than the number of cores, which would appear to violate traditional Amdahl's law. However, this behavior is due to the experiments run on a processor with Turbo Boost technology. It increases the running frequencies from 3.06 GHZ to 3.46 GHZ. Therefore, the traditional maximum Amdahl's speedup multiplied by $H = 3.46/3.06 \approx 1.1307$ (Meneses-Viveros et al. 2020). For one thread, it means that for one thread must be 1.1307, for two threads is 2.2614, for four threads is 4.5228 and six threads are 6.7842.

4.3 Heterogeneous Implementation

The heterogeneous parallel implementation used a GPU and CPU, and Table 4 shows the execution times for the GTX 960M card and the Fermi Tesla 2070. This table observes that although the transfer time is lower for the M690 card, the execution time is better on the Tesla 2070. Besides, the memory size of the M690 is not sufficient for problems of size greater than 256. A comparison of the execution of bifactorization on both cards shown in Fig. 4. We can observe how the same experimentation shows a considerable reduction in the execution time depending on the card on which it is executed.

Table 4. HouseHolder bifactorization execution time using only GPUs.

n	GTX 690M - Times(ms)			
	Data Exchange(CPU-GPU)	kernel Execution	Total	Speedup
128	49.25	42357.80	42407.05	
256	186.18	385910.47	386096.65	
512	764.07	3827876.50	3828640.57	
	Tesla 2070 Times(ms)			
	Data Exchange(CPU-GPU)	kernel Execution	Total	Speedup
128	65.59	5554.12	5619.71	
256	253.98	51 127.34	51381.32	
512	1027.45	542 280.13	543 307.58	
1000	3914.59	6 260 953.50	6264868.09	
2000	15671.66	63 241 900.00	63257571.66	

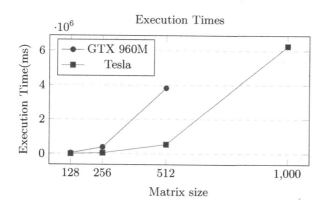

Fig. 4. Householder bifactorization execution time on GTX M690 and Tesla 2070.

4.4   PahHousholder Implementation

The parallel heterogeneous hybrid (HH) implementation uses multiple CPUs and GPUs. Table 5 shows the performance when the bifactorization runs on more than one GPU. This approach has two main advantages: firstly, there is a reduction in the execution time, and secondly, we can increase the size of the problem. Figure 5 shows the decrease in execution time as the number of GPUs used increases.

Table 5. Execution time for HouseHolder bifactorization runs in two and three GPUs cards.

n	Two GPUs - Times(ms)			
	Data Exchange(CPU-GPU)	kernel Execution	MPI Communication	Total
1 000	13 565.85	1 724 308.75	5 232.46	1 743 107.06
2 000	71 268.21	28 066 792.00	42 426.12	28 180 486.33
3 000	177 776.97	120 106 832.00	135 439.37	120 420 048.34
4 000	348 623.71	268 435 456.00	287 675.46	269 071 755.17
	Three GPUs - Times(ms)			
	Data Exchange(CPU-GPU)	kernel Execution	MPI Communication	Total
1 000	15 875.75	1 101 020.00	35 200.49	1 152 096.24
2 000	70 530.17	18 481 052.00	69 298.65	18 620 880.82
3 000	191 979.02	92 628 416.00	206 430.76	93 026 825.78
4 000	354 307.13	253 067 424.00	314 666.45	253 736 397.58

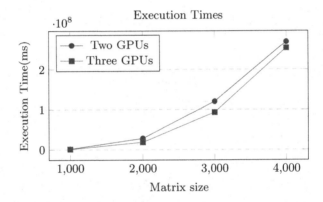

Fig. 5. Execution time for PahHousholder uses two and three GPUs.

The bifactoring process shows an increase of the GPU numbers in the same proportion that occurs in the experimentation with OpenMP. The cards do not have the same characteristics and affect the experiment's performance differently, as shown in Table 4.

Table 4 shows that the same implementation has a faster execution time on the Tesla card than on the GTX card.

Figure 6 shows a comparison between the accelerations obtained for the different experiments. The runtime decreases when more GPUs are used. Although the program executes on a single card, the experiment on the CPU is faster.

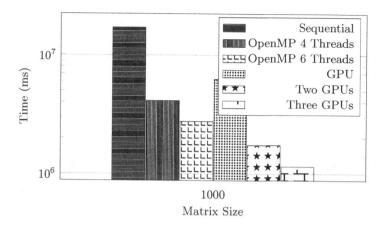

Fig. 6. Comparision of differents experiments for Householder bifactorization.

As the number of GPU cards increases, the time required to exchange data between the MPI processes increases. However, the time for communication between CPU and GPU decreases, as shown in Fig. 7.

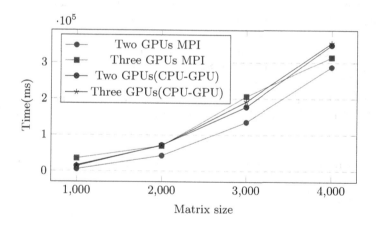

Fig. 7. Data Transfer Time for PahHousholder experiments.

Figure 8 shows the data exchange times between the CPU and GPU. The number of communications between processes and the time for execution for the matrix size is accelerated 4000 × 4000. We note that there is a decrease in the kernel runtime when there is an increase in communication between processes and a decrease in the exchange time between CPU and GPU.

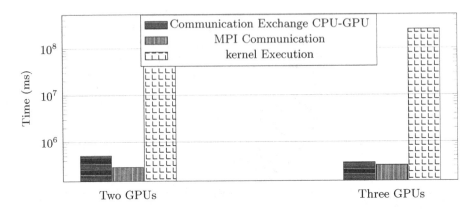

Fig. 8. Data transfer and execution for PahHousholder experiments.

5   Conclusion and Discussion

The results presented above demonstrate the performance enhancements achieved through the use of the PahHousholder implementation, which significantly reduces execution times for bifactorization and bidiagonalization.

The OpenMP implementation was for sizes of matrices greater than 1000×1000, but these tests were incompleted due to the continuous creation and destruction of execution threads involved.

Since the method for bifactorization of matrices requires $n - 2$ iterations, this may affect the implementation's performance with OpenMP.

This implementation shows that its possible get the bifactorization process in multiple GPU cards to process large matrices that are difficult to compute in a single GPU card. Also, the speedup is consistent with the number of GPU cards used.

Conflict of Interest. The authors declare that they have no conflict of interest.

References

Bowgen, G., Modi, J.: Implementation of QR factorization on the dap using householder transformations. Comput. Phys. Commun. **37**(1–3), 167–170 (1985)

Chen, Y., Davis, T.A., Hager, W.W., Rajamanickam, S.: Algorithm 887: Cholmod, supernodal sparse cholesky factorization and update/downdate. ACM Trans. Math. Softw. (TOMS) **35**(3), 22 (2008)

Choi, J., Dongarra, J.J., Ostrouchov, L.S., Petitet, A.P., Walker, D.W., Whaley, R.C.: Design and implementation of the scaLAPACK LU, QR, and Cholesky factorization routines. Sci. Program. **5**(3), 173–184 (1996)

Cosnard, M., Muller, J.-M., Robert, Y.: Parallel QR decomposition of a rectangular matrix. Numer. Math. **48**(2), 239–249 (1986)

Cosnuau, A.: Computation on GPU of eigenvalues and eigenvectors of a large number of small hermitian matrices. Procedia Comput. Sci. **29**, 800–810 (2014)

Golub, G.H., Loan, C.F.V.: Matrix Computations, 4th edn. Johns Hopkins University Press, Baltimore (2012)

Householder, A.S.: Unitary triangularization of a nonsymmetric matrix. J. ACM (JACM) **5**(4), 339–342 (1958)

Lahabar, S., Narayanan, P.: Singular value decomposition on GPU using CUDA. In: IEEE International Symposium on Parallel & Distributed Processing, 2009. IPDPS 2009, pp. 1–10. IEEE (2009)

Leininger, M.L., Sherrill, C.D., Allen, W.D., Schaefer, H.F., III.: Systematic study of selected diagonalization methods for configuration interaction matrices. J. Comput. Chem. **22**(13), 1574–1589 (2001)

Liu, F., Yu, C., Meng, W.: Personalized web search by mapping user queries to categories. In: Proceedings of the Eleventh International Conference on Information and Knowledge Management, pp. 558–565. ACM (2002)

Meneses-Viveros, A., Paredes-López, M., Hernández-Rubio, E., Gitler, I.: Energy consumption model in multicore architectures with variable frequency. J. Supercomput. **77**, 1–28 (2020)

Osinski, S., Weiss, D.: A concept-driven algorithm for clustering search results. IEEE Intell. Syst. **20**(3), 48–54 (2005)

Press, W.H., Teukolsky, S.A., Vetterling, W.T., Flannery, B.P.: Numerical Recipes in C: The Art of Scientific Computing, 2nd edn. Cambridge University Press, Cambridge (1992)

Sachdev, G.S., Vanjani, V., Hall, M.W.: Takagi factorization on GPU using CUDA. In: Symposium on Application Accelerators in High Performance Computing, Knoxville, Tennessee (2010)

Sameh, A.H., Kuck, D.J.: On stable parallel linear system solvers. J. ACM (JACM) **25**(1), 81–91 (1978)

Sunderland, A.G.: Parallel diagonalization performance on high-performance computers. In: Parallel Scientific Computing and Optimization, pp. 57–66. Springer, Heidelberg (2009). https://doi.org/10.1007/978-0-387-09707-7_5

Author Index

C. J. Barrios H. et al. (Eds.): CARLA 2023, CCIS 1887, pp. 227–228, 2024.
https://doi.org/10.1007/978-3-031-52186-7

Printed in the United States
by Baker & Taylor Publisher Services